Distant Markets, Distant Harms

Distant Markets, Distant Harms

Economic Complicity and Christian Ethics

Edited by

DANIEL K. FINN

OXFORD
UNIVERSITY PRESS

OXFORD
UNIVERSITY PRESS

Oxford University Press is a department of the University of
Oxford. It furthers the University's objective of excellence in research,
scholarship, and education by publishing worldwide.

Oxford   New York
Auckland   Cape Town   Dar es Salaam   Hong Kong   Karachi
Kuala Lumpur   Madrid   Melbourne   Mexico City   Nairobi
New Delhi   Shanghai   Taipei   Toronto

With offices in
Argentina   Austria   Brazil   Chile   Czech Republic   France   Greece
Guatemala   Hungary   Italy   Japan   Poland   Portugal   Singapore
South Korea   Switzerland   Thailand   Turkey   Ukraine   Vietnam

Oxford is a registered trademark of Oxford University Press
in the UK and certain other countries.

Published in the United States of America by
Oxford University Press
198 Madison Avenue, New York, NY 10016

© Oxford University Press 2014

Library of Congress Cataloging-in-Publication Data
Distant markets, distant harms : economic complicity and Christian
ethics / edited by Daniel K. Finn.
pages cm
ISBN 978-0-19-937099-3 (hardcover : alk. paper)—ISBN 978-0-19-937100-6
(pbk. : alk. paper)—ISBN 978-0-19-937101-3 (electronic text)   1. Consumption
(Economics)—Moral and ethical aspects.   2. Commerce—Moral and ethical
aspects.   I. Finn, Daniel K., 1947-editor of compilation.
HB835.D57 2014
174'.4—dc23
2013036449

1 3 5 7 9 8 6 4 2
Printed in the United States of America
on acid-free paper

Contents

List of Contributors

Paul Appiah Himin Asante is the Personal Secretary of Cardinal Peter Turkson, the president of the Pontifical Council for Justice and Peace. He earned his Ph.D. in anthropology from the Catholic University of America, Washington, D.C. He did other graduate studies at Loyola University of Chicago, the University of Illinois at Chicago, and Pontificia Universidad Catolica de Puerto Rico at Ponce.

Margaret S. Archer is Professor in Social Theory at École Polytechnique Fédérale de Lausanne and Directrice of its Centre d'Ontologie Sociale. She was Professor of Sociology at the University of Warwick from 1979 until 2010 where she wrote over twenty books, including (published by Cambridge University Press), *The Reflexive Imperative in Late Modernity* (2012), *Making Our Way Through the World: Human Reflexivity and Social Mobility* (2007), *Structure, Agency and the Internal Conversation* (2003), *Being Human: The Problem of Agency* (2000,) and *Realist Social Theory: The Morphogenetic Approach* (1995). She took her first degree and Ph.D. at the London School of Economics and was a post-doctoral student at the École Pratique des Hautes Études in Paris. She was president of the International Sociological Association (1986–1990), is a founder member of the Pontifical Academy of Social Sciences (1994 to date) and is a trustee of the Centre for Critical Realism.

Albino Barrera, O.P., is a Professor of Economics and Theology at Providence College, Rhode Island. A member of the Order of Preachers, he earned his Licentiate in Sacred Theology from the Pontifical Faculty of the Immaculate Conception in Washington, D.C., and his Ph.D. in economics from Yale. His publications include *Market Complicity and Christian Ethics* (Cambridge University Press, 2011), *Globalization and*

Economic Ethics: Distributive Justice in the Knowledge Economy (Palgrave MacMillan, 2007), *God and the Evil of Scarcity: Moral Foundations of Economic Agency* (University of Notre Dame Press, 2005), *Economic Compulsion and Christian Ethics* (Cambridge University Press, 2005), and *Modern Catholic Social Documents and Political Economy* (Georgetown University Press, 2001).

John A. Coleman, S.J., a sociologist and ethicist, was for many years the Charles Casassa Professor of Social Values at Loyola Marymount University, Los Angeles. Coleman is the author of *One Hundred Years of Catholic Social Teaching* (Orbis, 1991), *Globalization and Catholic Social Thought* (Orbis, 2005), and *Christian Political Ethics* (Princeton University Press, 2007). He has contributed some sixty chapters to various books and has edited about fifteen books.

Pierpaolo Donati is Professor of Sociology at the University of Bologna. He is past-president of the Italian Sociological Association and Counsellor of the Board of the International Institute of Sociology, and since 1997 he has been a member of the Pontifical Academy of Social Sciences. Founder and editor of the journal *Sociologia e Politiche Sociali*, he has directed many national and international surveys. He is known as the "founding father" of the Italian relational sociology, which was first advanced in *Introduzione alla sociologia relazionale* (FrancoAngeli, 1983) and shortly presented in *Building a Relational Theory of Society: A Sociological Journey*, in M. Deflem (ed.), *Sociologists in a Global Age: Biographical Perspectives* (Ashgate, 2007). Further theoretical and empirical developments of his approach appear in many subsequent books, such as *Teoria relazionale della società* (FrancoAngeli, 1991) and *Relational Sociology: A New Paradigm for the Social Sciences* (Routledge, 2011).

Daniel K. Finn is Professor of Theology and William E. and Virginia Clemens Professor of Economics and the Liberal Arts at St. John's University, Collegeville, Minnesota. He earned his M.A. and Ph.D. at the University of Chicago. He is a past-president of the Society of Christian Ethics, the Catholic Theological Society of America, and the Association for Social Economics. His books include *The Moral Ecology of Markets: A Framework for Assessing Justice in Economic Life* (Cambridge, 2006), *The True Wealth of Nations: Catholic Social Thought and Economic*

Life (Oxford, 2010), and *Christian Economic Ethics: History and Implications* (Fortress, 2013).

Mary Hirschfeld is an Assistant Professor of Theology and Economics in the Department of Humanities at Villanova University. She earned a Ph.D. in economics from Harvard University in 1989 and a Ph.D. in moral theology from the University of Notre Dame in 2013. Her research focuses on the dialogue between economics and theology, using Thomas Aquinas in order to construct a theological economics that challenges neoclassical economics while remaining sympathetic to many of its best insights. Her work has been published in the *Journal for the Society of Christian Ethics, History of Political Economy, Faith and Economics, Journal of Economic Education*, and *Review of Economics and Statistics*.

Brian J. Matz is Assistant Professor of the History of Christianity at Carroll College in Helena, Montana. He researches Christian literature in late antiquity and the early Middle Ages, especially the corpus of Gregory Nazianzen, texts concerned with social ethics, and the manuscripts of the Carolingian theological controversies. He earned his first Ph.D. in early Christian studies from Saint Louis University. He earned a second Ph.D. in social ethics from the Katholieke Universiteit Leuven. He also was a research fellow with the Centre for Catholic Social Thought in Leuven from 2005 to 2009. His publications include *Patristic Sources and Catholic Social Teaching: A Forgotten Dimension* (Peeters, 2008), the jointly edited *Reading Patristic Texts on Social Ethics: Issues and Challenges for 21st Century Christian Social Thought* (Catholic University of America Press, 2011), and various articles in *Studia Patristica, Greek Orthodox Theological Review, Journal of Catholic Social Thought*, and elsewhere.

Douglas V. Porpora is a Professor of Sociology at Drexel University in the Department of Culture and Communication. He has written widely on social theory. Among his interests is the role of moral emotions and moral reasoning in public discussion and behavior. His books include *How Holocausts Happen: The United States in Central America* (Temple, 1980) and *Landscapes of the Soul: The Loss of Moral Meaning in American Life* (Oxford University Press, 2001). He is co-author of *Post-Ethical Society: The Attack on Iraq, Abu Ghraib, and the Moral Failure of the Liberal American Public Sphere* (University of Chicago Press, 2013).

Cristina L. H. Traina is Professor of Religious Studies at Northwestern University in Evanston, Illinois, where she has taught Christian ethics and theology since 1992. She earned her Ph.D. in theology from the University of Chicago Divinity School. Her publications include _Feminist Ethics and Natural Law: The End of the Anathemas_ (Georgetown University Press, 1999) and _Erotic Attunement: Parenthood and the Ethics of Sensuality Between Unequals_ (University of Chicago Press, 2011). Her current interests include children's moral agency and the ethics of child work.

Introduction

CHRISTIANS HAVE MANY warrants for the obligation to assist others in their suffering even if the believer played no role in causing those harms. This volume, however, explores a different issue, one posed dramatically in a globalized economy: how can we account for a causally rooted moral responsibility of consumers for harms that markets cause to distant others.

The discipline of ethics, whether in philosophy or theology, has traditionally identified individual causal efficacy as the primary reason for one's moral responsibility for harms caused in the lives of others. Putting it briefly, if I caused a problem, I am responsible for it. But my impact in global markets is vanishingly small. Thus our challenge is to articulate the moral responsibility that arises from our participation in markets even though none of us makes a perceptible difference in the harms caused.

Mainstream economics has been notoriously individualist in its conception of economic life, and as a result, social structures of all kinds—whether firms, families, government, or markets—are undertheorized within economic science. Sociology is the discipline where there has been a consistent and careful analysis of social structures and their impact in people's lives. Thus Christian economic ethics has much to gain from a conversation with sociological colleagues.

Out of this conviction, the True Wealth of Nations Project of the Institute of Advanced Catholic Studies organized a conference in June 2012 that brought together sociologists, economists, and theologians to reflect on this theme of causal and moral responsibility for the harms that market cause to distant others. Papers were written and circulated ahead of time to allow maximum time for conversation about the issues. This volume presents the fruits of that gathering by presenting the various papers, as they were modified in light of those conversations.

Contributions of this Volume

Sociologist Douglas Porpora orients the conversation by making clear that any use of sociological insight by outsiders to the discipline will have to entail a choice among different approaches (or schools) within sociology. As a member of the "critical realist" school of thought within both the philosophy of science and the practice of sociology, Porpora emphasizes the important of the notion of "emergence" in both nature and social life. Emergence occurs when elements at a "lower level" of reality combine to form something new that possesses properties not present in those lower-level elements. The classic example here is water, which could never be understood simply by analyzing hydrogen and oxygen, as it will extinguish a fire while each of its two constituents will feed the flames. Emergence explains the errors of an individualistic interpretation of social life that sees social structures as nothing more than the combined actions of individual agents. Understanding social structures as relationships among preexisting social positions, Porpora cautions that simply putting more virtuous managers in place of unprincipled CEOs will not make much difference, because the constraints and incentives implicit in the role of CEO will lead the next person who holds that position to make largely the same decisions.

Sociologist Margaret Archer addresses the process by which the market, like all structures, provides "structural conditioning." In critical realist sociology, only persons are agents, but structures have a causal impact on those agents, often unintended by the persons whose actions caused those structures to emerge in the first place. That causal impact occurs not by some sort of "hydraulic pressure" but by shaping the situation in which people find themselves. Whether CEOs, elementary school teachers, or college students, the social position that an agent takes on influences what they do by means of the vested interests, opportunity costs, and "situational logics of action." Thus an attempt to explain the moral responsibilities of persons within the market individualistically—without attending to the structural conditions that markets impose—can only lead to failure. Archer goes on to report the results of her recent study of four dominant "modes of reflexivity" (styles of interaction with one's social environment) that typify people now, identifying where hope may lie for confronting many of the problems we face in society today, including those that markets cause for distant others.

Sociologist Pierpaolo Donati addresses the shortcomings of the intellectual foundations of social-democratic holism and individualistic liberalism, the two main political options in Western industrial democracies. These two options, he argues, have come to a strange convergence in relieving individual persons of their moral responsibility for the harms markets cause. The holistic explanations (that unfortunately predominate in sociology) attribute causal force to structures or systems and emaciate the moral responsibility of individuals. One might expect that the individualist explanations (that unfortunately predominate in economics) would at least preserve the individual's moral responsibility. However, Donati argues, economics and individualist liberalism in the end attribute the harms caused by markets not to individual participants but to long chains of (individually justifiable) exchanges, leaving the individual blameless. What is needed, he argues, is a relational understanding of economic life that looks inside the "black box" of the market and calls for a change of social relations that constitute the market. He calls us to begin to think of all the persons involved in and affected by any particular set of market decisions as together forming a "relational subject." Thus, for example, firms need to think of their personnel policies not simply as standing between management and the employees but within the broader context that includes those employees' children or elderly parents for whom they have responsibility. Applying these notions to social dumping, human rights issues, capital flight, and the involuntary creation of poverty, Donati calls for changes that would "civilize" the market.

Historian and theologian Brian Matz examines the question of moral responsibility for harms caused to others during the early centuries of the Christian church. Examining a wide variety of patristic sources, Matz employs the metaphor of a "marketplace" for philanthropic help to the poor provided by the well-to-do. This *"philanthropia* marketplace" becomes a way to describe a fundamental theme in patristic teaching: that both the rich and the poor have something to offer each other in accord with God's plan. The wealthy are called to share from their surplus with those who are unable to meet their own needs, and the poor provide to the wealthy a spiritual service, assistance in demonstrating to God that the wealthy man is indeed a good person and an appropriate recipient of God's mercy and eternal life. Matz goes into detail in describing both the historical conditions of social classes in the early centuries of the Church and the structures for assistance to the poor developed by the bishops, abbots, and other religious leaders of that era. Examining both the structures of the *philanthropia* marketplace and the preaching (and rhetorical devices) that elicited financial support for it, Matz concludes that the early Christian church recognized the moral responsibility of the prosperous for harms caused to others in the economy of the day and that church leaders took active steps to mitigate those harms in light of faith.

Economist and theologian Mary Hirschfeld asks whether and how the traditional Catholic moral framework arising from the work of Thomas Aquinas can address issues of social causality that have only come to general awareness through modern social science. Examining the Thomistic account of private property as including both a benefit to the property owner and a duty to share one's surplus with the needy, Hirschfeld contrasts this Catholic account of property with the more individualist understanding of property rights arising from the work of John Locke and others. She then addresses Adam Smith's insight about a social dividend of increased wealth that arises from specialization ("the division of labor," as Smith put it), benefits that run parallel to harms caused by the same economic system. "Regnative prudence" was, for Aquinas, "the practical reason exercised by a king, directing the kingdom toward its own good." In a democratic society, Hirschfeld argues, this same regnative prudence must characterize the decisions of individual persons, who are not simply market participants but also citizens responsible for the common good. This extension of Aquinas echoes the calls of the earlier sociological chapters that all persons need to take responsibility for the character of the social structure of the market within which economic life occurs.

Theologian Christina Traina steps outside of theology to examine the contributions of feminist philosophers to this volume's theme of moral responsibility for harms that markets cause to distant others. Traina describes several methodological principles of such a feminist approach to these issues: the use of standpoint theory (where our experience and interests affect what we see), a future orientation (with less interest in assigning praise or blame for what has already happened), a focus on the reality of injustice (rather than on ideal notions of justice itself), a self-critical awareness of our own participation in exploitation, and an understanding of those harmed by markets not as passive victims but as active agents. Feminist philosophers argue that an "ethic of care" is in many ways more fundamental than justice and is all too often ignored in theories of justice. They also examine the ways in which human agency is constrained by one's social setting. Traina illustrates all of these concerns through "global care chains," in which, for example, a highly paid professional woman in the United States hires a nanny from the Philippines to care for her children while she is at work. This immigrant, drawn to the United States by attractive wages, in turn hires a nanny to care for her own children while she is out of the country, and this nanny, by far the poorest in this chain of care, turns to her own mother or sister to provide care for her own children, typically without charge. The moral ambiguities so frequent in such a global care chain provide a vivid illustration of the challenges facing those who recognize their moral responsibility for the harms that markets cause to distant others.

Sociologist Fr. Paul Appiah compares the notions of community and individual in Western social science with analogous traditional African conceptions of these basic human realities. He illustrates the differences by examining the Akan people, a matrilineal tribe in Ghana, beginning with fundamental conceptions of personhood rooted in a mother (who transmits her blood), a father (transmitting spirit), and God (providing the soul). This fundamental anthropology generates a view of the human person as both uniquely individual and deeply communal. This, he argues, makes the Akan "ontologically religious" and renders community life and values central to daily life, even in a modern economic system whose logic of individuality nonetheless threatens to undermine these traditional understandings. Employing examples such as the billions of dollars in remittances sent "home" by Africans living elsewhere in the world, Appiah argues that African culture maintains the fundamental conviction about human life summarized in the saying, "I am because we are, and since we are, therefore I am."

Theologian and economist Albino Barrera, O.P., provides a counterpoint to the analysis in most of the other chapters in this volume. Employing the insights of traditional Catholic moral theology and legal philosophy, he provides a framework for assessing an individual's share of collective responsibility for the harms that markets cause to distant others. Distinguishing causal responsibility, moral responsibility, and liability, Barrera argues that our common responsibility to alter the social structure of the market needs to be "individuated" not only to identify individual responsibility but also because collective action is always initiated by individuals. He then provides a helpful framework for thinking through this process, focusing on the nature and severity of harm by markets, the nature of the economy, the character of causal relations within the economy, the diverse capabilities of different agents, and the philosophical commitments any of us may bring to this conversation.

Sociologist John Coleman, S.J., applies the social scientific analysis of the earlier chapters in this volume to the concrete case of global warming, viewing it as a pressing example of harms that markets cause to distant others without anyone's intending them. He begins with the vivid example of the island nation of the Maldives, whose very existence is already threatened by rising sea levels. Coleman reviews the various dimensions of global warming and the well-orchestrated campaign of a small number of scientists who are climate-change skeptics, largely funded by economic interests tied to fossil-fuel production. Examining the prospects for structural change to address the issue, Coleman describes the options facing the industrialized world and relates both the challenges and prospects for addressing global warming to the social scientific and moral analysis presented in this volume.

The final chapter, which as editor I have written in light of the discussions at the conference, demonstrates how mainstream economic presumptions about the function of prices in the market can be related to the sociologist's understanding of the market as a social structure. Employing the notion of coercive power as a threat employed to change another person's behavior, the standard economic notion of prices—as quickly and efficiently leading market participants to change their behaviors—can be deepened to understand prices as exerting a coercive power, just the sort of "restriction" or incentive that critical realist sociology describes as the causal effect of social structures. Employing Albino Barrera's analysis of market coercion, we can distinguish those ordinary, efficient, and beneficial constraints that markets impose on us all from other constraints, which are deeply threatening to the well-being of particular individuals and groups, typically the poor and powerless.

Conclusion

This volume as a whole seeks to provide an interdisciplinary analysis emerging from sociology, economics, and Catholic social thought. Such an initiative holds out the promise of a morally and empirically adequate appreciation of both the benefits of economic markets and the harms that they frequently and unintentionally cause to so many in the world. When so much discourse about economic life arises from those who un-self-critically endorse or oppose markets, both the Christian community and the larger world stand in need of this sort of intellectual development.

There is no attempt here to catalogue the harms markets cause or the particular changes in the structure of markets that could reduce or prevent those harms. The particular aim of this volume is to sharpen and deepen the ethical analysis of harms markets cause to distant others by drawing on a diverse set of intellectual resources from various disciplines. The hope of all involved is to contribute to making the world more just and to help those many currently harmed by markets attain greater human flourishing, in all its dimensions.

Acknowledgments

This book is the fruit of the efforts of many people to whom I am deeply grateful. The authors, of course, stand in first position, but even prior to their work, Mr. Paul Caron, co-director with me of the True Wealth of Nations Project, worked to plan the conference from which these chapters arose. With a lively intellect and nearly half a century of experience in European banking, he has continually generated creative insights to broaden the reach and deepen the focus of this project. Fr. James Heft, S.M., the third member of our steering committee and president of the Institute for Advanced Catholic Studies, has been a constant source of insights and support. Dr. Gary Adler, Director of Research for the Institute, contributed with lively participation in the conference and assisted in its planning and execution.

All of us involved are indebted to Sheila Garrison whose administrative work made the June 2012 conference possible. And once again I owe much to Judy Shank for her careful preparation of this manuscript.

As editor, I am also indebted to several very able people who have made this book possible at Oxford University Press, including Cynthia Read, Charlotte Steinhardt, Stuart Roberts, Saranya Rajkumar, and Kari Lucke.

Daniel Finn
Collegeville, Minnesota
December 2012

PART ONE

Sociological Resources

I
_____

Who is Responsible?

CRITICAL REALISM, MARKET HARMS, AND COLLECTIVE RESPONSIBILITY

Douglas V. Porpora

EARLY IN THE 2012 U.S. presidential election campaign, *The Washington Post* issued a report critical of candidate Mitt Romney.[1] The *Post* commented how Romney's opponents tried for years to tie him to the outsourcing of American jobs. Now, the *Post* reported, it was clear that Romney's financial company, Bain Capital, "invested in a series of firms that specialized in relocating jobs done by American workers to new facilities in low-wage countries like China and India."

The American public was not amused. In fact, this news report initiated a media storm with calls for Romney to clarify his relationship with Bain. Subsequent polls showed widespread public disapproval of Romney's business practices.

Romney's political opponent, President Barak Obama, was quick to seize on the weakness exposed. "There is a new study out by a non-partisan economist," Obama said. "Governor Romney's economic plan would in fact create 800,000 jobs. There's only one problem. The jobs wouldn't be in America."[2]

Pundits were equally critical of Romney. Writing online for the *Huffington Post*, political analyst Elizabeth Parisian was characteristically scathing:

Decimating American jobs through offshoring is a main element of what we'll call the Romney Economy, an economic ideology that focuses exclusively on enriching America's wealthiest individuals via tax cuts for the rich, and a business ideology centered on taking over companies, siphoning off the profits, laying off workers, and leaving crummy low-wage jobs for everyone else. Exemplified by Bain Capital, the Romney Economy involves sacrificing the jobs, security and well being of working Americans in order to funnel wealth to a relatively few extraordinarily rich folks in the financial industry.[3]

Outsourcing and offshoring refer to management decisions to relocate facilities to places where business costs are lower, both because wages are lower and because labor and environmental regulations are more lax. Romney has not been the only one to be vilified for such activity. Michael Moore's first blockbuster movie, *Roger and Me*, similarly made it seem as if the outsourcing and offshoring of General Motors plants was all due to the personal greed of GM president, Roger Smith.

The implication is that with different managers, with a better mentality than Romney and Smith had, different decisions would be made. But is that so? Greed is always the popular explanation for unpopular executive decisions. If greed is the explanation, responsibility is narrowly contained and the solution rather easy: Get more virtuous managers.

But suppose the real problem is less personal greed than it is the basic nature of the economic game we all have agreed to play, the game we call "the market" or "capitalism." If market harms created by outsourcing and offshoring derive less from the particular executives in charge and more from the basic nature of our economic system, then the responsibility is more diffuse and the requisite solution more demanding. This brings us to the aim of this book and of the conference that generated the papers presented here. Authors were invited to think together about what causes market harms and who bears moral responsibility for them.

Due to those conversations, this paper is now different from the one I originally presented. Although I am a practicing Catholic, I discovered at the conference that I had been more steeped in liberal Protestant thought than in the Catholic tradition. I found the insights of the Catholic tradition very helpful, especially its emphasis on relationality and the specifically Thomistic understanding of the market as a human institution embedded differentially in wider political and cultural fields. I incorporate and refer to these insights in this chapter.

Critical Realism and Emergence

My own initial charge as one of the sociologists at the conference was to recount how a sociological perspective, particularly one informed by critical realism, would explain in causal terms both how market harms arise and the nature of our individual responsibility for them. This, it was hoped, would provide a better understanding of causality than the covering law model of scientific explanation employed by many philosophers of science and by most economists.

Critical realism is a school of thought within the philosophy of science that is an alternative to the positivism that dominates the social sciences, particularly psychology and economics. In its nondeterminism and relationality, critical realism's conception of causality certainly accords better with Catholic thought than does the focus on abstract scientific laws in the covering law model. Also, critical realism's focus on causal mechanisms rather than abstract laws is more helpful in understanding social processes; thus part of this chapter presents a brief introduction to critical realism.

As the conference dialogue proceeded, one particular element of critical realism took on central importance: the principle of emergence. Critical realism is not the only perspective to uphold emergence, but emergence is one of the chief positions critical realism upholds against positivism, which tends toward reductionism.

Basically, emergence and reductionism refer to the "levels" of reality that make up our world and to the corresponding sciences that study them: for example, the level of elementary particles studied by physics, the level of compounds studied by chemistry, the organic compounds studied by biology, and the level of intelligence studied by the human sciences. Reductionism holds that ultimately all levels and all sciences can be reduced to physics, at least in principle. We may not know enough to accomplish that reduction now, but as science proceeds, we will one day achieve that knowledge, or so reductionists believe. If reductionists are right, then insofar as human behavior is ultimately reducible to the laws of physics, it is deterministic. Free will is an illusion.

In contrast, emergentists hold that as elements at each level of reality combine, the new wholes that emerge often possess new, "emergent" casual properties not previously present in the world and certainly not present at the lower levels of reality. Water, for example, is an emergent from hydrogen and oxygen and has characteristics very different from theirs. (For one, it extinguishes a fire while they intensify it.) If emergentism is true, not everything can be reduced to physics. Consciousness and free will in particular emerge out of more basic physical processes. Emergentism clearly is a view more consistent with Catholic thought, which recognizes in the human person unique capacities and a unique dignity.

Emergence plays a critical role in this book, because the theme of the volume—individual responsibility for the collective harms of the market—spans two levels of reality: the level of the individual actor and the level of the collectivity. Traditional ethics has tended to approach the problem of collective harms in an exclusively aggregative way, depicting them as an aggregation of individual contributions. It then follows that our personal responsibility for a collective harm is commensurate with our own individual causal contribution to it, what Christopher Kutz calls the "difference principle."[4] Thus, if I contribute little to an overall effect and if, moreover, that effect would still occur more or less the same without my input, I cannot personally be held very responsible for it.

Consider this aggregate approach in relation to the issue of global warming that John Coleman addresses in this volume. Each of us in our individual consumer behavior contributes to the combined effect of global warming. Nevertheless, our individual causal contribution to the whole is so slight that in aggregate terms our personal causal responsibility is negligible. And if our personal responsibility is negligible, then seemingly negligible as well is the moral obligation of any of us to change our ways. Such a conclusion is not very satisfactory.

The value of the emergentist view is the way it avoids the aggregative logic and reframes the considerations at issue. As a social structure emerging from the interactions of economic actors, the market has emergent properties, properties that generate global warming and unsafe Asian factories beyond our individual market behavior. Our contribution to such a collective harm thus enters now at two levels. First, there is our individual market behavior, which, assessed in aggregate terms, is slight. Second, at a higher level, there is the matter of our participating in and sustaining the market as an institutional whole and what we are or are not prepared to do about its governance. This second level of analysis is not well understood if we employ just an analysis in the aggregate. Our responsibility instead is a matter of our orientation in moral space.

The two levels of responsibility show up in our earlier discussion of outsourcing and offshoring. From a purely business perspective, moving operations abroad often makes good sense. It increases a company's profit. Is this nonetheless bad? Americans may think so, but they generally are neither theologians nor economists. Economists in particular note that outsourcing and offshoring make products less expensive for consumers, and for economists that result is undeniably good. This is why so many economists support looser restrictions on international trade.

Catholics, however—even Catholic economists—cannot support cheaper prices for everyone without further consideration. In the first place, however beneficial cheaper prices may be for us collectively as consumers, we are also workers. And without the money we earn from work, we cannot consume, regardless of how inexpensive consumer goods become. Workers and even entire communities left behind by plant shutdowns can be truly devastated. Parisian reports that, even as she penned her article on Romney, this sort of devastation was being faced by 170 employees of a Bain-owned firm in Freeport, Rhode Island, that was to relocate operations to China by year's end.[5] Even if outsourcing cannot be described as bad, the effect on workers and communities left behind is certainly a market harm, one that should concern socially responsible Catholics.

But we are not done yet. If factories move to where pollution controls are looser, then even if the ensuing prices for our goods are lower, the net effect can still be harmful. The outsourcing contributes to exactly the adverse market effects on the environment that Coleman describes.

Finally there is the issue of wages. Is any price afforded labor a just one? Moral economy is a term of art used to describe economic exchanges grounded not only in profit and market efficiency but also in justice. The idea goes back to Catholic teaching on the notion of a just price. Here, one virtue of Catholic thought going back to Thomas Aquinas is a relativizing of the market system. The basic idea is addressed in Mary Hirschfield's chapter.

Aquinas's thought on moral economy is quite sociological. For him, a market is not a unitary natural thing. Instead, markets are diverse human creations and as such must be not only judged for their contribution to human good but also governed so that they do so contribute. Aquinas's thought is thus an ocean away from today's neoliberalism, which tends to fetishize the market as something that must be allowed to operate without any human constraint. Instead, for Aquinas, because the market is a human creation, it is imperfect and thus in continual need of human stewardship. The American Protestant theologian Reinhold Niebuhr made a similar argument.

One of Aquinas's more explicit principles was the idea of a just price, a notion crucial to our situation. Today, in America, with the hyper-individualism that governs our lives, the very notion of a just price is trivialized. Because interactions between buyer and seller are considered voluntary, both parties being formally able to walk away from any market transaction, any price that receives mutual agreement is considered fair. If a party considers a proposed price unjust, it is up to them simply to decline the offer.

This principle, enshrined in Chicago economist Milton Friedman's *Free to Choose*, is completely devoid of any wider relationality.[6] It overlooks, in other words, the wider nexus of relations in which individual transactions are proposed and accepted. In particular, the principle assumes a balance of power and resources between buyer and seller that often does not obtain. Such balance specifically does not obtain when for whatever reason the urgency for the transaction is much greater for one party than for the other.

In this situation, the party with greater urgency may be forced to accept a trade that, far from just, is actually exploitative. We react with indignation, for example, at what we consider the price gouging of the inland motel in Florida that triples the usual nightly price during a hurricane—knowing that many families living on the coast will have to move out of their homes temporarily. Why? Because, Milton Freidman notwithstanding, we instinctively recognize that the justice of a price is not determined solely by whether or not we accede to it. In contrast to Friedman, Aquinas was very sensitive to this point:

> Yet if the one man derive a great advantage by becoming possessed of the other man's property, and the seller be not at a loss through being without that thing, the latter ought not to raise the price.[7]

Here, Aquinas is saying explicitly that we are not to take advantage of others' extenuating circumstances to extend to them an unfair price. Yet is that not what is happening when plants close down in places where employees are paid a good wage, due to strong unions and labor laws, and moves to where those protections are absent?

Certainly, the workers in other countries may desperately need the work and eagerly agree to the wages and working conditions offered. Yet, as Aquinas observes, the wage offered does not necessarily thereby become a fair one. A year before the 2012 presidential race, there erupted another mini-media storm about the pay and working conditions at China's Foxconn factory, where, it turns out, all Apple iPhones are made. At a single factory employing some 400,000 workers, each iPhone is apparently made by hand—some 300 pairs of them—over the course of five days. Workers labor at 12-hour shifts and live in cramped, on-campus dormitories. At salaries in the range of $300 a month, none of these workers can afford to buy the very products they themselves labor so hard to make.[8]

Are those workers receiving a just price for their labor? It is a complicated question that goes beyond Foxconn and Apple's iPhones. Only 2% of all the clothing we wear is made here in the United States. The rest is produced abroad by cheap labor in other countries. Once again, a great deal of our clothing is made in China. Evidently, one town alone—Datang—makes a third of the world's socks, the workers there earning about what workers earn at Foxconn.[9]

The privilege we enjoy in America to buy as much as we buy—from our jeans to our iPhones (I own both)—depends on the production of these goods by people earning far less than would be paid to Americans for similar labor here. Were the workers in those other places not making so little, a lot of the products we buy would perhaps not even be made. But maybe products like the iPhone should not be made, if making them entails an unjust wage.

In short, whatever good comes of the market transactions described, there also seem to be some definite harms. Who is responsible for those harms? Just Mitt Romney and Roger Smith and other business executives like them? What I have tried to delineate in the foregoing is a global way of life from which we in America all disproportionately benefit. Although it is the business executives who decide to move their operations to places that allow unjust wages and greater contribution to global warming, we all benefit from the lower prices that result. But the unpaid costs of our benefits are not fully accounted for by tallying up the labor and environmental harms entailed. There is, in addition, our accession to the entire way of life for which we must assume responsibility, and that point returns us to the discussion of Mitt Romney.

Romney's critics, particularly Obama and Parisian, fault Romney on two counts, one narrow and one broader. The narrow complaint focuses on Romney's role as a business executive who moves jobs overseas. Here, whatever Romney's personal responsibility, we need to understand his behavior also as a response to the demands of his social position as a business executive, playing by the rules of the game. To the extent that

Romney's behavior is a response to that social position and those rules, the responsibility is not Romney's alone. It is also the responsibility of those who authorize the rules and the existence of such a social position, and that means all of us.

The wider criticism of Romney relates to the rules of the game, which again returns us to the thought of Aquinas and Niebuhr. If, as both would argue, we think of markets as embedded within various political systems, then we are all also responsible as citizens for the constraints we do or do not impose on the market. In other words, we are also responsible for what we stand for politically relative to the market. According to Obama, the current rules of the game actually give companies tax breaks for moving operations overseas. He wants to end that policy and instead give companies tax breaks for bringing jobs back to America. Romney opposes such moves.

We too are responsible for where we stand on such matters, and, again, it is not a responsibility that can be measured in aggregate terms. Nor do our responsibilities end with just determining the appropriate tax code. As custodians of the market, we are responsible for the entire way the market behaves, including the pressures it exerts on corporate executives to do things we actually might prefer them not to. That responsibility requires us to reflect more closely on social causality in general and market causality in particular.

Understanding Causality

With its emphasis on econometric regression equations, standard economics remains under the grip of the positivist covering law model of causality. According to this model, a causal explanation is basically a deductive argument in which the event to be explained, the *explanandum*, is logically deduced from some antecedent conditions and events and from a covering law linking the prior situation to the event to be explained. For example, to explain why the book I was holding hit the floor, a covering-law explanation in physics cites the law of gravity and my losing my grip. It is such law-like, "if-then," relations among events that econometric equations putatively express.

There are multiple problems with the covering law model of causality, even in the physical sciences but most certainly in the social sciences. The biggest problem is that it is untenable. To work, the model requires deterministic laws or, at a minimum, statistical laws in which there is at least a constant probability that one event will follow from some prior event or conjuncture of events.

Were there deterministic laws governing human behavior, then we could not even speak of moral responsibility for any harms we cause. Instead, whatever harm we did we were causally determined to do. We could not have done otherwise. True, as compatibilists say, we might have done otherwise had we chosen otherwise, but if we could not have chosen otherwise, it is hard to see how we can be held responsible for choosing as we did.

In fact, however, no deterministic laws in the social domain have ever been found, nor even any statistical laws with constant probabilities. Found at most are the statistical generalizations captured by econometric regressions that have nothing deterministic or constant about them so as to enable the logical deductions required by the covering law model.[10]

Nor is it likely that we will ever find even statistical generalizations with the requisite determinacy. The reason is that such determinacy is likely only in closed causal systems where only a single causal mechanism operates without interference. In the causally open world outside the laboratory, multiple causal mechanisms are always interfering with each other so as to prevent any constant conjunctions among events, what Roy Bhaskar terms event regularities.[11] If, moreover, as I argue, human thought is an ever creative and, therefore, intrinsically un-closable system, then no thought will ever follow with any constancy from any finitely specifiable set of antecedent thoughts and conditions.[12] No laws, then, will ever be found with the degree of determinacy necessary for the covering law model to work. Instead, in those social science fields like economics that remain tied to a positivist philosophy of science, the covering law model will continue to function only as a polite fiction, justifying an unreflective use of statistics.

But let us consider a primary alternative approach to these issues. Going back to Wilhelm Dilthey, many humanist scholars have argued for a distinction between the human and natural sciences, with deterministic laws operating only in the latter. In the former domain, humanists say that they seek not causal explanation but interpretative understanding.[13]

The problem with this humanist view is that our interest is *not* just interpretation. We want to know how harms are caused by the market and how we individually are causally responsible for them. The humanist denial of social causality would thus stop us before we even began. Such humanists deny social causality because they too conceptualize causality according to the covering law model.

Yet because critical realism completely breaks with the covering law model and its implicit determinism, it has no need to deny that reasons, too, can be causes. And indeed, reasons certainly function like causes, supporting both counterfactuals and subjunctive conditionals.[14]

As it turns out, contrary to both positivists and humanists, a fully deterministic understanding of causality fails even in the physical sciences. As Nancy Cartwright has shown in both *How the Laws of Physics Lie* and *The Dappled World*, the laws of physics likewise do not so much specify the events likely to occur in the real world as they point to the causal powers operative in various real-world mechanisms.[15]

It is a "powers view" of causality to which Cartwright's work points and a powers view of causality that underlies the view of critical realism. In a sense, the covering law model sucks the power or agency from the world's things and assigns it instead to laws.[16] On the covering law view, laws are the motivating force for things. Dispensing with laws, the critical realism causal powers view puts the motivating force back into the things of the world. Critical realist Ruth Groff states this position well:

> The standard alternative is to think of laws as themselves being efficacious in some sense; it is because they are in place that things are as they are. Realism about causality shows this to be backward. Laws register regularities ex post facto; they don't produce them. Stephen Mumford goes a step further, suggesting that if the causal work in question is being done by powers, then at the level of explanation the concept of laws is superfluous.[17]

For critical realism, as for other powers understandings of causality, the things of the world are not inert but alive with causal agency. They have active capacities to produce changes and passive capacities to be changed.[18] A knife, for example, has the active capacity to cut and paper the passive capacity (or what is sometimes called a liability) to be cut.[19] Similarly, water has the causal capacity to dissolve certain solids like salt, which, correspondingly possess the causal capacity or liability of being dissolvable by water.

Instead of the covering law model's colorless and unilinear understanding of causality, critical realism's powers view makes sense of our entire, rich vocabulary of causative verbs: pushing, pulling, attracting, repelling, corroding, binding, killing, reproducing, exiling, redeeming. These verbs and so many others like them are the textured ways we speak of causal processes in concrete situations. Causality is a multiform reality.

Similarly, for critical realism, causality is not understood in terms of necessitated events but more in terms of forces that can be counteracted or functions that things can serve, whether or not they actually do so. A gun, for example, has the functional capacity to shoot bullets, whether or not it actually does so. Thus, for critical realism, as opposed to the understanding that follows the covering law view, causality is not only about what actually happens (*actualism*) but also about what could potentially happen, even if it never does.[20]

It should also be clear now that for critical realism, causality is not primarily a relation among events. Certainly, some events can cause other events. In the event that a baseball, flying through the air, breaks a window, it could be said that one event caused the other. But more fundamental than events are the ontological particulars involved—the baseball and the window—and their causal properties. It is the hardness of the ball, its projectability, and its momentum that gives it the power to break and the brittleness of the window that disposes it to breaking.

In each case, the causal powers of the particular derive from its basic properties, which in turn derive from its internal structure. What makes glass brittle, for example, is the lack of long-range structure in its molecular makeup.[21]

From a critical realism point of view, causal analysis enters in different ways in two different moments. In a first moment, we try to explain why things have the particular causal powers they possess. The causal features of things are explained by the constitutive structures of those things, that is, by describing the mechanism that generates the causal feature. In the second moment, we try to explain why in a particular case a conjunction of mechanisms, each having its own causal powers, combine to cause a particular, perhaps nonrepeatable event.

It is in critical realism's attention to mechanisms that relationality and emergence come to the fore, as it is often relations among lower-level elements that give rise to the emergent causal powers of the whole they generate. As indicated earlier, the emergent properties of water are not possessed by either the oxygen or the hydrogen that produce it. Rather, the special properties of water arise from the way in which oxygen and hydrogen combine to form it. Similarly, the ability to tell time is an emergent power of a clock taken as a whole rather than of any of its parts separately.

What gives rise to the emergent properties are not just the particular parts, although they are important too, but the way those parts are arranged, their structure, which is to say, their interrelations.

Relations are also distinctively central to what critical realism means by *social* structure. In fact, in contrast with most other sociological views, for critical realism, social structures are social relations among (preexisting) social positions, relations like power, competition, cooperation, exploitation, and the like.

Relations in this sense are not the same as interaction. Interactions are behaviors among actors, and they are important too. However, as structures, relations are not behaviors but ontologically distinct. Think, for example, of the capacity of a high school principal to expel students from classes. This capacity itself is an important causal power. As noted, one crucial point for critical realism is that causal properties like the principal's can exist and exist consequentially even if they go unexercised. Thus the principal retains the capacity to expel students even when he or she does not exercise it. The capacity or power to expel is not reducible to the event of its exercise. As an ever-present threat, even unexercised, the power to expel hovers like a shadow over the interaction between students and principal. The principal's power to expel thus becomes *power over* students, and as *power over* it is not just an individual's capacity but also a social relation. Insofar as the principal's relational power over students shapes the entire interaction between principal and students, the interaction cannot be fully understood apart from that power and the capacity in which it inheres.

Notice also that the principal's power over students exists whether or not anyone notices it. Employing the notions of restrictions and enablements outlined in Margaret Archer's chapter in the volume, we can say that this power constrains the students and enables the principal. To the extent that this power is noticed, however, it also motivates both the principal, who can deploy it, and the students, in whose interests it is to beware of it. Thus, social relations can exist even if the actors related by them are unaware of them. For example, it is not as if economic exploitation does not exist until the exploited come to see themselves as such. Were that true, we could make exploitation disappear simply by convincing the exploited that they are not.

From whence does the principal derive the objectively real causal power over students? From his causal capacity to expel them. And from whence derives this capacity? From the constitutive rules of the educational system, which establish what it means in the first place for someone even to *be* a principal. Some of those rules have legal standing in society as they may be written by the school board (a governmental body), but other rules—in schools and all social structures—are simply widely accepted ways that things should be done. So the final important point to notice is that objectively real social relations (i.e., relations that exist and exist consequentially regardless of their notice by actors) are themselves a phenomenon that emerges from constitutive rules (i.e., rules that establish what social things are).

The central way in which critical realism analyzes social behavior is via a model that posits dialectical relations among actors, cultural rules, and social structures. Actors always act from a context established by the rules and relations that structure them, the relations deriving from the rules. As Margaret Archer's chapter explains, the rules and relations typically produce vested interests (interests tied to particular positions in the systems) that motivate people to act in certain ways. That is, the rules and regulations are causes in people's lives, but the causality here is not deterministic. Actors always remain free to ignore their interests or, if they act on them, to do so in creative ways that often cannot be predicted. And part of what people do is alter the rules and relations that govern them. Thus, from a critical realism perspective, causal explanation is not a deductive argument but must ultimately take a narrative, historical form.

Understanding Market Behavior and Market Harms

As just seen, critical realism thinks of causality in terms of mechanisms. So what is the "market mechanism"? It is usually described as the law of supply and demand, but supply and demand is no law in any strict sense, and, to the extent that it holds, it is actually the effect of a mechanism. It is an underlying mechanism of competition that actually comprises the market's so-called invisible hand. Competition is the motor that makes the markets run. As Adam Smith put it:

> It is not from the benevolence of the butcher, the brewer or the baker, that we expect our dinner, but from their regard to their own interest. We address ourselves, not to their humanity but to their self-love, and never talk to them of our own necessities but of their advantages.[22]

What Smith is saying is that it is not out of benevolence that the butcher, the brewer, or the baker deliver us good products at fair prices. They do so because it is in their interest to do so. And only one thing makes it in their interest to do so: the fact that they are in competition for our purchases with other venders of the same kind.

The "mechanism" of competition functions as a relation. Relations are ontologically real, but they are abstract. Thus people tend to think of competition more as a concrete behavior, something that individual sellers *do*. They compete. But before competition is a behavior engaged in by individual sellers, it is first a relation in which individual sellers mutually find themselves positioned. It is this competitive relation that causes the competitive behavior.

Again, the causality here is not deterministic. The competitive relation merely creates vested interests. Individual incumbents of the position can choose to ignore those interests, but because the interests are objective, incumbents who ignore them will pay an objective price. In a competitive market place, a butcher who consistently charges too much or delivers less satisfactory meat will not long remain a butcher. The butcher's customers will all go elsewhere.

The idea behind the invisible hand is that the competitive relations of the market channel private self-interest into collective good. It is out of their own interest that sellers seek to offer their customers the best that they can; in many respects the market works this way as well. In the *Communist Manifesto*, Karl Marx himself acknowledged the awesome efficiencies of the market, which "knock down all Chinese walls."

Of course, Marx also understood that competitive market systems are unstable. In fact, they contain the seeds of their own destruction. As time goes on, as in the board game of Monopoly, competition eliminates competition. Indeed, were the process not stopped by government regulations, (i.e., social rules—antitrust legislation—structuring the market), the end result would be as in the children's game: the survival of a single competitor.

Even with such rules, the process has gone on and is now far advanced. Early competitive capitalism has largely been eclipsed by our current conglomerate phase of capitalism. Thus, the trend in the United States is for there to be fewer individual butchers, bakers, and brewers, their numbers replaced by supermarkets that combine all three—and more. Giant conglomerates now dominate, owning multiple firms in diverse market sectors that used to be distinct industries: hotels, food, oil, and so on. Thus, today in the United States, the largest four one-hundredths of 1% (.04%) of all American corporations account for 69% of corporate income and 75% of corporate assets.

In this new conglomerate phase of the market, where the competition is now global, the competition is likewise ever more intense. In this environment, the rule is "grow or die." To grow, profits need to be generated.

But it is not enough just to generate profits and grow. To survive, it is necessary to grow faster than the competition. That requires not just profits but more profits than the competition. Thus, even as I write, the corporate giant Caterpillar is in dispute with its union in Jolliet, Illinois, over a wage freeze that Caterpillar wants to impose over the next six years—a pay freeze even while Caterpillar profits are at an all-time high. Is this not greed? How much profit is enough? These are the wrong questions. It is not greed because the motive is not personal aggrandizement. The motive is structural and corporate: exceeding the competition. If Caterpillar does not generate more profits than its now worldwide competitors, then, relative to those competitors, Caterpillar's position is vulnerable.

The very thing that makes the market efficient is the mad scramble among producers, induced by competition, to cut costs. Costs can be cut by better technology necessitating fewer workers (producing fewer jobs). Costs can be cut, as at Caterpillar, by pressuring workers who do remain to accept lower salaries or fewer benefits. Costs can be cut, as by Mitt Romney and Roger Smith, by relocating operations to where labor sells for a lower price, with fewer labor and environmental protections.

Thus, like the Force in the movie *Star Wars*, market competition has both a light and a dark side. The light side gives us better products at lower prices. The dark side is the disregard for how those effects are achieved.

Who Is Responsible for Market Harms and in What Way?

From a sociological point of view, we are who we are not just as isolated individuals. Instead, we are who we are in relation to both social space and moral space. In social space, we are the occupants of certain ontologically real social positions, apart from which we would not be who we are. We are, for example, someone's son or daughter. We are members of a certain race and gender and social class in a certain society. While some of these category designations could be different without altering fundamentally who we are (e.g., we might change employers), other changes would alter us essentially (and just which changes would be so fundamental might vary depending on the person).

Because we exist in social space and derive our identities in part from the groups or categories to which we belong, we share a part of both the pride and the blame that attaches to those social designations. If we are proud to be Americans, it is because we are a part of what America is, so that America's doing is also our doing.

How much of what America is are we each? How much pride are we each entitled to feel over what America does? According to an aggregate analysis, the answer to each question is clear: not much. This conclusion only serves to show how inadequate an aggregate analysis can be. Our identification with America is more qualitative than quantitative. America's identity and fate and our own are intertwined and inseparable, and that relationship cannot be measured numerically.

The same is true with moral space. We exist in a space of rival moral values, and an essential part of who we are is determined by how we orient ourselves in that space. To which values and ideals are we committed? Which do we repudiate? Our answers to such questions also define who we are. Again, those answers cannot be computed numerically, are not given to parceling out. They are instead relational.

Both individuals and collectivities exist in moral space. Collectivities too are often engaged in morally laden actions. Even when we are not members of those collectivities, their doings can implicate us morally. In some cases, like the Holocaust, it is shameful enough just to be a nonresponsive bystander to what is happening. In such situations, we have an obligation to act even if we ourselves made no causal contribution to the proceedings.

How much more are we obligated to act when we ourselves are members of an immorally acting collectivity whose identity and our own are intertwined?

Once again, we can approach this question at two levels. As Paul Caron has noted,[23] we tend to approach the question too much at a first level, a level that reflects the perspective of tort law, which takes an aggregative approach to such questions. How much did one of Adolph Eichmann's lower-level bureaucrats contribute to the Holocaust? In quantitative terms, not much. Certainly the Holocaust would have carried on even had that bureaucrat, at whatever risk to his life and career, resigned his position.

In terms of such first-level analysis, as we have noted, the same might be said of the individual contributions we make to aggregate market harms. As executives in a market economy, making decisions about plant closings and relocation, Mitt Romney and Roger Smith definitely play a nonnegligible causal role in the harms produced, but within a global GDP of some $70 trillion, even their contribution is minor. For each of the rest of us, the percentage share of any causal contribution is infinitesimal.

But there is a second level of approach to the question of moral responsibility for harm done exemplified in criminal law, which operates on logic different from tort law. In criminal law an accomplice, such as a lookout or the driver of the get-away car, shares the same guilt as the principal, who may have uniquely conducted the holdup or murder. What matters in criminal law is not the magnitude of an individual's causal contribution to a crime but that individual's shared intention to carry it out. Stated otherwise, it is the individual's "yea saying" to the crime that is decisive.

At this second, higher level of analysis, it is the logic of criminal law that more aptly applies to our individual responsibility for market harms. At this level, that for which we must assume responsibility is not primarily our particular consumer behaviors or our particular business decisions that we may make even in an executive role. Instead, that for which we must assume responsibility is our yea saying to the whole market system we participate in and sustain, including the deleterious causal relations it generates. We have laid enough groundwork to make brief the unpacking of this formulation. First, we need to consider that according to the previous section's analysis of the market, many of the harm-causing business decisions are themselves caused not by personal greed but by the exigencies of the very business competition that generates the market's vaunted efficiencies.

Thus replacing Mitt Romney or Roger Smith at the helm will not change the outcome. Their replacements would end up making the same harm-causing decisions. It is not that the causality here is deterministic. Any one executive *could* simply refuse to make the decision called for. He or she might even choose to resign. But if the executive does not resign, the corporate board will force him or her to make the economically wise decision, for otherwise the company's position will suffer too severely. Conversely, if the executive does resign, the same fateful decision will be made by someone else.

So whether we are talking of plant closings or a financial crisis, replacing the people will not change things. Without there necessarily being any determinism, the exigency of competition is the pivotal cause. But remember, we are talking here of competition not as a behavior but as a relation, and that relation is an emergent phenomenon arising from the rules we set in place. Thus whereas the behavior is caused by the relations, the relations are caused by or emerge from the rules.

While basic rules of trade and property ownership may be endemic to all markets, they do not constitute natural law. They can vary considerably and have. "The land is mine," says the Lord in Leviticus, "so you shall not sell it in perpetuity." While likely never practiced, the Jubilee passage set definite limitations on ownership. Such limitations can always be set as conditions on competitive practice or labor relations. Antitrust legislation represents the former and the National Labor Relations Act the latter.

Market harms are caused by certain behavior, which is caused by certain relations, which emerge from the rules. Because the pivotal cause is an emergent phenomenon, there is no proper way to approach responsibility in an aggregative fashion. It is not that we each make some quantum contribution that added up to a market's governing relations. The causality does not work like that. Instead, the relations emerge naturally all at once from the rules. The rules in turn come into being all at once when we collectively agree to them. Rules are social by nature. There are no private rules. They exist when enough of us say yes to them that they govern the interactions of the whole.

When we talk of these broader rules within which markets are embedded and by which markets are concretely constituted, we are back to Thomas Aquinas and Reinhold Niebuhr. What we are being held responsible for here at this second, higher level of analysis is actually nothing directly economic but rather something political. We are responsible for our orientation to the market-governing rules: Which rules are we willing to accept, for which are we willing to fight, and which will we resist or refuse? How we decide is a matter of personal orientation. It is a matter of personal integrity.

Conclusion

If we return to the beginning of this chapter and read closely, we see that it is more at this higher, second level of analysis rather than at the first that

Obama and Parisian are criticizing Romney. They are criticizing Romney less for the business decisions he made or endorsed as an executive than for his continued support of the very rules that promote and encourage such business behavior. It is for Mitt Romney's general political orientation to the rules of our economy that he is being held accountable.

In this regard, we are no different from Romney. We are all held to the same account. The industrialized nations are in the midst of a great moral struggle over the rules of our economy. In the United Sates the New Deal consensus that once governed our economic transactions has, over the past thirty years, been substantially dismantled. It is continuing to be dismantled now and replaced by a neoliberal vision of the market as something natural, that runs on its own, that should be left free from all human intervention.

Where do we stand on this great debate? It is on this question in the realm of politics that our greater responsibility resides. Whatever we decide, the particular markets that govern us are in the end the creation of our own rules. Collectively, we remain responsible for how those markets behave and for the harms they cause near and far.

NOTES

1. Tom Hamburger, "Romney's Bain Capital Invested in Companies That Moved Jobs Overseas," *The Washington Post*, June 21, 2012. Accessed September 26, 2012: http://www.washingtonpost.com/business/economy/romneys-bain-capital-invested-in-companies-that-moved-jobs-overseas/2012/06/21/gJQAsD9ptV_story.html.

2. Roger Madhani, "Obama Says Romney Plan Will Send 800,000 Jobs Overseas," *USA Today, The Oval*, July 16, 2012. Accessed September 26, 2012: http://content.usatoday.com/communities/theoval/post/2012/07/obama-says-romney-policies-will-send-800000-jobs-overseas/1#.UB7K3EI1aFJ.

3. Elizabeth Parisian, "Welcome to the Romney Economy—Making Millions by Shipping Our Jobs Overseas," *The Huffington Post*, 2012. Accessed September 26, 2012: http://www.huffingtonpost.com/elizabeth-parisian/welcome-to-the-romney-eco_b_1688286.html.

4. Christopher Kutz, *Complicity* (New York: Oxford University Press, 2001).

5. Parisian, "Welcome."

6. Milton Friedman, *Free to Choose* (New York: Avon, 1981).

7. Thomas Aquinas, *Summa Theologica*, Edited by Kevin Knight. New Advent, 2012, q.77, a.1. Accessed September 16, 2012: http://www.newadvent.org/summa/.

8. Huff Post Tech, "Nightline Tours Apple Supplier Foxconn," *Huff Post Tech*, 2012. First Posted 2/22/12. Accessed November 3, 2013: http://www.huffingtonpost.com/2012/02/22/nightline-apple-supplier-foxconn_n_1293393.html?ref=technology.

9. Bradley Blackburn, "Clothing 'Made in America': Should U.S. Manufacture More Clothes?" *ABC News*, March 10, 2011. Accessed September 26, 2012: http://abcnews.go.com/Business/MadeInAmerica/ made-america-clothes-clothing-made-usa/story?id=13108258#.UB7HBEl1aFJ.

10. See Douglas Porpora, "On the Prospects for a Nomothetic Theory of Social Structure," *Journal for the Theory of Social Behaviour*, 13 (1983):243–264; and Porpora, *The Concept of Social Structure* (New Haven, CT: Greenwood Press, 1987).

11. See Roy Bhaskar, *A Realist Theory of Science* (Leeds, UK: Leeds Books, 1970).

12. See Porpora, "Prospects." Also see Porpora, "How Many Thoughts Are There? Or Why We Likely Have No Tegmark Duplicates $10^{10^{115}}$ Meters Away," *Philosophical Perspectives*, 163 (2013):133–149.

13. See Martin Hollis and Steve Smith, *Explaining and Understanding International Relations* (New York: Oxford University Press, 1991).

14. See Joseph Margolis, "Puzzles About Explanation by Reasons and Explanation by Causes," *Journal of Philosophy* 67 (1970):187–195; and Margolis, "Action and Causality," *Philosophical Forum* 11 (1979):47–64.

15. See Nancy Cartwright, *How the Laws of Physics Lie* (Oxford: Clarendon, 1983), and Cartwright, *The Dappled World: A Study of the Boundaries of Science* (Cambridge, UK: Cambridge University Press, 1999).

16. Brian Ellis, "Powers and Dispositions," in Ruth Groff (ed.), *Revitalizing Causality* (New York: Routledge, 2008), 76–92; and Stephen Mumford, "Powers, Dispositions, Properties or a Causal Manifesto," in Ruth Groff (ed.), *Revitalizing Causality* (New York: Routledge, 2008), 139–151.

17. Ruth Groff, "Introduction: Realism and Causality," in Ruth Groff (ed.), *Revitalizing Causality* (New York: Routledge, 2008), 1–10.

18. Ellis, "Power and Dispositions."

19. Ellis, "Power and Dispositions."

20. See Roy Bhaskar, *The Possibility of Naturalism: A Philosophical Critique of the Contemporary Human Sciences* (Sussex, UK: Harvester, 1979).

21. Mumford, "Powers."

22. Adam Smith, *An Inquiry into the Nature and Causes of the Wealth of Nations* (New York: Cosmio, 2011). Accessed September 26, 2012: http://geolib.com/smith.adam/won1-02.html.

23. In discussion at the June 2012 True Wealth of Nations Conference, Los Angeles, California.

REFERENCES

Aquinas, Thomas. *Summa Theologica*. Edited by Kevin Knight. New Advent, 2012. Accessed September 16, 2012: http://www.newadvent.org/summa/.

Archer, Margaret. *Realist Social Theory: The Morphogenetic Approach*. Cambridge, UK: Cambridge University Press, 1995.

Bhaskar, Roy. *A Realist Theory of Science*. Leeds, UK: Leeds Books, 1970.

———. *The Possibility of Naturalism: A Philosophical Critique of the Contemporary Human Sciences*. Sussex, UK: Harvester, 1979.

Blackburn, Bradley. "Clothing 'Made in America': Should U.S. Manufacture More Clothes?" *ABC News*, March 10, 2011. Accessed September 26, 2012: http://abcnews.go.com/Business/MadeInAmerica/ made-america-clothes-clothing-made-usa/story?id=13108258#.UB7HBEI1aFJ.

Cartwright, Nancy. *How the Laws of Physics Lie*. Oxford: Clarendon, 1983.

———. *The Dappled World: A Study of the Boundaries of Science*. Cambridge, UK: Cambridge University Press, 1999.

Ellis, Brian. "Powers and Dispositions." In Ruth Groff (ed.), *Revitalizing Causality* (pp. 76–92). New York: Routledge, 2008.

Friedman, Milton. *Free to Choose*. New York: Avon, 1981.

Groff, Ruth. "Introduction: Realism and Causality." In Ruth Groff (ed.), *Revitalizing Causality* (pp. 1–10). New York: Routledge, 2008.

Hamburger, Tom. "Romney's Bain Capital Invested in Companies That Moved Jobs Overseas." *The Washington Post*, June 21, 2012. Accessed September 26, 2012: http://www.washingtonpost.com/business/economy/romneys-bain-capital-invested-in-companies-that-moved-jobs-overseas/2012/06/21/gJQAsD9ptV_story.html.

Hollis, Martin, and Steve Smith. *Explaining and Understanding International Relations*. New York: Oxford University Press, 1991.

Huff Post Tech. "Nightline Tours Apple Supplier Foxconn." *Huff Post Tech*, 2012. First Posted 2/22/12. Accessed on November 3, 2013: http://www.huffingtonpost.com/2012/02/22/nightline-apple-supplier-foxconn_n_1293393.html?ref=technology.

Kutz, Christopher. *Complicity*. New York: Oxford University Press, 2001.

Madhani, Roger. "Obama Says Romney Plan Will Send 800,000 Jobs Overseas." *USA Today, The Oval*, July 16, 2012. Accessed September 26, 2012: http://content.usatoday.com/communities/theoval/post/2012/ 07/obama-says-romney-policies-will-send-800000-jobs-overseas/1#.UB7K3EI1aFJ.

Margolis, Joseph. "Puzzles about Explanation by Reasons and Explanation by Causes." *Journal of Philosophy*, 67 (1970):187–195.

———. "Action and Causality." *Philosophical Forum*, 11 (1979):47–64.

Mumford, Stephen. "Powers, Dispositions, Properties or a Causal Manifesto." In Ruth Groff (ed.), *Revitalizing Causality* (pp. 139–151). New York: Routledge, 2008.

Parisian, Elizabeth. "Welcome to the Romney Economy—Making Millions by Shipping Our Jobs Overseas." *The Huffington Post,* 2012. Accessed September 26, 2012: http://www.huffingtonpost.com/elizabeth-parisian/welcome-to-the-romney-eco_b_1688286.html.

Porpora, Douglas. "On the Prospects for a Nomothetic Theory of Social Structure." *Journal for the Theory of Social Behaviour,* 13 (1983):243–264.

———. *The Concept of Social Structure.* New Haven, CT: Greenwood Press, 1987.

———. "How Many Thoughts Are There? Or Why We Likely Have No Tegmark Duplicates $10^{10^{115}}$ Meters Away." *Philosophical Perspectives,* 163 (2013):133–149.

Smith, Adam. *An Inquiry into the Nature and Causes of the Wealth of Nations.* New York: Cosmio, 2011. Accessed September 26, 2012: http://geolib.com/smith.adam/won1-02.html.

Structural Conditioning and Personal Reflexivity

SOURCES OF MARKET COMPLICITY, CRITIQUE, AND CHANGE

Margaret S. Archer

THIS VOLUME SETS out to investigate harms that markets cause to distant others. This task requires that we address human agency, social structures, and moral responsibility. Before proceeding further, we must accurately understand all three of these realities. Consider three inadequate approaches.

First, there are the theories based on structural, cultural, or technological determinism that regard human agents as *träger*, the carriers of "forces" above and beyond them, pushed as if by hydraulic pressure. Were this the case, then there could be no talk of moral responsibility, either individual or collective. No one can be held responsible for the effects of something they do not have the capacity to alter. From this perspective, social determinism is a matter of *force majeure;* human agents can no more be held morally responsible for social outcomes than they can for the weather.[1]

Second, some theories make a discussion of moral responsibility impossible because they deny that we can talk about the properties and powers of human agents in any way separately from the social structures they inhabit. These types of theory—such as those of Pierre Bourdieu and Anthony Giddens—insist that every action entails drawing on structural factors and contributes to their reproduction or transformation: "Structure is both medium and outcome of the reproduction of practices."[2] Structure is thus both the condition and the consequence of action. This causes two problems. Agents and structures are so closely elided that responsibility for outcomes cannot be apportioned to them. They are, as it were, jointly responsible—causally and morally—for each and every state of affairs found in society at any time. In addition, as agents, they cannot be disentangled from their circumstances, and that also nullifies moral discussion.

Third, some theoretical approaches regard social structure as nothing more than the aggregate effect of human doings. As an aggregate outcome, structural (or cultural) forms may or may not be held to have further consequences, but in any case these are reducible to the individuals that produced them. Here it might seem to follow that moral responsibility can be directly attributed to the human agents present and their doings. For example, in representative democracy you cast your vote, contributing to the result of the election, and are generally held to be morally bound to accept the outcome even if this is not the one for which you voted. But there is a problem here. Structure cannot be eliminated as easily as this because it affects precisely *how* aggregation itself takes place. An identical pattern of voting in two counties with different electoral systems (e.g., one using "first past the post" and the other proportional representation) could result in different political parties coming to power in the two. Who can take moral responsibility for that? Not the individuals who just voted, because they did not create the electoral process but had to work within it. It is a serious mistake to view structures as nothing more than the sum of individual doings.

The conclusion is that we cannot discuss human agency, social structures, and moral responsibility unless all three terms are at least understood to be separable; conflating agency and structure in any of the above three ways suspends moral discourse. Moral discussion is predicated on regarding "social structures" and "human agents" as being different in kind (i.e., ontologically different) because they have distinct properties that are (or can be) exercised as their distinctive causal powers. Consider the difference. A structure, for example a business firm, can be "centralized" or "hierarchical," which is impossible for a person, but people can be "emotional" or "reflexive," which is not a capacity of structures.[3] Although a structure may be held "undesirable," it cannot itself be blamed for it. Culpability and moral censure are reserved for human beings, individually or collectively.

Both structures and agents exercise causal powers, though in quite different ways. Only persons are agents, but structures have casual effects in that they constrain, enable, and motivate what agents do. In turn, agents create, sustain, and transform structures by their actions and interactions. Agents and structures are ontologically different, but they are intertwined and together they account for the state of social affairs at any time and place. However, saying only this is unhelpful for two reasons.

First, it does not explain why, in Max Weber's words, social matters at a particular time and place are "so" rather than "otherwise." It doesn't yet provide what we need for moral discussion of these issues. Although all structural (and cultural) properties found in any society are continuously activity-dependent, we must distinguish "structure" and "agency" analytically in order to examine their interplay and to account for the sustaining and transforming of structures over time. Structure operates over different time periods because (a) structure necessarily predates the action that transforms it and (b) the transformation of structures necessarily follows after those actions.[4] (My explanatory framework is presented by Douglas Porpora and used by Pierpaolo Donati, both in this volume.)

Both sociologically and morally it is necessary not only to highlight the ontological differences between structure and agency but also to have an explanatory framework that accounts for how the elements are intertwined such that they generate the particular state of affairs in question. This means examining the interplay of structure and agency, which, in turn, involves accounting for how structures influence agents and how agents maintain or change structures. The explanatory framework needs to be able to specify the "who," the "when," the "where," under "what" circumstances, and by means of "which" actions and inactions specific social changes came about or the status quo was maintained. Without such explanations, the discussion of the moral responsibility of market participants for harms markets cause to distant others cannot get off the ground.

First, because we all live within that large structure we call global capitalism, we are all structurally conditioned by it. What does this conditioning mean, and how does it work if, as indicated above, this is not determinism? Second, because structure conditions everyone, it is empirically inaccurate to think of the actions of persons as arising from some sort of pure "free choice." The first part of this chapter unpacks conditioning and argues that its effects are matters of collective responsibility and not of aggregate individual intentionality. The second part is devoted to the agents and their intentions—to why and how they reflexively take different stances toward the harms done to distant others.

As we will see, the economic system has its causal, conditioning effects through restrictions, enablements, and incentives, which affect different people differently, to foster support or opposition to the economic status quo. Considerations about distant others do not figure in the conditioning process. The only way in which they can impinge is if agents (individuals, whether singly or in groups) introduce them through the "projects" they are pursuing in that structural context. This is where intentionality comes in.

This sociological approach is quite different from Albino Barrera's chapter, outlining a legal individualistic method of assigning personal responsibility. His method could hypothetically form the basis for arraigning particular culpable individuals in a court of law; the sociological approach of this chapter holds the majority of us guilty but is not designed for prosecuting anyone.

Structural Conditioning by the Market

Attention to social structure is unavoidable because all social action takes place within a social context; there is no such thing as a context-less action. What is contested (particularly by interpretive and hermeneutic theorists) is whether the social context that agents confront at any time can properly be described as consisting, in part, of social structures. In other words, the dispute is about what a structure is.[5] (We should note that this debate about social structures—how to describe the actual relationship among people—runs parallel to another, which this chapter ignores due to limitations of space in, namely, the character and effects of culture: the ideas, symbols, beliefs, etc., that people hold).

Rather than examine the debate about the character of social structures here, I refer readers to Douglas Porpora's economical classification of four meanings of the term "structure"[6] and endorse his conclusion that, for critical realists, a structure refers to relationships between (pre-established) social positions: master/slave, manager/worker, teacher/student. These are internal or necessary relations in the sense that, although one might have the credentials to teach, to be a teacher one needs students.

As a context of action, such positional relations are neither of the making nor of the choosing of the "contemporary" subjects who literally inherit them. This is fairly uncontroversial for newborn infants, who open their eyes in a context that includes not only parents, family rules, and traditions but also schools, the legal obligation to attend them, and a subordinate relationship of pupils to teachers within them. A new teacher is in a similarly preexisting context: Entering the profession at some particular time when the position of teacher entails, say, specific relations with school administrators, a school board or local authority, officially imposed definitions of the curriculum and accreditation, and so on. The new teachers neither made nor chose the learning and teaching context and might view it with anything from approbation to outright critique.

In either case, they ought not praise or blame their older colleagues for the context they now encounter. Those colleagues, as individuals or as members of a professional organization, may themselves have wanted matters to be otherwise but lost out in a struggle; they may have had no say in the decision making involved, or they may have been ideologically misled about the nature and consequences of changes introduced. In any case, they too exercised their own agency within an earlier context, structured in a somewhat different way. No amount of historical regress can return to a time when there was a completely unstructured context of action; there was no time when individuals were solely the cause of (or solely responsible for) their own social situations.

Social structures have their own causal powers: to constrain, to enable, and to motivate. How do they do this without our having to invoke hydraulic mechanisms—pushes and pulls—and thus slipping into determinism? They do it by shaping the situations in which people find themselves (like the previously mentioned teachers entering a school). Such situations exert constraints (e.g., teachers cannot teach whatever they please), and they create enablements (e.g., to more education and promotion). They are also sources of motivation, giving some people vested interests in maintaining the status quo (e.g., if it rewards their particular expertise) and others in bringing about change (if, for instance, they wish to see the compulsory teaching of religion removed from the curriculum or "creationism" put into it). The maintenance or change of any organizational characteristic is completely dependent on what people do: how they ally and conflict and whom they can mobilize in supporting or resisting change. However, as Andrew Sayer points out,

> One of the most pervasive illusions of everyday thinking derives from the attribution of the properties of the position, be they good or bad, to the individual or institution occupying it. Whatever

effects result, it is assumed that particular *people* must be responsible; there is little appreciation that the structure of social relations,
together with their associated resources, constraints or rules, may
determine what happens, even though these structures only exist
where people reproduce them.[7]

This mistake is why people so often search for guilty parties, the "per-
sonalization" of banking fraud or corporate malpractice (someone's
head must roll), even though this serves to foster "business as usual."
This is also part of the reductionist fallacy that the greed of capitalism
simply results from capitalists being greedy people. From this follows
the erroneous conclusion that if business executives simply became
more virtuous individuals, the market would be reformed. Instead,
we need to understand how the market as a social structure conditions the actions of market participants, confining them to proximate
considerations and thus detracting from potential concern for distant
others.

All structural influences are *transmitted* to people by the way the structures shape the situations in which people find themselves and are *mediated* by what people make of these situations. At any given time, structures
are the results of past social interaction, including the results of previous results of such interactions, and those resulting structures may have
been unintended, unwanted, or even unacknowledged. As such, they are
dependent on past activity and irreducible to current activity alone. Given
that it already exists when new participants enter the market (in whatever
capacity), global capitalism crucially shapes the socioeconomic environment to be inhabited. Through restriction, enablement, and incentive, it
shapes what is produced and how it is distributed; it conditions the character of employments currently available and the benefits, harms, and business practices associated with them.

To understand how structures have such causal effects in the lives of
persons (and why that typically eclipses any concern for harms caused to
distant others), it is helpful to examine three particular effects that structures have in people's lives—by endowing them with *vested interests*, by
attaching *opportunity costs* to following or rejecting those interests, and
by associating a *situational logic of action* to what agents do in the context.
This clarifies why harm done to distant others tends to be of little concern
in global capitalism.

Vested Interests

To call an interest "vested" is to say that it is integral to occupying a particular position in relation to others. Since social structures are, as we have seen, relations among preexisting social positions, we all hold positions within various structures and we all have vested interests. In the context of the economic system, such a position can be occupational or one of the many of positions often referred to as "stakeholders." To occupy such a position in the current market is not equally accessible to all, for vested interests arise out of scarcity, through social processes of unequal distribution.

Typically, structures divide most people into two groups, some with a vested interest in maintaining the inherited status quo and others in changing it. Such interests are objective and should not be confused with an agent's subjectivity; a vested interest in being sufficiently competitive not to go out of business is different from a subjective feeling of competitiveness. And a person's vested interest may or may not conflict with his or her real interests, such as the circumstances necessary for expressing and developing his or her capacities.[8]

Agents' vested interests are objective features of their situations that predispose them to general courses of action—either to maintaining the benefits associated with their positions or to seeking to overcome related disadvantages. As Porpora has put it,

> Among the causal powers that are deposited in social positions are interests. Interests are built into a social position by the relationship of that position to other positions in the system....[Thus], capitalists have an interest in maximising profit because they are in a competitive, zero-sum relationship with all others occupying the position of capitalist.... In other words, actors are motivated to act in their interests, which are a function of their social position. Again, this doesn't mean that actors always with necessity act in their interests, but if they don't they are likely to suffer. A capitalist who shows no concern to maximize profits is liable to cease being a capitalist.[9]

The promotion of vested interests, be it by seeking social reproduction or transformation, has the effect of negating and neglecting responsibility for consequences on distant others. This derives quite simply from the proximity of the vested interest itself—it is, after all, the structurally rooted interest of the self—and it works in the same way whether that interest is to defend or to transform structures based on their interests.

This is fairly obvious for those defending the benefits they currently derive from their occupational positions. Motivationally, the last question they will raise is "should this position exist at all?" For example, in the 1980s, the British procedures for assigning children to special education involved a combination of agencies (at least six) that had historically established a place for themselves in the process[10] and exerted themselves to maintain it. Benefit to the recipients seems to have been a subordinate consideration and, significantly, Caribbean boys were overrepresented among those deemed to need the special treatment. The same dynamics of institutional preservation characterize multinational corporations, football teams, and all other organizations.

Less obviously, the vested interests of those seeking change can display the same formal type of "proximate privileging," of which the unionized closed shop is the most obvious example. In fact, it is outside the market and its vested interests that social movements pursuing human rights for all are typically located, among those without material interests at stake in whether human rights are protected around the globe (though, of course, those gainfully employed in those movements have vested interests related to their own jobs within human rights organizations). In the final section of this chapter, it will be important to ask whether or not such movements, voluntary associations, and charitable initiatives concerned with the well-being of distant others can retain independence from vested interest groups in market and state.

Opportunity Costs

Social structures entail vested interests in response to which those experiencing benefits tend to seek to retain them and thus work for social stability, while those experiencing restrictions tend to seek to eradicate them and thus work for change. These are truly causal forces, but they compel no one. Objective opportunity costs are associated with different responses to frustrating or rewarding situations, and those costs condition (but don't determine) the interpretations people place upon them. These costs represent the next link between the structured shaping of agents' situations and their reactions to them.

Opportunity costs constitute "good reasons" for many people to pursue their vested interests. Nevertheless, this does not justify the empirically inadequate portrayal of persons in mainstream economics as *homo economicus*: individuals trying to maximize their expected utilities, making them simply bargain hunters.[11] In this view, those who appear to turn their backs on material incentives are held to be motivated not by an un-self-interested concern but by some other, nonmaterial form of self-interest. This eclipse of altruism blocks exploration of other reasons that can outweigh the cost to self of one's willingness to pay opportunity costs.

In most situations, opportunity costs do not have to be great for interested parties to find sufficient reason not to pay them. Thus this frequently prolongs social injustice. In the late 1960s, for example, if a male colleague at my university had dropped dead, his wife and children would have received "death in service" payments from the compulsory contributory system for all academics. Had the same happened to me, as a female, my family would have received nothing, despite the parity of our financial contributions in support of the system. When rectification of this injustice was put to a secret ballot among the association of university teachers on campus, where men had a large majority, the result endorsed maintenance of the status quo. In this case, a vote for fairness would have cost each member £4 a month. A secret ballot allowed the majority of male academics to regard their female colleagues as "distant others": faceless, nameless, stripped of relations to them, which seemingly facilitated taking no moral responsibility for perpetuating unfairness toward them.

Those with the greatest freedom in the market—those with the greatest influence over decision making and the least to lose in opportunity costs to themselves—bear a higher moral responsibility for the harms done by their corporations. It is one they do not take. The defense of patents in the pharmaceutical industry keeps the price of drugs prohibitively high for the developing world and constitutes an obstacle to relief agencies. The targeting of markets in terms of profitability (e.g., Brazil as the target for soft drinks because of its youthful demographic distribution) positively creates harm. The operations of finance markets in bringing about the Great Recession in 2008 led to no root and branch reforms; the harms done have only been acknowledged in proportion to the specific scandals revealed. Even when that occurs, the response is personalized and symbolic; a chief executive of a bank refuses his annual bonus, and "business as usual" is resumed.

But such responses are inadequate. They see those in charge as simply immoral individuals for whom the suitable treatment is a course in business ethics or a dose of virtue ethics. After all, this has been the popular response, and Catholic Church leaders have been rather vocal in its favor. But this is to endorse the very individualism that is at the heart of the crisis, and it employs the preferred mode of explanation of neoliberal economists themselves. It rests on the old fallacy that good people make for a good society, which denies emergent structures any role in shaping societal outcomes.

Instead, it is necessary to introduce the third mediating process that induces ordinary people as well as captains of industry and finance—persons likely to be morally no better or worse than their peers—toward individualist behavior that entails disregard for others but especially distant others, who usually have no voice with which to issue a reproach. This is the "directional guidance" provided by the *situational logic of action*.

Situational Logics of Action

The discussion of causal effects of structures above does not yet address what courses of action would serve to sustain or transform them. It would seem as if the strategic means for either aim relies only on the discretion and ingenuity of the agents concerned. So far, we have focused on only one structural influence, that of the market and its constituent positions and relations. However, in social life there are always two other factors in play. On the one hand, there are other structured institutions—especially the state—and their (second-order) relationships to the market, which can be one of compatibility or incongruence; on the other hand, cultural emergents (beliefs, theories, values) may be supportive of or challenging to the material array of institutions. These potential compatibilities or strains are themselves relational properties and important ones for fostering stability or change: Complementarities serve to reinforce social reproduction, and the incompatibilities augment the potential for transformation.

Once again, structures operate by shaping the situations in which people find themselves, by providing directional guidance for action. This operates by supplying good reasons for particular courses of action, in the form of premiums or penalties associated with following them or ignoring them, embodied in vested interests.

The point here is that the major social institutions, including the media engaged in cultural diffusion, dissemination, and legitimation, are usually compatible and mutually supportive in fostering the same situational logic of competition as that emanating from the market. Capitalism is inherently competitive (see Douglas Porpora's chapter in this volume); it generates winners and losers and is a zero-sum system among producers and among consumers. Thus a landlord has degrees of freedom about how fairly he will treat his tenants, yet he is constrained to extract enough rent to cover maintenance and leave a profit or he will cease to be a landlord. Similarly, tenants have good reason to press for improvements to the property but also not to make demands that would lead to the termination of their leases. Competition is about doing the best for oneself (and one's own) *against others*. A disregard for effects on others is in-built, which is all the easier when those others do not have to be confronted face to face but remain anonymous and distant.

Agent's Personal Powers: Their Social and Moral Implications

This section turns from the ontological question of how social structures exert causal impact in people's lives (and thereby play a role in sustaining harms and unjust relationships) to the sociological question of who takes responsibility for the harm done.

Human agents have their own very different kinds of properties and powers: commitments, intentionality, and evaluation. All of these depend on reflexivity, which is defined as "the regular exercise of the mental ability, shared by all normal people, to consider themselves in relation to their (social) contexts and vice versa."[12] All constraints, enablements, and sources of motivation, whether structural or cultural, work by being mediated through agents. Structures are only influential *through social subjects,* since a constraint requires someone to constrain and an enablement needs someone to enable. If no agent ever conceived a project—a course of action with an intelligible goal—then no agent could ever be constrained or enabled. But of course, given our biological constitution and our life in society, we quite naturally conceive of courses of action— from thinking about what to eat today to what employment to seek in the future. Since the response of the agent to a constraint (or enablement) is a matter of reflexive deliberation, it can take very different forms: from compliance, to evasion and strategic action, to subversion. It is because of reflexive deliberations that a complete uniformity of response on behalf of every agent who encounters the same constraint or the same enablement is rarely, if ever, found.

Therefore, it is essential to distinguish between the objective existence of structural or cultural properties and the exercise of their causal powers, since the realization of their causal powers requires them to be activated by agents. Hence, the efficacy of any social emergent property is at the mercy of the agents' reflexive activity (although actors may be oblivious or mistaken about many aspects of sociocultural organization and will pay an objective price for such epistemological shortcomings). Outcomes vary enormously with agents' creativity in dreaming up new responses, even to situations that may have occurred many times before. Ultimately, the precise outcome varies with agents' personal concerns and degrees of commitment, as well as with the costs (in various currencies) that different agents are willing to pay to see their projects through in the face of structural obstacles and cultural hindrances.

Equally, they vary with agents' readiness to avail themselves of enablements. Therefore, the examination of the subjectivity and reflexive variability of agents becomes even more important in order to understand differences of response under the same conditions, such as within the market and the legitimacy claimed for it.

People deliberate about their relationship with their social "context," although most would speak in terms of "the situation" in which they find themselves. Whatever the vocabulary used, it is the process through which reasons become causes of the actions adopted by social subjects. Agents' reflexive decisions are appropriate matters for moral consideration. It is through agents' subjective internal deliberations—"internal conversations"—that those objective structural factors have their (conditional) influence on social action.[13] Although reflexivity is indispensable to any social system, it does not follow that its properties and powers or its mode of influence remain unchanging. On the contrary, reflexivity has a long history, and it has a future of increasing social importance, as will be seen below.

All of these arguments are illustrated in the dominant modes of reflexivity that have been empirically distinguished in my trilogy of books about reflexivity.[14] Each mode of reflexivity is a particular way of deliberating about oneself in in relation to one's social context. The different modes are fundamentally the outcomes of two elements. On the one hand there are the personal "concerns" that subjects develop, namely, their priorities—what they care about and what matters to them most. On the other hand, they also develop an orientation toward their social settings, depending on whether these satisfied their concerns, how they selectively evaluated their natal context, whether they sought a radical change in their social circumstances, or if they found themselves disoriented when attempting to put the two together. The four dominant modes of reflexivity practiced are not reducible to psychological "personality types," and the dominant mode for any one person might change.[15]

- Communicative reflexivity: Internal conversations need to be confirmed and completed by others before they lead to action.
- Autonomous reflexivity: Internal conversations are self-contained, leading direction to action.
- Meta-reflexivity: Internal conversations critically evaluate previous inner dialogues and are critical about effective action in society.
- Fractured reflexivity: Internal conversations cannot lead to purposeful courses of action but only intensify personal distress and disorientation.

These distinct orientations mediate subjects' encounters with structure and cultural constraints, enablements, and sources of motivation. Their alignment to them varies with the mode of reflexivity practiced most frequently (for we all use each of the modes some of the time). The four combinations of "concern + context," which were found to be closely related to the type and quality of subjects' relationships in their families, represented very distinctive stances toward the social order. These four "stances" entailed different moral outlooks: judgments about what was worthy of pursuit within the social order and practical reasoning about what should be done to live out personal commitments.

The point of introducing these modes and their associated stances is that they also represent different moral outlooks on the social order. The moral values to which subjects subscribed were frequently adopted from external sources (school, media, movements) in self-conscious resistance to the moral tenor of their family and natal environment. Socialization is no longer a matter of passive internalization, if it ever was. These distinctive moral outlooks are important because they are the prisms through which agents view the social structures that they encounter. Each ethical stance influences which elements of the contemporary social system are selectively supported, rejected, or critiqued by subjects—sometimes overtly, but always by the actions they take and by those on which they turn their backs.

"Communicative reflexives" live out a moral communitarianism. Their concerns are firmly located in interpersonal relations (family and friendship), and their aim is effectively to replicate their natal context within their own generation. Communicative reflexives are "investors in people," and the expression of their concerns implies deep embedding in a localized social context. The very practice of their mode of reflexivity—the way they think of themselves in relation to their social context—depends on a secure relational anchorage. Through sharing reference points, experiences, and biography, "similars and familiars" can become interlocutors, capable of completing and complementing the person's own reflexive deliberations. Communicative reflexives take a stance of evasion toward constraints and enablements, neither confronting the former nor taking advantage of the latter. Thus, in the subjects studied, objective enablements to social advancement were shunned and their associated motivation discounted in favor of fostering a familial life world. Correspondingly, their most active common denominator of political action was to vote in general elections.

"Autonomous reflexives" are moral libertarians, endorsing individualism in politics and the free market in economics and social policy. They come from families where divorce, separation, and negative relations predominated. Independence has largely been enforced on them when growing up, and these subjects vested their concerns in various types of performative achievement—sporting, mechanical, artistic—but eventually looked toward work and employment for their expression. They are individualists who work hard, cogitating about their tasks and how to overcome the problems they present, thus contributing considerable "surplus value" to the organizations employing them. They welcome responsibility and assuming control, and often prefer the freedom of self-employment. These are neither team players nor traditionalists but competitive individualists. In the economy, autonomous reflexives contribute to economic development, in the polity to neoliberalism, and in the community they operate as minimalistic citizens, who eschew involvement and prefer to "pay as they go" for whatever facilities they use. Since little ethical value is attached to human relations, interactions with others tend to be subject to administrative regulation or commodification, and human value is often reduced to exchange value.

"Meta-reflexives" are the most committed to pursuing cultural and moral ideals that cannot be accommodated by the current socioeconomic structure. They regard the amalgam of "lib/lab" politics—the narrow options offered by the dominant liberal and labor parties in so many industrialized nations today—as poverty-stricken. They refuse political centrism's trade-off between justice and efficiency, repudiating the governments' favored executive instrument, the performance indicator. To them, this dehumanizes people and robs tasks of their intrinsic worth. They counterpose an ideal in which social integration and economic development are reciprocally related rather than mutually compromised. Common ethical themes and practices are subsidiarity, cooperative organization, voluntary association, community service, intergenerational solidarity, social inclusiveness, and other constituents of a robust civil society and civil economy.

Their ideals are ones that cannot be accommodated by the current socioeconomic structure. Their social stance is subversive, meaning that they resist constraints and enablements by walking away, accepting occupational volatility, displaying indifference toward social mobility, and thus paying the price for their social critique. They animate an ethical ideal of how the social order could be otherwise, thus restocking the pool of salient social values and exposing the aridity of current politico-economic compromises. Although the practices of individual agents are not intentionally geared toward producing societal effects, there are important aggregate consequences that derive from exercising their personal reflexive powers that have cumulative significance.

"Fractured reflexives" are those fundamentally disoriented by the tensions and contradictions of their social context. For them, the internal conversation serves only to intensify personal distress and disorientation because their reflexive deliberations go round in circles without enabling them to define any purposive courses of action to lead out of their difficulties.[16] The resulting moral passivity of fractured reflexivity is examined later.

Communicative and autonomous reflexives exert opposing influences. Since the ultimate concerns of communicative reflexives are vested in interpersonal relations (family and friendship), their main effect is to strengthen social integration. Because the ultimate concerns of autonomous reflexives are vested in work and employment, their main effect is to increase economic productivity, performance, and development. Communicative reflexives foster social integration at the expense of economic and financial growth.[17] Autonomous reflexives intensify such growth at the cost of reducing social integration. Communicative and autonomous do not share moral values and are in fact associated respectively with two mutually hostile sets of values: collectivism and individualism.[18]

Fundamentally, the communicative reflexives and the autonomous reflexives pull society in two different directions. Because the aggregate effect of the meta-reflexives constitutes a critique of both tendencies, there is no sense in which society at the start of the new millennium is underwritten by shared values.[19]

Reflexivity in the New Millennium

In recent decades, a synergy has developed between the structural and cultural domain that was responsible for reflexivity becoming imperative for all.[20] The key structural dynamic was the rise of multinational enterprises and finance markets, whose global interests were epitomized in the abandonment of foreign exchange regulations in 1980. The central cultural dynamic was the invention of the World Wide Web in the same decade, which progressively severed most of the links between intellectual property and its geolocal ownership.

Increasing connectivity and later globalization were among the consequences of this growing synergy from World War I onward. Synergy works by positive feedback, increasing change, and the rate of change. It results in social transformation, as opposed to the stability generated by negative feedback, which restores structure (or culture) to the status quo ante.[21] In other words, globalization is an effect of this synergy and not a primary cause of anything.

A major consequence was that the state of *the social* ceased to be of concern to the market at the national level. In the developed world, the postwar formula of "social democracy and the welfare state"—which served to put the "neo" into capitalism—meant that economic success depended on national social integration.[22] But the new synergy burst national bounds before the end of the twentieth century. The leading and increasingly intertwined economic and informational organizations—at the transnational and eventually the global level—no longer had such a single national population on which they depended for recruitment, retention, legitimation, or performance. Instead, increasing synergy proffered opportunity, not merely opportunity narrowly understood as positions or openings in proliferating transnational enterprises or information services, but the open invitation to join in the process of stimulating yet further innovations.

This synergy increased from the 1980s onward, multiplying the variety of alternatives available, especially in terms of work and employment. It also burdened people with exercising their personal reflexivity more inten-sively in order to make choices in uncharted territory. The previous guide-lines, functioning in a slowly changing context, were rapidly becoming outdated. The occupational pattern of sons following their fathers or peers joining their mates was shattering. In place of such guidance, subjects were increasingly thrown back upon their own personal concerns as the only compass to guide action. This is the "reflexive imperative."

Fast and penetrating change is fundamentally destructive of a stable context. It destroys the ways of life continuous from the past and defies the reestablishment of new continuities on the basis of residence, com-munity, occupation, religion, or kinship, which were frequently the basis for stability in modernity's past. For the majority in developed nations, the name of the new game is "transferable skills" and "serial retraining" because "human resource development" has become a lifelong enterprise. In this morphing context, there are no jobs for life but only a succession of changing posts, change of postings, and intercontinental changes of addresses.

For the first time, the situational logic of opportunity (to make what one will of new knowledge and new applications as opposed to competing over old ones) is starting to predominate at both corporate and individual levels. The tendency for variety to spawn more variety has consequences for newly available positions that take generic names—systems analysis, finance management, informatics or logistics—whose common denomi-nator is synergy. All of this requires intense reflexive activity on the part of the subject; he or she has no alternative but to engage in it because the old routine guidelines are no longer applicable and new ones can-not be forged because rapid social change is inhospitable to any form of routinization.[23]

When reflexivity has to be exercised against a shifting horizon, in novel situations where routine no longer recommends a particular course of action and socialization does not supply a dispositional orientation,[24] indi-viduals must become both more self-critical and more socially evaluative, which are the hallmarks of meta-reflexivity. The prime task of internal conversation[25] is for subjects to design courses of action that will enable them to realize what they care about most and to establish a satisfying and sustainable *modus vivendi*, enabling them to thrive within the social order. In short, agents' commitments become their compass for making their way through their fast-changing social environment. This can be summa-rized as the need to complete the sequence shown in Figure 2.1.[26]

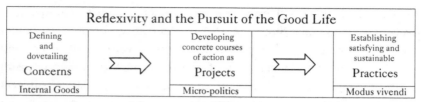

FIGURE 2.1 Reflexivity and the Pursuit of the Good Life

Under modernity, completing this sequence was at the mercy of contingency and human fallibility, but the way of life sought could still be envisaged clearly. Economic employments were relatively durable (jobs for life), and the prospects offered were fairly predictable, as were the routes toward them (e.g., investing in private education). In all institutional areas, the situational logic of competition, rooted in capitalism, represented clear sociocultural guidelines.

However, with increasing synergy, the situational logic of opportunity placed a premium on innovative action; not only can there be no guidelines about how to innovate but also, logically, there can be no knowing where an innovation will lead. In other words, the sequence becomes much more difficult to complete and requires frequent revisions and reformulations, as contexts continue to change. Not only do more and more subjects have to monitor themselves and their shifting social contexts to establish a livable relation between them, but they must also do so repeatedly. This means that their reflexivity is continually on call, critically evaluating their present *modus vivendi* and evaluating opportunities for superseding or sustaining it. To the contingencies of life in an open system has to be added the fact that the social system itself has become quintessentially transformatory. As a result, the incidence of fractured reflexivity is expected to rise, especially in the light of reduced social integration.

Changes in Reflexivity and Outlooks on Moral Responsibility

It appears[27] that the landscape with which the baby boomers grew-up was the last in which the modern social order presented autonomous reflexivity in clear ascendancy (because of its enduring association with capitalism). Communicative reflexivity is quietly but slowly losing ground, and meta-reflexivity, still a minority practice, is largely confined to idealist, both religious and secular. The proportions between them are changing, and, with this, their aggregate macroscopic social consequences are undergoing a parallel transformation.

In this last section, I attempt to track the consequences of these changing proportions for taking up moral responsibility, especially toward distant others. Communicative reflexivity appears to be in decline and autonomous reflexivity to be stable, while both meta-reflexivity and the various kinds of fractured reflexivity are anticipated to be on the increase. Were these expectations found to be broadly correct, the final question I want to raise is whether or not this holds out any hopes for the development of an integrated civil society and civil economy.

The Moral Consequences of Declining Communicative Reflexivity

The demise of the communicative reflexives seems to be irreversible. The speed and penetration of change in the advanced parts of the world is fundamentally destructive of the "contextual continuity," the decline of the community upon which communicative reflexivity depends. If their progressive demise is indeed the case, then normativity is fast losing its social anchorage in a group whose notions of rectitude once stood as a firm reminder to others. The "decencies" for which the communicative collectivity used to provide aggregate support—loyalty, respectability, mutual assistance, responsibility—are losing their strongest protagonists and exemplars and, most important, so has the moral practice of "living within one's means," in which older communicatives took pride, and so too the reliance on the family, rather than credit agencies, for financial support or assistance.

The structural bastion of the communicative reflexives was the traditional family, but those who still seek to replicate their natal backgrounds have become a small minority. Moreover, they find replication difficult, in large part because their partners often do not share the same background but also because job location draws them away from it. One result is the seemingly enhanced importance of friendship networks for young people. Yet friendship is often perceived as a precarious effort and cannot be taken for granted in the way that the family once was. They resort to mobile phones, socially interactive websites, and those sad Facebook entries addressed to "my 1,000 friends" but, in fact, to one in particular. Others are symptomatic of the loss of social integration spelt by the diminution in the conditions necessary for communicative reflexivity.

(Actually, the spread of these devices is probably more damaging to other modes of reflexivity, given the solitude and loss of silence they entail.) Communicative reflexives make generous responses (donations) in cases of natural disaster of humanitarian crisis but take no sustained responsibility for the plight of distant others.

The Moral Passivity of Fractured Reflexives

Every society includes some (unfixed) portion of fractured subjects who become disoriented in encountering the contingent adversities of life in an open system. Where societies differ is not only in the incidence of fracturing of this kind but also in society's relational capacities to provide support rather than neglect for these people. Of even greater concern in the downward plunge in social solidarity is the fact that "underdeveloped" reflexivity, which is expressive rather than deliberative, typically accounts for most of the fracturing among the young cohort.

The subjects in this study appeared to be products of a lifelong "relational deficit," becoming "loners" whose inclinations toward their own particular "concerns" did not connect up with a network capable of nurturing them into commitments. They never became full-fledged members of any normative group, because even if they were on the periphery of several, they formed insufficiently close relational bonds to experience the relational goods deriving from engagement that encourage resilient dedication to a group or "cause." Instead, they retreated into *événementalisme*, where responses to (what are perceived as) discrete situations are guided by "gut feelings" and justified by selective perception of their consequences. This condemns them to the agential and moral passivity of "presentism," where each event is tackled in isolation from events that precede and follow it. In these people, gut feelings may prompt moral outrage about child labor and sweatshops, but this doesn't develop into sustained and organized protest action.

Autonomous Reflexivity: Corporate Social Responsibility or Moral Complicity?

If autonomous reflexivity remains proportionately stable in the immediate future, does this mean it will counteract any expectation about the transformation of modernity? These agents compete for positions in finance capitalism, in the multinationals, in corporate life in general and now have expanded outlets in the public services, since these have often became run on lines of managerial performance. Is there any question mark hanging over their future role in perpetuating the situational logic of competition, foundational to modernity's institutions with their winners and losers? Since this logic is fundamentally socially divisive, should these subjects not automatically be seen as the prime agents who will foster future social division? One recent development could hold promise.

Young autonomous subjects, unlike older autonomous reflexives, claim to uphold a new "spirit of social enterprise." If this is not dismissed as ideological "bad faith" on their part, we should not slip into a facile nominalism that assumes them to be the same group as their employers and predecessors simply because they occupy many of the same posts, reap many similar advantages, and appear to be seeking the same objective material rewards. This would be to disregard the social, cultural, and structural crises that have confronted modernity's main enterprise during young subjects' lifetimes—the countermovements and collective critiques that have bombarded capitalism in the past two decades.

Until the 1990s, the main ideological challenge to liberal economics came from different parts of the socialist spectrum and was defused by the political incorporation of unionism and the expansion of welfarism. The varied oppositional groupings developing from the late 1980s onward were dealt with in similar fashion.[28] This is not the place to attempt even a rough sketch of these intricate forms of protest and ideological critique. The only point I want to make here is that while capitalist enterprise and liberal interests would initially make the most minimalist concessions to their critics and opponents, their survival compelled them toward more "generous" forms of response throughout Europe.

The point is not about good faith or bad but concerns corporate practice and its practitioners.[29] Very quickly "personnel departments" turned into "human resources," taking "human bonding" exercises into schools and melding them with heroic-sounding survivalist weekends, living on lichen and camaraderie; business schools spawned "business ethics" curricula; multinational accounting firms adopted schools for the underprivileged; global corporations paid for access to computers for street kids, and corporate charitable initiatives mushroomed. In short, corporate social responsibility took its place on capitalism's agenda.

In part, the autonomous reflexives' new "spirit of social enterprise" arose from the very firms they were inclined to join, as young recruits took the new corporate rhetoric in good faith. An equally important cause was the arguments of the social movements that had increased in social salience throughout their schooldays. Although such movements didn't make converts from among the autonomous reflexives, they did normalize the lowest common denominator of their charters: antiracism, a light green tint, and ubiquitous concern for "the most vulnerable."[30] In other words, a positive feedback loop had developed here too, with consequences for change. In sum, the legitimate expression of autonomous reflexivity is now significantly different from its postwar versions. Yet does this shift make a real difference to social integration? Is it a shift in an increasingly divided social order that is sufficient to induce concern for distant others harmed in global capitalism?

Structurally, the recent economic crisis lays bare the vacuity of talk about "liquid society" made up of shapeless, evanescent, and, above all, unstructured flows. It should have been a painful lesson about the interlocking financial structures of late modernity had it not been deflected into the relative trivialities of bankers' bonuses. Now that Europe is scrambling to return to "business as usual," evidence points to the poorer sectors bearing the brunt of politico-economic retrenchment.

Nevertheless, as time passes, young business recruits will gain promotion and the firm itself will become an increasingly interesting place of division over the divisive and unbridled "logic of competition." The stability in the proportion of autonomous reflexives anticipated for the immediate future will serve to inject their spirit of social enterprise into corporate life, sandpapering away the rougher edges of the profit motive and bringing corporate social responsibility into the company rather than, as now, looking benignly on the voluntary extramural activities of employees. If so, the newly recruited autonomous subjects will be predisposed to make some incremental contribution, offsetting the prospects of a divided social order. But for now, those distant others harmed by markets occupy the lowest place on the agenda of corporate social responsibility.

Meta-Reflexives and Moral Vision

More important, however, than civilized corporatism is the effect that increasingly rapid social change will have on already outdated notions of vested material interests—objective ones, of course, remain. Vested interests have such a weight and length of history as hierarchical, functional, and stratified givens that it takes a reflexive mental shake—even from academics—to recognize that we ourselves no longer have them. In short, we now live by relational and not positional, let alone material, goods. We have a "cause," or, as Weber rightly called it, a "vocation." Yet most of us are not utopians. What is encouraging is that the young meta-reflexives understand that this kind of life is possible and preferable to modernity's zero-sum game plan. They are personally unmoved by class, status, and power because their aim is "to make a difference." As critics of market and state, they are protagonists of civil society who manifest a distinct predilection for work in the Third Sector, regardless of its rewards or lack of them. Thus, practitioners of meta-reflexivity show a greater willingness to consider, if not to opt for, employment in the voluntary sector. However, an intrinsic part of national political centrism is an increased reliance on the voluntary sector to reinforce both market and state.

Meta-reflexives have already turned their backs on these two old and ailing leviathans of modernity. They reject the confines while valuing the benefits of "friends and family." They recognize that it is only in between the macro and the micro, with like-minded others, that they can be both generators and beneficiaries of the relational goods they hold worthwhile: solidarity in pursuit of a common cause, multifaceted friendship, meaning and purpose in daily life, and making a communal contribution that exceeds their aggregate exertions. Another way of putting this is that they use the situational logic of opportunity to discover congenial "corporate agents" with whom they can live and work. Meta-reflexives furnish the overseas volunteers who go (if only temporally) to promote educational, medical, and sustainability projects. Without yet being able to undermine corporate malpractice, they do demonstrate the viability of alternatives.

Conclusion

The central concern of this volume is to specify the causal role of social agents (singular or plural) in the creation and sustaining of markets and their consequent moral responsibility for what they have contributed to making and maintaining. Even though social movements and collective action are usually and rightly given most credit for the instigation of significant social change, they have to recruit members and activists who are positively disposed toward them.

My argument had two parts. The first described how markets—like all social structures—have causal efficacy through restrictions, enablements, and incentives that shape the contexts in which market participants find themselves. These make a difference only in the actions of agents (both individuals and groups) who take decisions in light of those deeply conditioned contexts. The second part of the argument focused on reflexivity, that ongoing reflection by persons about their relationship to the contexts in which they live. Personal commitments and the dominant mode of reflexivity practiced by subjects canalize who will be drawn toward them and toward working in different social institutions. This explanation is significantly different from another that stresses the cumulative impact of virtuous *individuals*—the view that all we really need is more virtuous market actors. Ironically, that other argument pits individual virtue against the individualism inherent in the capitalist markets of the late twentieth century, overlooking the causal effects of social structures and the reflexive stances people take in response to them.

In the new millennium, the struggle between the autonomous reflexives and the meta-reflexives, with their distinctive commitments and moral values, will shape the form of structural change to take place. Of course, the result will not likely be what either of these groupings wants. This is precisely what keeps change going in the social order: the fact that agents continue to counterpose cultural values and structural changes that are mutually antipathetic.

That is the situation at the moment. Global finance capitalism, whose structure becomes (temporarily) open to serious scrutiny only during economic crisis, will fight on under its banner of "there is no alternative," but it will also adopt an increasingly civilized face. This will spell growing internal tensions within corporations, particularly between those at the extremes: recruits with a genuine spirit of social enterprise and the criminal entrepreneurs who now sit round boardroom tables, when they do not simply own the enterprise. It will continue to be opposed by variants of the Third Sector, but the latter is vulnerable to both colonization (take over by the market) and to becoming counter-organizations (modeled on their market opponents).

"Colonization"[31] by the market is indisputable. Many activities that were successfully pioneered by voluntary initiative have been turned into business ventures, floated on the stock market (as in chains of Care

Homes). Similarly, "green" and "organic" have been profitably assimilated into marketing strategies. Attempts to create a "cyber commons" through Peer2Peer exchanges were promptly appropriated by *Wikinomics*[32] as a method for harvesting free technical solutions under what was euphemistically termed "dispersed production." The trick consists in taking over voluntary innovations and turning them into for-profit firms.

Counter-organizations perform the trick the other way round. Charities become charitable enterprises, as was already presaged several decades ago by the commercialized "plate dinner," where the self-promotional opportunity to have one's picture taken with some famous person displaced free giving as a motive. More recently, employing commercial fundraisers has become standard (competitive) practice of nonprofits, as has media promotion, lobbyists, and celebrity representation.

This fundamental antinomy between the for-profit and not-for-profit sectors cannot be eliminated by attempts to blur the different structural contexts in which they thrive. It cannot be done by putting corporate social responsibility inside the for-profit enterprise or business ethics into management schools. The point is that multinationals remain competitive and business schools reflect competition between universities, which are now financialized enterprises whose best seller is the MBA. The situational logics of competition and of opportunity remain antipathetic. Those who evade this scene—the shrinking ranks of communicatives reflexives— also withdraw from their old role of producing the social cement. As social integration continues to decline, represented by the growing number of "expressive reflexives", these constitute an undirected but potentially disruptive force.

Perhaps the best that can be expected in the immediate future will be living with gradualism and even encouraging it. Terms and practices such as corporate social responsibility and social enterprise have been placed on the agenda of global capitalism, and for-profit enterprises are aware they will be held to account. The Third Sector—voluntary or social-private—is growing and diversifying, and if it is subject to colonization and regulation, it can then exert some influence from within and respond with further new initiatives from without. Maybe we should look at it as the research and development agency for a future civil society and civil economy, whose interim task is to make the "logic of the gift" less abnormal within economic activity.

However, moral responsibility for the poorest in the market seems likely to be confined to the most proximate and most visible poor, where offering a "better deal" can, with suitable media exposure, even become a new form of market competition. The word "fairness" need never be used. It seems probable that concern for harms caused to distant others will remain a moral charge for which only the voluntary associations *sans frontières* will assume responsibility.

NOTES

1. For a detailed discussion of the three types of conflationist theory, see Margaret S. Archer, *Culture and Agency: The Place of Culture in Social Theory* (Cambridge, UK: Cambridge University Press, 1988), chapters 2–4, pp. 25–100. Determinist theories are instances of what I have called "downward conflation" in social theory, because what agents do is attributed to powers working on them from "above." The second type of theory listed represents "central conflation" and the third, "upward conflation."

2. Anthony Giddens, *Central Problems in Social Theory* (London: Macmillan, 1979), 69.

3. Frequently, these ontological differences attract a different moral vocabulary: "Hierarchy" in an organization may be deemed "undesirable"; someone being "understanding" may be considered to be "good," although the semantics can cross over—as in "structural sin."

4. This framework is spelled out in Margaret S. Archer, *Realist Social Theory: The Morphogenetic Approach* (Cambridge, UK: Cambridge University Press, 1995), 165–194.

5. Margaret S. Archer and Dave Elder-Vass, "Cultural System or Norm Circles? An Exchange," *European Journal of Social Theory*, 15 (2011):1–23.

6. Douglas V. Porpora, "Four Concepts of Social Structure," *Journal for the Theory of Social Behaviour* 19.2 (1989): 195–212.

7. Andrew Sayer, *Method in Social Science: A Realist Approach* (London: Routledge, 1992), 92–93.

8. Stefano Zamagni, "Reciprocity, Civil Economy, Common Good," in M. S. Archer and P. Donati (eds.), *Pursuing the Common Good: How Solidarity and Subsidiarity Can Work Together* (Vatican City: Pontifical Academy of Social Sciences, 2008), 467–502.

9. Porpora, "Four Concepts of Social Structure," 208.

10. Sally Tomlinson, *Educational Subnormality—A Study of Decision Making* (London: Routledge and Kegan Paul, 1981). The apparent reason for this was an interested preference for having undisrupted classrooms in mainstream schools rather than assuming any responsibility for harms done to those perceived as culturally distant others (who were usually British born).

11. See Martin Hollis, *The Cunning of Reason* (Cambridge, UK: Cambridge University Press, 1988), and Margaret S. Archer and Jonathan Q. Tritter, (eds.), *Rational Choice Theory: Resisting Colonization* (London: Routledge, 2000).

12. Margaret S. Archer, *Making Our Way Through the World: Human Reflexivity and Social Mobility* (Cambridge, UK: Cambridge University Press, 2007), 4.

13. Margaret S. Archer, *Structure, Agency and the Internal Conversation* (Cambridge, UK: Cambridge University Press, 2004), ch. 4. However, the "internal conversation" was first conceptualized by the great American pragmatists, especially Peirce and Mead.

14. Archer, *Structure, Agency and the Internal Conversation; Making Our Way Through the World; The Reflexive Imperative in Late Modernity* (Cambridge, UK: Cambridge University Press, 2012).

15. In Archer, *Making Our Way Through the World*, the following dominant modes of reflexivity were estimated, using the Internal Conversation Indicator (ICONI) for the small, stratified sample of Coventry inhabitants: Communicative Reflexives = 21%, Autonomous Reflexives = 27%, Meta-Reflexives = 23%, and Fractured Reflexives = 22% (figures rounded up), 335.

16. See Archer, *Structure, Agency and the Internal Conversation*, ch. 9: "Fractured Reflexives."

17. To appreciate the consequences for social stability and change of the actions taken by the different kinds of reflexives, use will be made of the distinction between "social integration" (the orderly or conflictual relations between members of society) and "system integration" (the orderly or conflictual relations between society's constitutive institutions). David Lockwood, "Social Integration and System Integration" in G. K. Zollschan and W. Hirsch (eds.), *Explorations in Social Change* (Boston: Houghton Mifflin, 1964).

18. As Donati has emphasized, the compromise between them is the hallmark of "lib/lab" politics and policy. Pierpaolo Donati, *Teoria Relazionale della Società* (Milan: Franco Angeli, 1996), ch. 8.

19. "Fractured reflexives," who may later recover, are temporarily too self-preoccupied to make any systematic contribution to social change or stability.

20. Archer, *The Reflexive Imperative*.

21. See Walter Buckley, *Sociology and Modern Systems Theory* (Englewood Cliffs, NJ: Prentice-Hall, 1967).

22. This refers to the views of their controllers and proximate beneficiaries.

23. Margaret S. Archer, "Routine, Reflexivity, and Realism," *Sociological Theory* 28.3 (2010): 272–303.

24. Archer, *The Reflexive Imperative*, ch. 3, deals with the need to revise theories of socialization.

25. This is from the point of view of social theory. Subjects themselves may see the "task" of their internal conversation in whatever terms they please, including not having a "task" at all. Nevertheless, all of those interviewed agreed that some of their internal conversation was devoted to the deliberations under discussion.

26. See Archer, *Making Our Way Through the World*, 87–90. For a more extensive discussion, see Archer, *Being Human: The Problem of Agency* (Cambridge, UK: Cambridge University Press, 2000), ch. 7.

27. From interviews with young subjects, followed up over their three years as undergraduates, which form the basis of Archer, *The Reflexive Imperative*.

28. Feminism could initially be addressed by "tokenism" but not to eliminative exclusion with more than half of women now working; likewise the Greens, as ongoing consumers, received minor concessions such as restrictions on the use of plastic bags; similarly the advocacy of more family-friendly policies was met at least gesturally since all workers had families.

29. Christine Hemingway shows how variable this was among corporate executives, although only a tiny minority overtly challenged it. "The Conditions and Character Traits of Corporate Social Entrepreneurship: Insights From a UK-Based Multi-National Corporation," paper presented at the 23rd European Business Ethics Network Annual Conference, University of Trento, Italy, 2010. See also C. A. Hemingway, *Corporate Social Entrepreneurship: Integrity Within, Business, Value Creation, and Society* (Cambridge, UK: Cambridge University Press, 2013).

30. The new mantra about "vulnerability" focuses attention on a minority who evoke sympathy but also distracts attention from the deteriorating socioeconomic circumstances of the bulk of the population.

31. J. Habermas, *The Theory of Communicative Action* (Cambridge, UK: Polity Press, 1989).

32. Don Tapscott and Anthony Williams, *Wikinomics: How Mass Collaboration Changes Everything* (London: Atlantic Books, 2008).

REFERENCES

Archer, Margaret S. *Culture and Agency: The Place of Culture in Social Theory.* Cambridge, UK: Cambridge University Press, 1988.

——. *Realist Social Theory: The Morphogenetic Approach.* Cambridge, UK: Cambridge University Press, 1995.

——. *Structure, Agency and the Internal Conversation.* Cambridge, UK: Cambridge University Press, 2004.

——. *Making our Way Through the World: Human Reflexivity and Social Mobility.* Cambridge, UK: Cambridge University Press, 2007.

——. "Routine, Reflexivity, and Realism." *Sociological Theory* 28.3 (2010): 272–303.

——. *The Reflexive Imperative in Late Modernity.* Cambridge, UK: Cambridge University Press, 2012.

——, and Dave Elder-Vass. "Cultural System or Norm Circles? An Exchange." *European Journal of Social Theory*, 15 (2011):1–23.

———, and Jonathan Q. Tritter (eds.). *Rational Choice Theory: Resisting Colonization*. London: Routledge, 2000.

Buckley, Walter. *Sociology and Modern Systems Theory*. Englewood Cliffs, NJ: Prentice-Hall, 1967.

Donati, Pierpaolo. *Teoria Relazionale della*. Milan: Franco Angeli, 1996.

Giddens, Anthony. *Central Problems in Social Theory*. London: Macmillan, 1979.

Habermas, J. *The Theory of Communicative Action*. Cambridge, UK: Polity Press, 1989.

Hemingway, C. A. "The Conditions and Character Traits of Corporate Social Entrepreneurship: Insights from a UK-Based Multi-National Corporation." Paper presented at the 23rd European Business Ethics Network Annual Conference, University of Trento, Italy, 2010.

———. *Corporate Social Entrepreneurship: Integrity Within*. Business, Value Creation, and Society. Cambridge, UK: Cambridge University Press, 2013.

Hollis, Martin. *The Cunning of Reason*. Cambridge, UK: Cambridge University Press, 1988.

Lockwood, David. "Social Integration and System Integration." In G. K. Zollschan and W. Hirsch (eds.), *Explorations in Social Change*. Boston: Houghton Mifflin, 1964, 244–57.

Porpora, Douglas V. "Four Concepts of Social Structure." *Journal for the Theory of Social Behaviour*, 19.2 (1989): 195–212.

Sayer, Andrew. *Method in Social Science: A Realist Approach*. London: Routledge, 1992.

Tapscott, Don, and Anthony Williams. *Wikinomics: How Mass Collaboration Changes Everything*. London: Atlantic Books, 2008.

Tomlinson, Sally. *Educational Subnormality—A Study of Decision Making*. London: Routledge and Kegan Paul, 1981.

Zamagni, Stefano. "Reciprocity, Civil Economy, Common Good." In M. S. Archer and P. Donati (eds.), *Pursuing the Common Good: How Solidarity and Subsidiarity Can Work Together Pontifical Academy of Social Sciences*. Vatican City: Vatican City Press, 2008, 467–502.

3

The Morality of Action, Reflexivity, and the Relational Subject

Pierpaolo Donati

THE CENTRAL QUESTION of this volume asks, "Who is responsible for the harm that market agents[1] bring to bear on distant others in an impersonal and unintentional way?" The "others" can be single individuals, vast social groups, and even entire populations.

Moral responsibility can be direct or indirect. It seems relatively easy to identify direct moral responsibility when, for example, a financial trader directly sells tainted financial products without informing clients of the elevated risk of loss, or when the owner of a sweatshop exploits female workers, violating basic human rights. In these cases, *ego* inflicts direct harm on *alter*, who is nearby.

But what can we say when the economic action is done with the intention of harming no one yet causes negative effects? Take the example of the decision to move investments in order to create work and wealth in one location when this decision involuntarily causes unemployment and poverty in other locations.

Traditional moral theory usually applies the principle of *double effect*. As commonly formulated, this principle establishes that it is possible to legitimately allow or tolerate a bad effect that comes about through an act of choice if four conditions are met: (1) the action in itself, apart from the harm caused, is good or at least indifferent; (2) the good effect of the action is what the agent directly intends, the bad effect being unintended; (3) the good effect must not be obtained by means of the bad effect; and (4) the path must be the only one possible or, in any case, there must be a proportionately grave reason to let the negative effect happen.[2] If these criteria are met, the individually honest investor can feel at ease. But is this really how things are?

The moral criterion of the principle of double effect presupposes a "linear" society where the intentionality and causality of social action can be established with certainty. However, in a society in which interactions and relations are increasing out of all proportion, with marked circularities and long causal chains, this principle goes haywire.

A society in the process of globalization increases the frequency of cases in which the morality of action is problematic because action has a multiplicity of effects that, for the most part, are not grasped by the individual subject of the action.[3] The reason for this resides in the fact that the complexity of society is increasing significantly; the production of effects that are the outcome of complex social networks is increasing.

There was a time when people wondered whether the moral responsibility for poverty should be attributed to the fact that the poor are lazy, incapable, or maladapted or, instead, to certain economic and social structures. Put in these terms, the question today appears naïve and simplistic. The social sciences have demonstrated that a reciprocal influence exists between structure and agency: Indeed, there is a real and complex interplay between these factors,[4] so that the problem of knowing who or what is responsible for the condition of poverty of particular individuals and social groups becomes one of knowing how the acting subjects and social structures influence one another. The social sciences have demonstrated for some time now that agents' (direct or indirect) moral responsibility can never be separated from the societal structures[5] within which they operate.

Who bears the moral responsibility for the fact that broad strata of society do not have equal life opportunities as compared to those who enjoy more favorable positions? It is easy to impute the cause of this social fact to societal structures that were produced in the past, for which no one in the present is responsible. Yet structures do not think or act by themselves. They are not imposed on the human mind, as, for example, Mary Douglas asserts. As the chapters by Margaret Archer and Douglas Porpora explain, the causality exerted by structures is always mediated by agency—they have no effects except when some person's plan of action is influenced by those structures. Nevertheless, structures do count for at least two broad orders of reasons: (a) They define the field of immediately accessible opportunities, and (b) they place constraints on agents in terms of incentives and sanctions.

This is our problem: Because the responsibility of agents is proportional to their freedom, we must investigate what freedom agents enjoy
vis à vis market structures, the exercise of which could prevent the harm
that their actions bring to bear on distant others as a result of the causal
mechanisms inherent in the market. Obviously, it is to be supposed that
the agents are not immoral or amoral subjects, in which case they would
have a direct moral responsibility.

Ostensibly, phenomena such as unemployment, poverty, and unde-
served inequalities in life are phenomena that individuals reproduce but for
which they cannot be imputed to have direct moral responsibility because
these are effects that do not depend on their intentions and individual wills.
But is it really thus? To whom or what should we attribute the moral responsibility for harm caused to distant others by actions that the agents carry out
in a licit and rational way from the point of view of the market?

The Prevailing Answers on Offer

The answers generally offered by economists consist in claiming that we
are dealing with the unintentional consequences of free market "laws."
Harm is conceptualized as a "side effect" or "negative externality." Harm
caused to distant others is held to be the inevitable consequence of freedom as the guiding value of the social institution of the market and, thus,
a contingency that is intrinsic to it. Redress can be thought of only ex post
once rock bottom has been reached.[6]

In democratic regimes, one expects that ex post consequences will be
tempered and countered by political systems. In effect, this is what the
master plan of Western nations says: On the one hand, it is necessary
stimulate interaction between forces of the free market and of competition, while, on the other hand, equality of opportunity must be guaranteed
to all citizens.[7] The state is assigned the task of redressing the free market's
failures by means of legislation that regulates economic transactions and
compensates those who are harmed through public welfare interventions
(in a collective and impersonal way). This is the societal arrangement that
I call "lib-lab," characteristic of the interaction of liberal and labor parties
in so many industrialized nations.[8]

The social sciences, however, point out that the market is a structure
(or system) endowed with an ontological reality[9] that, in a necessary and
intrinsic manner, unintentionally harms distant others in a variety of

ways, whether within single nations or in the relationship between developed and developing countries. These effects are called "unintentional structural effects," precisely to indicate that they depend on mechanisms that elude the power of individuals. When they deviate from the actors' intentions, they are called "perverse effects."[10]

Yet is it really true that these mechanisms are inevitable and the effects unexpected? If it is true that these structures do not depend on the power of individuals, can we assert, for this reason, that harm to distant others are not the moral responsibilities of the agents?

The prevailing answers on offer see responsibility falling to the structures that condition the agents. Western societies, inasmuch as they are founded on the compromise between individualistic liberalism and social-democratic holism (the lib-lab configuration), abundantly legitimate these answers. In these societies, the welfare state arose and grew precisely in order to render individuals' responsibility collective and impersonal. Liberal culture and socialist culture ended up converging as they relieved agents of their moral responsibility. How and why did this strange convergence come about?

My explanation is that, although they have different conceptions of the social, liberals (individualists) and socialists (holists) end up attributing the moral responsibility for the harm we are discussing to structures and not to agents, due to the fact that both standpoints lack a relational view of society.

On the one hand, the holists understand the social realm in a positivistic way, that is, as a structure that overshadows relations and interactions among human beings and conditions them as if by a physical or biological law. For this reason, they believe that single agents do not have moral responsibility—whether direct or indirect. The preferred solution is to consider agents' market action as free of moral responsibility. As to the harm inflicted, one can only exclaim: *c'est la vie!* This explanation is a form of downward conflation[11] from structures to agents: The structures are the cause and the agents have no say in the matter.

On the other hand, individualists understand the social realm as an arbitrary and conventional construction in the minds of individuals. Social causality, societal structures, and moral responsibility are considered to be merely contingent ideas[12] and, thus, always susceptible to modification. Harm to distant others is conceived as pure "possibility" that goes beyond the subjective responsibility of agents. The explanation for societal structures that generate harm (such as poverty, unemployment, unjust inequalities) takes on the form of an unintentional upward conflation. According to this view, the answer regarding the role of social structures becomes purely nominalistic. No single agent can assume responsibility for the final outcome.

Hard (holistic) conceptions and weak (individualistic) conceptions of the social structure both end up nullifying the moral responsibility of agents. Holists shift responsibility on to societal structures, defined as amoral. The theorists of individualism undermine the concept of structure; they eclipse social facts and thereby sabotage agents' moral responsibility for them. Both of these explanations are inadequate.

The Relational Perspective

Social structures have causal effects (such as harm to strangers), but that causality does not determine agents' behavior in a compulsive or nominalistic way. Social mechanisms are relational in the sense that they are made of social relations that are enacted by individuals and by the super-individual social subjects that individuals create. Societal structures are institutionalized social relations, which are the product of networks of relations.[13] For this reason, there exists a moral responsibility on the part of individual and collective subjects for outcomes, even for the unwanted outcomes produced in the processes of the transformation of social structures. However, in order to see what is at stake, it is necessary to understand what is meant by the fact that social structures are made *by* individuals but are not made *of* individuals, since they are *made of relations*, and it is here—in the relational dynamic—that the problem of moral responsibility is to be found.

For example, poverty, unemployment, and inequality brought about involuntarily are the product of networks of social relations; indeed, they are themselves social relations in which all actors, whether close at hand or distant, share some moral responsibility, in different forms and degrees.

The Causes of Impersonal Harm to Distant Others
Prevailing Explanations of Causality Imputable to Social Structures

Emergent structural effects can have various sociological and economic explanations. The comparison almost always takes place between holistic explanations and individualistic explanations, although for years now theories have been proposed that reject this alternative in favor of "relational" explanations.[14]

Holistic explanations predominate in the field of sociology.[15] The most widely held version explains and justifies structural effects as products of system requirements in the sense that unintentional effects fulfill certain functions that are necessary to the social system.[16] The paradigmatic theory in this regard is functionalism (in its various versions). In this view of things, there is no responsibility of single social actors, whether individual or collective. If the law of competition demands that the prices of merchandise be kept low, the individual entrepreneur has no choice but to pay lower wages and resort to lay-offs—and cannot worry about the consequences for workers' families.

Impersonal social harm brought to bear on distant others is seen as inevitable, and even morally indifferent, because it is essential to the good functioning of social systems. A certain number of unemployed and poor workers is considered to be an inevitable systemic fact for which market agents do not bear responsibility because the economic system functions only if there is the mechanism constituted by a certain quota of the workforce that is always available to enter or exit the labor market needed.[17] But this holistic point of view is not acceptable on the scientific level because the so-called functional imperatives (or the alleged "laws") of the system are neither necessary nor inevitable.

Individualistic explanations predominate in the field of economic theory, inspired by some version of methodological individualism. A great many mainstream economists hold that structural effects are "perverse" (i.e., unexpected and unintentional) due to (a) deviations from "perfect competition" in the market and (b) defects in the appropriate regulations that political systems should provide (with legislation on the labor market and the redistribution effected by the welfare state). According to prevailing economic theory, a perfectly competitive market would not *produce* negative structural effects such as poverty. Such problems only reflect *pre-existing* structural characteristics such as deserved inequality. Harm to distant others is considered an effect of deviation from economic norms. The recipe for avoiding social harm thus consists in correcting those market mechanisms that do not correspond to perfect competition and correcting welfare state mechanisms that do not guarantee equality of opportunity for individuals in the market and that, on the contrary, generate poverty traps and other harms.

In short, a great deal of social thought holds that impersonal harm brought to bear on distant others is the product of long chains of exchanges in which each single exchange can be rational and legitimate, in keeping with market rules.[18] The "responsibility" for such phenomena is assigned to "mechanisms" that produce an allocation of resources that is inefficient and/or inequitable. If the market system functioned correctly ("perfectly") in accordance with Adam Smith's mercantile ethics,[19] inequality would be only what is deserved by the individual. Poverty would be caused by factors such as illness, handicaps, and old age, which could be countered solely by means of policy, that is, by assigning the responsibility to redress these problems to the welfare state and to private charity (whether religious or secular). This is also what the Catholic Church's traditional social doctrine recommends.[20]

Negative outcomes (poverty, unemployment, unjust inequality) are imputed to ethically wrong individual behaviors and to unjust rules, while it is assumed that, if agents are "ethical" and rules just, ethically good outcomes will automatically be produced. However, this is not true. From this error stems the fact that redress for the social harm produced by actions that are licit and rational in themselves is sought in a different distribution of resources (rectification after the fact), rather than in a change in the network of relations (within the market) that produces the harm at a distance. People ask for compensation for those who are harmed by means of a more generous welfare state, that is, through redistributive measures by public means. In general, this is also the proposal of Catholic bishops' conferences around the world, including the U.S. bishops and, in particular, the Pontifical Council for Justice and Peace.[21] The responsibility for harm brought to bear on distant others that are caused by behaviors that are ethically legitimate in themselves is considered ex post and shifted on to impersonal mechanisms of public welfare. This responsibility is not understood as a call to alter those mechanisms that produce negative outcomes from individual actions that are ethically valid in themselves.

The outcome of this logic is always to resort once again to compromise between state and market (the lib-lab arrangement). According to this reading, individuals do not bear either direct or indirect responsibility for the impersonal harm brought to bear on distant others. The responsibility for social evils falls to the political collectivity, which should provide redress through impersonal measures (*l'État-Providence* is a safeguarding principle that lightens the burden of individuals' personal responsibility or completely relieves them of it).

This solution is not satisfactory for many reasons. First, it risks making single agents unaccountable. Individuals do not have to change their logic of preferences and can shift their personal responsibility on to the collectivity. Second, it is not satisfactory because, as the history of the welfare state demonstrates, the solution that proposes to redress social evils by socializing harm through a continuous broadening of social citizenship of a lib-lab type[22] multiplies the state's pervasive powers without civilizing the market, given that it reinforces these same market mechanisms.

Do Alternatives Exist?

We need to begin by acknowledging that markets have become complex systems that no longer answer to linear logics.[23] Systems develop networks that are "black boxes," so that the quality of social relation is regulated inside the system whose mechanisms and internal workings are invisible.[24]

Traditional ethics finds itself in a position of difficulty precisely because it is still anchored to linear thinking, that is, to goal-oriented (i.e., teleological) principles and to linear causality, while markets have no goal for the system and operate by means of functions and without a principle of linear causality.[25]

Confronted with the functionalistic behavior of globalized markets, one cannot but wonder whether there still exists the possibility of affirming a traditionally humanistic point of view that vindicates an active role for the human person and a capacity for modifying purely functional systems to serve higher goals. It is easy to see the conflict between the functionalist perspective (which holds that ethics pertains to individual's actions, which is possible for agents but not for restructuring the system)[26] and the humanistic perspective (which holds that social structures are the product of human persons and thus can be changed by them, giving them a goal based in ethics).[27] From the sociological point of view, the humanistic perspective seems to be losing ground and is impossible to maintain, not only because it presupposes an ethics that goes against the utilitarian primacy of the market but also because it does not take into account the market's perverse effects even when agents are honest and the market's rules respect ethical constraints.

What hope does the humanistic perspective have? Or, put another way, is it possible to alter market rules by introducing ethics as an independent variable that functions as a constraint on economic activity, considered not only in the single act but in the causal chain at a distance?

In my view, the answer is negative if we conceive of the markets as functional systems guided by ethics. This is true both for business ethics (recall the regulations introduced in national and international financial systems after the crisis of September 2008) and for an organic ethics of a traditional type such as that of the Catholic Church. In both cases, since they are functional in nature, they make no difference.

The answer can be affirmative if we recognize that markets can be understood not as functional systems (which are in crisis) but as systems of interdependence, characterized by a growing interactionality and relationality. This is what the relational paradigm proposes.[28]

In Which Direction Should Research be Taken?

Let us start over again with the question: Who bears moral responsibility for causing impersonal harm to others? The most helpful scientific paradigm for answering this question is provided by critical realism, outlined in the chapter by Douglas Porpora in this volume. The ontological answer given by critical realism is that the *interactions* among market agents bear that responsibility.[29] I agree. But exactly how do we define these interactions and their outcomes?

We must first reflect on the fact that the points of view of methodological holism and methodological individualism both lack relationality. As regards the holistic position, the functionalist theory of social systems encounters insurmountable limits and no longer functions beyond its own restricted domain because it eclipses the capacity of human persons to transform systems. Contrary to the holistic view, people possess the capacity for "reflexivity," defined by Margaret Archer as "the regular exercise of the mental ability, shared by all normal people, to consider themselves in relation to their (social) contexts and vice versa." [30] People assess and judge the mechanisms of social systems and can react reflexively on them through voice (pressing for change) or exit. Agents feel responsibility for the devices that run systems despite the fact that system mechanisms operate "impersonally."

The individualistic position is correct that markets do indeed encompass individuals who make decisions, but it fails to recognize that according to individualist assumptions these are not individuals who can act according to their wishes, and even less according to the rational choice theory. They cannot alter the network on the basis of their individual preferences and tastes. The network cannot be configured on the basis of a purely internal reflexivity of individual participants because it entails social relations as such. But reflexivity—both individual and social—can make a difference in the face of the endemic crisis of the capitalistic economy. It recognizes the outcomes of social networks as products of relations rather than of individual acts. In short, the moral responsibility of agents for the impersonal harm brought to bear on strangers becomes visible when the former are not considered as atoms but as "parts of a relational subject."

In such a case, it becomes plausible to understand that there exists a moral responsibility of agents if and to the degree that (a) agents consider the effects of their social relations and (b) they adopt a vision of the market that explicitly identifies the ethical criteria that should constitute the goal of the economic system.

The Market as a Black Box

In order to understand this sociological analysis, I propose the scheme depicted in Figure 3.1.

At the beginning of the process (time T^1), we observe agents, who are as always embedded in a social context that influences their opportunities and action preferences.[31] The context is a social structure produced by previous cycles of the process of structural transformation that

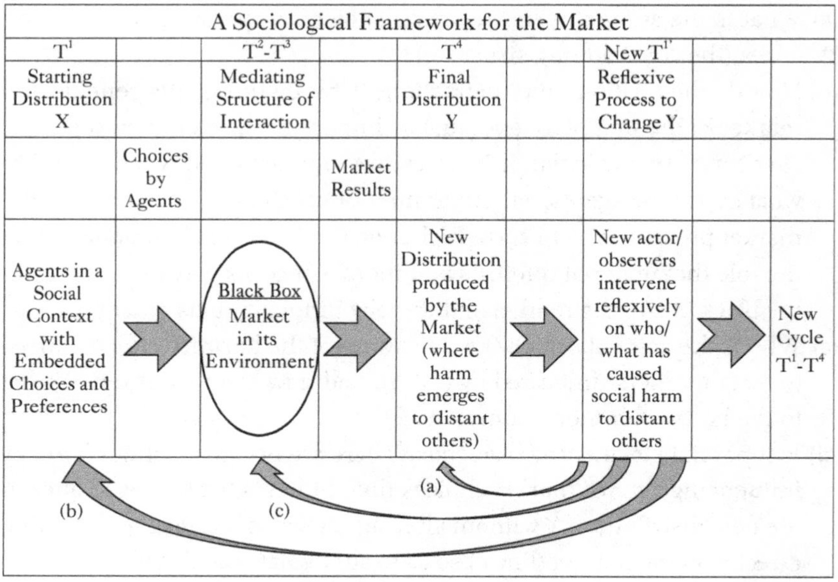

A Sociological Framework for the Market								
T^1		T^2-T^3		T^4		New $T^{1'}$		
Starting Distribution X		Mediating Structure of Interaction		Final Distribution Y		Reflexive Process to Change Y		
	Choices by Agents		Market Results					
Agents in a Social Context with Embedded Choices and Preferences		Black Box Market in its Environment		New Distribution produced by the Market (where harm emerges to distant others)		New actor/ observers intervene reflexively on who/ what has caused social harm to distant others		New Cycle T^1-T^4
(b)		(c)		(a)				

FIGURE 3.1 A Sociological Framework for the Market

Figure 3.1 describes.[32] This structure defines the positions and resources of the agents in the initial distribution X. The agents make individual, interacting choices in the market in the interval of time T^2–T^3. The choices combine with one another in the market, which is a network of relations among the agents. This network is a black box that transforms the initial distribution X into the new distribution Y (which emerges at time T^4). From this network arises the new configuration of resources, opportunities, and preferences Y. In distribution Y, we can find both relational goods and evils that the black box of the market produces, both among the agents under consideration as well as between them and distant others.

In order to see the harm generated by the market and to whom or what the responsibility should be attributed, "new" reflexive actors (who are also "observers")[33] intervene by interacting with the "old" actors (those who are present in the cycle T^1–T^4) in period $T^{1'}$.[34] Only under certain conditions do these actors/observers have some hope of explaining, understanding, and reflexively assessing the outcomes of the cycle and starting a new cycle T^1–T^4 aiming to stop producing the relational evils caused for distant others.

The problem that we must confront has four aspects requiring careful analysis:

(a) What is the autonomy of the acting subjects in pursuing their preferences (the conditioning structure)?

(b) How do the relations and interactions between the agents generate the market in the first place and, just as important, how do they sustain it over time? In particular, it is necessary to understand whether and to what extent the agents, with their intentional choices, can structure the market process so as to serve higher goals. This entails understanding the role that material interests and moral concerns play in configuring the black box of the market and thereby influencing its outcomes.

(c) Who is the actor-observer, the one aware of the harmful effects caused to distant others (indicated by line a), and how can this observer react to the harm with moral conscience?[35]

(d) Is it possible to alter the black box? There are two possibilities here: by influencing agents' market choices (line b) in such a way as to alter in the next distribution Y without altering the black box itself or by acting directly on the market (line c) so as to alter what it does with individual market choices, producing fewer harms to distant others.

Today's prevailing economic ethics considers agents as autonomous, rational, and generally free of social influences. They are considered ethical if they respect the laws covering economic transactions in the market. But the problem with this view is that subjects are not truly autonomous because they have social relations that they must take into account (leaving aside market regulations), their rationality is quite limited by the system's complexity, and there are many nonrational factors at play. It assumes that, on condition that the agents are honest and sympathetic, the black box operates as a beneficent system (brought about by an "invisible hand") that produces well-being for all participants. As a consequence, this view holds that the agents do not have any moral responsibility for the harm brought to bear on distant others because it considers the emergent effects as uncontrollable by the agents or, at least, as not dependent on agents' market choices.

This assumption is mistaken because it ignores the character of the emergence of those effects produced in the black box. Nonetheless, the prevailing economic ethics acknowledges agents' responsibility at the moment of their market choice (ex ante), without noting their responsibility for the market-mediated effects of those choices (ex post). The actor-observer that recognizes the harm brought to bear on distant others (and is thus able to react with moral conscience) can only be outside the market. The economy cannot observe and correct itself from the inside; ethics is considered to be an external constraint of a purely constrictive nature and not as an internal moral and social resource.

In this reading of things, redress for the damages caused by the market to distant others must be found elsewhere, generally in the intervention of the state and political systems in general, which must alter mechanisms of the black box (the market) with externally imposed regulations, devices, constraints, incentives, and sanctions.

In short, those who base their theory on methodological individualism counterintuitively end up embracing a holistic position in the sense that, once it is established that individuals' market decisions cannot be the cause of harmful market outcomes, it concludes that harm can be corrected only by the environment *outside* the market system. In contrast, the holists, after having maintained that individuals are victims of the system, end up appealing to creativity, reflexivity, or other characteristics of individuals in order to change society. Both intellectual positions lack the resources to understand the market and, in particular, the social processes capable of dealing adequately with the harms markets cause to distant others.

In order to find a solution to the problem, it is necessary to avoid seeing causes only in individuals or only in social, cultural, or economic structures. Both theories of exchange in the free market and theories of hierarchical structuring are losing their explanatory capacity. This reflects the fact that harms to distant others is increasingly caused by impersonal, remote networks in which agents' moral responsibility appears indirect or nonexistent. We must move beyond the mistaken focus on either free interindividual exchanges or organizational hierarchies and instead attend to "social networks."

The Moral Responsibility for Action and the Criteria for Imputing Responsibility
Reflexivity and Relational Ethics

Let us return to Figure 3.1 in order to understand the causal connections between a typical market agent's action and its effects.

In the case of lib-lab theories, things are quite clear. Agents make their choices from among the opportunities offered by economic structures and with the degree of freedom allowed by their resources and the rules of those structures. These theories emphasize the pressure of structures on individual actions;[36] the black box works in such a way that harmful outcomes are imputed to structures to the market itself, not to agents.

In reality, the typical person that participates in the market has more freedom than simply the degrees of liberty allowed by the social structure. Prevailing economic ethics limits itself to seeing responses to structural conditioning in terms of conformity or deviance. But there also exist "reflexive responses."

Those who discern that distribution Y in time T^4 is not morally acceptable have available to them the responses of voice or exit at time $T^{1'}$. At this point, to whom is responsibility to be attributed?

If ethics is to fulfill its obligation to alter the black box, it must make itself *reflexive*. In reflexive ethics, we must "turn back" and identify the responsibility of those persons and/or those processes operating inside the black box that produce the social evils. The box needs to be rendered transparent and its internal processes open to change.

There exist two paths to proceed from here. The first path is to impute responsibility *only* to the single agents (persons or firms) at the beginning of the process (time T^1, line b in Figure 3.1). This path is correct in the case of direct harm (e.g., sexual harassment of a vulnerable employee by a manager). In the case of indirect harm, however, it is necessary to see whether at time T^1 there existed different opportunities that the agent could have taken up instead of those contributing to the harm. Exercising such an option requires reflexivity reflecting back on one's context.

Consider the situation of a business owner who acts with honest intentions of saving his company by "moving" his manufacturing plant to a nation where wages are lower. Because this first path assigns causal responsibility for the unjust outcome in Y to individual agents (i.e., the firm) and not to the market itself, any owner who decides he must no longer contribute to the harm would have to exit from the market (allowing the firm to go bankrupt). Or consider individual consumers who would prefer not to buy products manufactured in factories in Asia that exploit their workers. They would prefer cooperative rather than competitive strategies, (e.g., buying from "fair trade" appliance companies), but this is not achievable by individuals and is only possible by taking the second path.

The second path consists in assigning responsibility to social relations among the agents acting *within* the black box of the market (line c). In fact, it is the play of relations and decisions that leads agents either to reproduce the same processes or to question and transform them. But in order to understand how structures can be changed, it is necessary to understand how they are causally generated.

Structures are relational; they are *made of* relations. Relations are made of reciprocal actions (with their intentions, norms, means, and values). What we call "market rules" are relational structures. Precisely due to their relational character, they generate an "other" reality distinguishable from the individuals and structures that we observe in any given time and place. This third reality emerges from this process, but traditional ethics does not see it, because it judges individuals and structures. It is here that ethics must make itself reflexive or, rather, meta-reflexive, in the sense that it must judge the morality of actions not simply by their effects on the distribution but also in light of how they configure relations, that is, how they sustain or transform the relations that makes the black box of market what it is.

This means that the ethical criteria that assess the functioning and effects of markets must begin with social relations[37] rather than with impersonal system mechanisms or individual preferences, even when systems provide incentives to act cooperatively.[38] In any case, causal imputations can no longer be of a deductive and conditional type: "If event A happens, judgment B then applies."

It is necessary that the ethical criteria for imputing moral responsibility concern agents not only as regards their individual subjectivity (internal conversation or personal reflexivity) but also as regards their social relations. Agents must reflect on the relations that condition them and on the relations that they sustain. They must assess the relation's good (the relation as a good) or the relation's evil (the relation as an evil).[39] Such relational good can transform itself into a relational evil in a context that lacks suitable social reflexivity. Ethics must make itself relational. What does this mean?

It means seeing good and evil even in relations and not only in the individual or in the conditioning structure. To understand the significance of this statement, think about the following examples. Traditional ethics considers poverty as a condition of insufficient resources that should rectified by a transfer from the prosperous to those who are in need. Relational ethics, instead, sees poverty as the product of relations that, even if enacted with good intentions, have objectively deprived some people of opportunities to which they had a right for reasons of reciprocity. Likewise, unemployment is seen as the product of policy that considers work as a commodity rather than as a social relation.[40] It is certainly true that for some years now the United Nations has understood of poverty as a lack of *capabilities*, which leads to exclusion from the circuits of productivity. Amartya Sen, whose thinking has contributed to this new view, has proposed that the conception of poverty as a pure and simple lack of income be superseded. Nevertheless, concepts such as a "lack of capabilities" or a "lack of flexibility in the job market" usually make reference to individuals as such; that is, they reflect an individualistic point of view (or for some they reflect a collective point of view, making reference to impersonal structures), rather than being expressed as forms of social relations. This is due to the fact that the common good is defined as a "total good" (a product of aggregation) rather than as a "relational good" (an emergent effect).

In general, involuntary, illegitimate inequalities must be seen as the product of a relationality among actors that lacks reflexivity in the mechanisms that distribute life opportunities, even if those who participate in the exchanges are individually honest.

At this point, a clarification of the concept of ethical good that I am proposing is called for. In Catholic moral theology, which was renewed after the Second Vatican Council and in the encyclical *Veritatis Splendor*, ethical good consists in the flowering of the human person in happiness and therefore in virtue, for the development of which ethical norms are needed that become the rules of the flourishing life. The human person's relationality is seen as part of this concept of ethical good since it presumes that in the relation are expressed the person's virtues that, if positive, generate a positive relation (the social relation is assumed to be configured in a certain way because it was *internally* desired by the person in that way, as Elisabeth Anscombe maintains).[41]

But the morality of the action requires a richer and more complex view of relationality. The social dimension of the morality does not only consist in the fact that the person is morally obliged to relate to others in a virtuous way. This is necessary but not sufficient. It also includes the person's responsibility for the moral good of the relation itself and therefore requires attending to the effects of one's own action on distant others, with whom the person has a relation within the market. In this consists the *social* nature of virtue.[42] To put it another way, the morality of an action does not consist only in the person's intentionality but also in the responsibility that the person bears toward the relation that the action supports, considering the relation as a good in itself and as constitutive of a structure that conditions the people involved.

For this reason, we can say that relational ethics joins together intentionality toward a good and responsibility toward the relational value of the good. The ethics of intentionality and the ethics of responsibility cannot be separated, precisely due to the relational character of the good. From the ethical point of view, the good that each entity possesses in itself[43] is not the same as the good that the entity in question has within the context of social relations. For example, the good that a building has in and of itself (as a thing that is there) is not the good considered from the market viewpoint or from the point of view of particular social groups, the local authorities, and so on. The building becomes a social good in as much as it becomes relevant (actually or potentially) to the people who use it in different ways. It can have a use value, an exchange value, a "bonding value" (the value attached to being an entity that bonds people together), and so on. It is the particular kind of social relation that people have with it, in a situated context, that makes it a social good and therefore a moral good having a particular value.

This claim that the moral responsibility for harm to distant others should be attributed to a *relational deficit* can seem vague and untenable. It certainly seems so from the standpoint of traditional ethics, which considers the concept of "relation" as a morally unimportant rational construct and assigns the responsibility for the character and effects of concrete social relations to individual persons.[44]

We are indebted to the modern social sciences for attributing a responsibility increasingly clearly to subjects, not simply for what they think or do individually but also for the social relations they generate. This means that the concept of relation has an ontological status when it is applied to the social realm. The morality of an action does not reside only in the conscience of the subject acting with an eye to a good in itself but in how that subject does or does not respond to the relational nature of the desired good.

The Relational Subject

The modern "discovery" of the reality of the social relation is a moral fact that requires a new ethical reflection.[45] Postmodern society and the globalized markets certainly have lost the classic ontological paradigm.[46] Nevertheless, they have also opened the way for the emergence of an ontology of the social relation based on a new critical realism as an alternative to a constructivist relationalism that manipulates responsibility, just as it manipulates social relations.

In Figure 3.1, we saw that relational good or evil is created in the interactive network (the market as black box) in the interval between times T^2–T^3. Let us now look at what happens inside the black box.

Moral responsibility changes relationally over time. It is not given, once and for all, in the initial decision. It does not only concern single acts in time but has to do with these acts in as much as they produce relational effects over the course of time. At the initial time T^1, individuals find themselves in a structure that conditions them, and they make their choices. These choices, at time T^2, enter into relation with the choices of other agents in the market. A network is constituted among nearby individuals (a proximity network). In this phase, moral responsibility concerns each agent due to the contribution that he or she makes to the network, that is, with respect to the constitution of a *we-relation*. But this network is not isolated; it has effects that go beyond it toward the outside (distant others).

Decisions in the proximity network affect the outside, often unintentionally, because there exist structural connections. For example, when in the early twentieth century white workers in the United States prevented blacks from joining labor unions, they did not do this to prevent them from working—or even due to racism—but because they believed that blacks would not be loyal to the union and, therefore, they thought that they were defending their legitimate interests. They had "good reasons" for their actions. Nevertheless, the emergent structural effect was to produce unemployment and poverty among blacks, as Merton has shown.[47]

From the standpoint of relational ethics, a morally responsible life requires knowledge of the relational connections of the networks in which the agent is integrated. Yet studies to this effect are quite rare, because the issue of knowledge of relations and their effects is fairly recent in social research. Nevertheless, it is possible to make several assertions that are validated by network analysis.[48]

For example, we can say that moral responsibility is proportional to the degree of the person's *centrality* in the network. For instance, whoever occupies the position of broker[49] has a supplementary responsibility, because the broker's responsibility is not only toward the network's individual nodes (each other person) but also toward the network overall inasmuch as what the network generates depends on the way in which brokers manage the structural wholes in which they are located.[50]

Ignorance is not an excuse for refusing to take responsibility. Undoubtedly, some connections are known and certain, while others are unknown or uncertain. In general, causal connections have a certain degree of probability. The morality of action in a network shares the problems of other dimensions of moral responsibility in facing risks.

It is considerably more difficult to address social phenomena and to speak of a relational ethics in social networks than to analyze individual moral decision making. What distinguishes the former is the fact that actors must act reflexively on the results of their own actions combined with others' actions and not simply on the consequences of their own individual actions. In order for this to happen, it is necessary that a moral relational subject, to which moral criteria are applied, be constituted. The morality of social action requires that agents be observed as parts of what can be called a *relational subject*.[51]

In many cases, the "remote" causality of the market's economic phenomena is identifiable only if we presuppose the existence of a relational subject with respect to which all agents involved are responsible. This is because it is with respect to this relational subject that an observer can assess the morality of those agents' actions, whether ex ante or ex post, in producing those causal chains that eventuate in harm to distant others.

For example, a company that hires women with no concern for their relations with their children is potentially responsible for the harm suffered by the children due to a lack of maternal care, which lies outside the company's organizational network. (Of course, the same holds true for men, because harm to children is an issue of parental care, not simply attributable to women.) The company did not have these intentions but can produce harm this way in the broad human environment within which it operates. Relational reflexivity on the process requires one to see the company, the employees, and their families as a relational subject.

A company has social responsibility vis-à-vis the inhabitants of its territory because it is part of a network that connects all of the stakeholders and constitutes a relational subject. In the same way, we say that employers have a responsibility toward their employees' families, which requires measures enabling family–work balance that lies outside the usual world of contracts in which a simple equivalence is assumed between services rendered and remuneration of the individual employee's work.

When conceived in a relational sense, moral responsibility is intrinsically reflexive. It is what leads from a simple moral judgment concerning harm (line a of Figure 3.1) to an alteration of the relational configuration acting on subjects (line b) and to a transformation of the structure of market relations (i.e., inside the black box, line c).

The relational perspective is not wishful thinking but has empirical corroboration in a number of new ways of structuring market relations in accord with relational ethics. For example, many companies prevent harm to distant others by building networks in which for-profit and nonprofit subjects cooperate and for this are called "socially responsible."

We are witnessing the birth of markets in which agents' behaviors and rules are being redefined from the point of view of the relational subject constituted by a broad spectrum of stakeholders (business owners and management, workers, and consumers). New forms of relational economy are being born, integrating for-profit and nonprofit sectors and holding as a value the social responsibility of business (corporate social responsibility, shared responsibilities) and the production of *commons*. More recent than the concept of corporate social responsibility is that of *shared value*, used by Michael Porter as well as Mark Esposito, Rosebeth Moss Kanter, and others, which has the advantage of using economic language in the sense that it underscores that the goal of business is value and not simply profit. Social and positive ecological effects are included in value. Running through all of these innovations is the observation that the company that pursues only monetary profit is destined to fail.

These developments introduce what I call "relational reflexivity"[52] into the black box. In this way, they civilize the market, while the typically capitalistic configuration based on an acquisitive reflexivity commodifies it. An example of innovation in this sense are the relational contracts between employer and employee that addresses not only services rendered and compensation, but also included are relations with the employee's family and the services that the latter may need, precisely in order not to harm those who are at a distance from the company. These contracts are not a form of philanthropy, charity, or a gift from the company but are another way to increase its social and human capital. In any case, they have a positive impact, both within the company as well as on the network outside of it.

Some Examples

If market participants do not understand harm brought to bear on distant others as a product of their actions, it is because they do not see, or refuse to see, the relations that connect them. The prevailing political economy of today immunizes them against these relations.[53] How can one respond to someone who refuses to consider relations? How can we address someone who wants to deal with us only for the things exchanged and refuses to consider the relations entailed by the exchange? Let us look at some examples.

Social Dumping

Social dumping (moving an enterprise to a nation with lower costs simply to increase profits)[54] is a practice considered in the economic world to be unfair. But in point of fact, in the United States it is a normal activity backed up by the laws on competition, and in the European Union it is a policy endorsed by the European Commission policy directives meant to foster market competition among member states. The lib-lab system imposes a market structure based on social dumping. And so one wonders: What responsibility does the individual businessperson who practices social dumping have in generating harm in those regions where it causes unemployment and endangers workers' social rights?

From the perspective of relational sociology, conformity to the rules of the market does not exhaust all of the entrepreneur's moral responsibility because the business has degrees of freedom in seeking alternative solutions if and when it wants to avoid unintentionally causing harm. Entrepreneurs can adopt cooperative strategies between the workers of the two regions involved, but for this they must promote the establishment of a relational subject that includes the participants in their market strategy. The entrepreneur's morality can and must come to terms with multiple criteria for justice. This entails not only the commutative justice of the market but also the redistributive justice of the state, the one based on solidarity in the Third Sector.

At the basis of everything, there is distributive justice as an ontological foundation, which consists in the recognition of the human person's rights. It is in this way that a civil economy arises that respects the ethical criterion of reciprocity as the moral rule of relations. Differently from other theoreticians of the civil economy, I would like to emphasize that avoiding causing harm to strangers is not a matter of introducing ethical principles that lie outside the market, such as one based on fraternity or love,[55] but rather of configuring relational networks within markets in accordance with their inner virtues.

Acquisition of Merchandise Produced in Violation of Human Rights

What moral responsibility does the consumer have when buying merchandise produced with the exploitation of child labor or with the low-paid work of women operating in sweatshops in developing countries?

The answer lies in the reflexive awareness of consumers. If they have no knowledge of the fact, we cannot impute moral responsibility to them. But if the network of corporate agents makes this reality public, and a consumer comes to know about it, the consumer has the freedom to choose what to do. The knowledge of exploitation is an element in the imputation of responsibility because the consumer often has the possibility of not buying sweatshop products.

Capital Flight

Let us take the case of a person who withdraws financial investments from a country in which there are risks of fiscal and financial instability. By acting in this way, the agent contributes to causing unemployment and economic recession in that country. Such an agent is generally perfectly aware of what he or she causes but imputes harm to the laws of the market. Something analogous happens when bank depositors, hearing a rumor that their bank is going to fail, rush to withdraw their deposits and thus effectively can cause the bank's failure even when there was never any real danger.

In these cases, in order to assess agents' responsibility, we can follow one of two paths: appealing to an ethics of risk or acting in such a way that the feared result does not come about. It is clear that the calculation of risk in these cases is quite difficult and often impossible. Moral irresponsibility lies above all in the refusal to alter the network of interactions, which can produce the bankruptcies and, consequently, the harm to distant others. Moral responsibility is thus proportional to the degrees of freedom available for altering the network of financial relations in such a way as to avoid both one's own losses as well as harm to others. Surely we cannot criticize a person who tries to save his or her modest savings.

On the other hand, from a moral standpoint one must reserve a negative judgment for rating agencies that, with their evaluations, contribute to increasing the difficulties experienced by those countries that already have weak economies and, thus, instead of helping these countries to get back on their feet, favor dynamics that lead these economies toward situations of even deeper crisis (as they are examples of self-fulfilling prophecies).

The Involuntary Creation of Poverty

From the standpoint of sociological analysis, the condition of poverty is not caused solely by certain individual characteristics but is above all the product of a relational system. It arises from a chain of social relations. Consider a related example, the notion of "economic capital," which usually is used as a synonym for valuable assets in production or finance. For relational sociology, however, economic capital is not the possession of a sum of money, a company, or real estate. It is, rather, a network of social relations that make possible the possession and use of those goods. Similarly, poverty is a context that hinders control of needed goods. Addressing poverty as an emergent effect of networks of relations completely changes the perspective as compared to an essentialist point of view that considers poverty as a condition caused by economic or physical factors that have determined a certain outcome (i.e., the lack of means).

Thus poverty is the result of a deficient relational structure, and the struggle against poverty in the market entails creating a new interactive network of a cooperative type.

Social causality is a relational causality. The conditions and opportunities of life are the outcome of a relational context that not only
conditions individuals' choices but also has its own logic of system interdependence. The category of interdependence is a moral category, not
only in that it refers to an appeal to the moral (and Christian) obligation of solidarity, as John Paul II affirms in the encyclical *Sollicitudo rei
socialis*, but in that it is inherent in the causality of social relations on the
empirical level.

The moral responsibility for the creation of poverty does not at the
most basic level have to do with the individual actions of individual market
participants but with the consequences of the relations that those actions
activate. People are responsible for the outcomes because they are responsible for the relations that generate them, even if these are emergent
effects that come about without their intending them.

The poverty of the homeless man or of the illegal immigrant is the
result of a long chain of actions that could have been individually legal
and honest but that did not take into account either aggregate or emergent
effects. When I see an old woman collect her pension at the post office,
she does not know that this money comes from me and from those who
are currently active in the workforce. But I know it, and I am responsible
for it. If I do not pay my taxes and other contributions to the collectivity, and if I do not share in the *we-relation* and the relational subject that
supports it, I am responsible for the failure of the collectivity to pay this
woman's pension.

Conclusion: Civilizing the Market

The idea that the market is a system of exchanges where the golden rule
is "pure" competition, that is, with no premises beyond the mere capacities of individuals,[56] is like the phoenix of myth. A model of market economy that is based on this type of competition is not a model with some
defects: It is an intrinsically erroneous model. This conception is a pure
illusion due to the simple fact that it erases the relations between market
participants. Competition is a social virtue if it means *cum-petere* (its Latin
root), that is, *to strive together* toward a good, vying to see who can reach
it first, who is best, on the condition that this does not entail actions that

voluntarily cause harm to those who are competing and, moreover, seeking to reduce involuntary harm.

The modern political economy that originated in the eighteenth century, which in general terms theorizes the market as "formally free" and, as much as possible, "deregulated," is based on the removal of social relations because it has a Protestant theological matrix.[57] This model has historically triumphed over the civil economy with a Catholic matrix, which is, instead, based on social relations. Although Adam Smith spoke of sympathy among market actors, all political economy from Ricardo onward is pervaded by an ethics of "immunization" of market agents *against* their relations.

Since the economy is essentially relational, its ethics must also be relational. Redistributive economies (based on a central authority) and the so-called social market economies (which are a form of state regulation of the market) do not have a relational character and, for this reason, fail in combating the harm brought to bear by the market on distant others. At most, they can bring some relief.

In any case, in order to avoid harm caused by the market to distant others, recourse to the state is neither sufficient nor appropriate. Rather, mechanisms of civil society are needed, if they are relational. An economy is relational not because it entrusts itself to the regulations of some political system but because it invests in solutions based on the social governance of civil society's networks.

With this we have reached the crux of the problem: The morality of actions in the market is essentially a problem of civilizing the market, considered as a system of interdependences and interactions.

Ethics can operate as an independent influence on economic activity if it is conceived according to reflexive criteria and no longer according to a linear logic (i.e., the conditional criteria such that, if X happens, then the norm Y is applied).

In a society that is expanding agents' subjectivity and creating always-new relations via the channels of globalization, it is no longer enough to say that the morality of action depends on the conscious intention to pursue something good in itself. Unfortunately, social evils do not derive only from behaviors that are dishonest, corrupt, driven by greed for money or power—though such behaviors are all too frequent. More fundamentally perverse processes are invisible to the naked eye and can be observed only with a suitable instrument—that of relational and reflexive observation.

The four fundamental principles of Catholic social doctrine (the dignity of the human person, the common good, solidarity, and subsidiarity) are not four pillars that stand separately from one another. They must be understood and must operate in a relational and reflexive manner. Each is defined *through* the others. But this presupposes having a relational and reflexive view of social reality. In this consists the civilization of the market.

From the time of Aristotle, traditional ethics has imputed the morality of action to the "acting subject." Over time and, in particular, with the advent of the modern social sciences, the social, economic, and cultural conditioning weighing on the subject have come to be better understood. The result has been to attribute moral responsibility to a "conditioned subject," that is, one that is constrained by existing societal structures. The increased importance of systems of interdependence, at the expense of functional systems, changes the epistemological frame in what we call global social order.[58] Moral responsibility encounters a process of ongoing change in the social structures conditioning individuals, and, as a result, the morality of action must make reference to a "relational subject," one that acts in a societal network and is required to know and configure "relationally."

Ethics must make itself relational, in the sense that the attribution of responsibility for acting for good or ill cannot be limited to a single act but invokes the reflexivity inherent in social processes. The morality of action must therefore make reference to the reflexive awareness that subjects have of how good and evil are produced by social relations and consist of social relations (relational goods and evils), within increasingly complex causal networks.

The ethics of intention is no longer sufficient. It must be integrated with an ethics of responsibility that is not restricted to the consequences of individual acts and is not purely instrumental in the means–ends relationship but takes into account the effects of relational networks. In a complex society, morality cannot be limited to the intrinsic goodness of aims but rather must make reference to an integrally relational view of human action.

The initial question, "Why should a person acting in markets be held responsible for the harm brought to bear on distant others due to impersonal market mechanisms?" thus has the following answer: because that person did not exercise his or her freedom, for which he or she is responsible in the first person. This freedom is not that of one's purely internal conscience nor is it freedom *from* external constraints. It is the freedom *to* act for the goods that can only be produced and enjoyed together by the participants in the market.

NOTES

1. With the term *agent*, reference is made to the subject's freedom. A second term, *actor*, would technically make reference to the social role covered by the subject. *Actors* are subjects that act in the roles of *functional* systems. *Agents* are subjects that act in systems of *interdependence*, both interactive and structural. The harm that market agents cause to distant others can come from functional systems as well as from systems of interdependence, but their moral responsibility is different. For simplicity, I use only the former term in this chapter.

2. See, W. May, "Double Effect," in W. T. Reich (ed.), *Encyclopedia of Bioethics* (New York: Macmillan, 1978), 316; J. L. A. Garçia, "Double Effect," in *Encyclopedia of Bioethics,* rev. ed. (New York: Macmillan, 1995), 637.

3. In my view, "subject" (Latin: *subiectus,* "lying beneath") refers to a human agent/actor who causes an action and therefore is causally and, under certain conditions, morally responsible for that action, whatever kind of action (internal or external to the agent/actor) may be. The subject can be an *individual person* or a social group having in common a social identity and therefore called *collective agent/actor.* The latter is constituted of a network of people belonging to each other for some publicly relevant reason and having joint liability to external agents (i.e., a "moral person," as defined by Thomas Aquinas; e.g., a family or a corporation). Both the single person and the collective agents are "relational subjects": I call the former "primary relational subject" ("primary" refers to the first-level agency) and the latter secondary relational subject' ("secondary" refers to the secondary-level agency, in its associational form). Sociologically, the notion of subject is necessary in order to attribute actions, which may be individual or collective, to a social (i.e., relational, not physical) cause. As a relational and critical realist, I assume that behind (or "beneath") an action—be it individual or joint—there should be a human agent, single or collective (properly speaking, animals do not "act," or have social relations). I am against the constructionists (like Luhmann) who maintain that the notion of "subject" is mystical, so that they reduce the "subject" only to a reference point for communication and only for communication (to them, "communication" does not mean to make a thing common—*co-munus*—as in classical philosophy but only to transfer of information).

4. M. S. Archer, *Realist Social Theory: The Morphogenetic Approach* (Cambridge, UK: Cambridge University Press, 1995), 324. D. Elder-Vass, "Searching for

Realism, Structure and Agency in Actor Network Theory," *British Journal of Sociology* 59.3 (2008): 455–473.

5. The term "societal structures" indicate, from now on, the structures of society in its various economic, political, cultural, and social articulations.

6. This is the logic clarified by G. Teubner, "A Constitutional Moment. The Logics of 'Hit the Bottom,'" in Paul Kjaer and Gunther Teubner (eds.), *The Financial Crisis in Constitutional Perspective: The Dark Side of Functional Differentiation* (Oxford: Hart, 2011).

7. In this way the master plan of the new European construction was formulated, based on the lib-lab ideology. But the statement also holds for almost all Western countries.

8. P. Donati, *Il lavoro che emerge: Prospettive del lavoro come relazione sociale in una economia dopo-moderna.* (Torino: Bollati Boringhieri, 2001).

9. D. Elder-Vass, *Towards a Social Ontology of Market Systems*, CRESI Working Paper 2009-06 (Colchester, UK: University of Essex, 2009).

10. The fact that Boudon designates these effects as "unexpected" evidently depends on the fact that he is not able to give an explanation for them. In point of fact, Boudon assimilates among themselves the unintentional, aggregate, and emergent effects, without distinguishing them in an analytical way. Cf. R. Boudon, *Effets perverse et ordre social* (Paris: Puf, 1989).

11. On the three forms of conflation (downward, upward, central), see cf. Archer, *Realist Social Theory*.

12. Contingency understood not as "dependence on" but rather as "being able not to be" and thus as "being always able to be otherwise" (differently, in another way).

13. There are many and diverse conceptions of social structure. See D. V. Porpora, "Four Concepts of Social Structure," *Journal for the Theory of Social Behaviour* 19.2 (1989): 195–211. I find interesting the essay by D. Elder-Vass, "Searching for Realism," in which he defines social structures through four dimensions: the dimension incorporated in the agents (embodied structure), the institutional dimension (institutional structure), the relational dimension (relational structure), and the emergent dimension (emergent structure). I think that these four faces of social structure are necessary, complementary, and interactive among themselves. In my opinion, they can be understood as the four dimensions that make up the structure according to the AGIL scheme, understood in a relational and not functionalist. See P. Donati, *Teoria relazionale della società* (Milano: FrancoAngeli, 1991), ch. 4.

14. However, a great deal of confusion reigns in the camp of relational theories. Many claim to be in favor of a relational approach, but very few focus on the social relation as such. As just one example, Bottero affirms that "Bourdieu's approach is *relational* but does not focus on *social relationships*, understood as social networks or as an interactional order"; W. Bottero, "Relationality and Social Interaction," *British Journal of Sociology* 60.2 (2009): 399. Personally,

I have analyzed the different conceptions of the social relation in the principle sociological approaches "society as a relation" and have reached the conclusion that almost no approach has a truly relational view of the social relation. See P. Donati, *Relational Sociology: A New Paradigm for the Social Sciences* (New York: Routledge, 2011a), ch. 2.

15. Holistic explanations derive to a great extent from the mechanistic interpretations contained in the theories of Karl Marx, Emile Durkheim, and Vilfredo Pareto.

16. We are reminded of the famous polemic between Kinsley Davis and Wilbert Moore on one side and Melvin Tumin on the other. Davis and Moore's thesis ("Some Principles of Stratification," 1945) was that, "social inequality is...an unconsciously evolved device by which societies ensure that the most important positions are conscientiously filled by the most qualified persons." Tumin criticized this functionalist explanation of inequality, maintaining instead that, "social stratification systems function to provide the elite with the political power necessary to procure acceptance and dominance of an ideology which rationalizes the status quo, whatever it may be, as 'logical,' 'natural,' and 'morally right.' In this manner social stratification systems function as essentially conservative influences in the societies in which they are found"; M. M. Tumin, "Some Principles of Stratification: A Critical Analysis," *American Sociological Review* 18.4 (1953): 387–393.

17. It is well known that Marx called it capitalism's "reserve army" and explained it as being the product of dominant economic laws. But this theory today appears simplistic and unacceptable.

18. If we observe attentively holistic and individualistic explanations for structural effects, we notice that they often become synergic and end up converging when the market is treated as a social system. Examples come from illustrious names, such as Raymond Boudon, Ralph Dahrendorf, Pierre Bourdieu, James Coleman, and many others. These authors converge in giving a system explanation for the perverse effects within the model of society that I have called lib-lab. See Donati, *Il Lavoro che emerge*. This model of society is built on the presupposition that individuals are relieved as much as possible of their personal responsibilities.

19. C. L. Griswold, Jr., *Adam Smith and the Virtues of Enlightenment* (Cambridge, UK: Cambridge University Press, 1999).

20. Not only in the encyclical *Rerum Novarum* (1891) of Leo XIII but also recently. See, for example, the second part of the encyclical of Benedict XVI, *Deus Caritas Est*, (2005), nn. 22–39.

21. See the document from the Pontifical Council for Justice and Peace, *Towards Reforming the International Financial and Monetary Systems in the Context of Global Public Authority* (Vatican City, 2011).

22. See Ralph Dahrendorf's theory of citizenship: R. Dahrendorf, "The Changing Quality of Citizenship," in B. van Steenberger (ed.), *The Condition of Citizenship* (London: SAGE, 1994): 10–19.

23. From *Stanford Encyclopedia of Philosophy*: "Linear logic is a refinement of classical and intuitionistic logic. Instead of emphasizing *truth*, as in classical logic, or *proof*, as in intuitionistic logic, linear logic emphasizes the role of formulas as *resources*. To achieve this focus, linear logic does not allow the usual structural rules of contraction and weakening to apply to all formulas but only those formulas marked with certain modals. Linear logic contains a fully involutive negation while maintaining a strong constructive interpretation. Linear logic also provides new insights into the nature of proofs in both classical and intuitionistic logic. Given its focus on resources, linear logic has found many applications in Computer Science."

24. According to Luhmann, "systems develop forms of access to complexity that are not available to scientific analysis and simulation" (black boxes, p. 14); "*every social contact is understood as a system*" (p. 15); "As soon as one goes beyond quantitative theory toward qualification, one can no longer forgo considering that and how systems qualify as elements the elements that compose them" (pp. 20f). N. Luhmann, *Social Systems* (Palo Alto, CA: Stanford University Press, 1995).

25. As Luhmann points out, "We can seek points of departure for increasing orientation to function, up to what is relatively improbable, in a stronger differentiation between action and observation...that at the same time does not question the communicative execution of self-observation. We thereby avoid teleological explanations, and also causal explanations...the hypothesis is that...it becomes probable that relatively improbable (more demanding, e.g., more specialized) functional orientations will take place and select corresponding structures." See, Luhmann, *Social Systems*, 302.

26. The most exemplary theory is that of Luhmann. See Luhmann, *Social Systems*.

27. Here are situated the theories of Margaret Archer, *Being Human: The Problem of Agency* (Cambridge, UK: Cambridge University Press, 2000), Donati (2009), Christian Smith, *What is a Person? Rethinking Humanity, Social Life, and the Moral Good from the Person Up* (Chicago: University of Chicago Press, 2010). Christian Smith has attempted to show that social institutions emerge as human products on the basis of an emergential vision of the human person and of social relations. The correspondence between the human characteristics of the person and of social institutions remains quite problematic, however, because society in the process of globalization tends to separate the human from the social.

28. This was explained on the basis of empirical investigations in two volumes that present the relational paradigm in sociology: see P. Donati and I Colozzi (eds.), *Il paradigma relazionale nelle scienze sociali: le prospettive sociologiche* (Bologna: il

Mulino, 2006), and in economics, P.L. Sacco and S. Zamagni, (eds.), *Teoria economica e relazioni interpersonali* (Bologna: il Mulino, 2006).

29. Elder-Vass, "Searching for Realism," and D. Elder-Vass, *The Causal Power of Social Structures: Emergence, Structure and Agency* (Cambridge, UK: Cambridge University Press, 2010).

30. Margaret Archer, *Making Our Way Through the World: Human Reflexivity and Social Mobility* (Cambridge: Cambridge University Press, 2007): 4. I call it *personal reflexivity*. In my approach, the concept of reflexivity can be extended to a social group (in this case it is called *social* or *relational reflexivity*) and—under very restrictive and dissimilar conditions—to social systems (*system reflexivity*). For details see P. Donati, *Sociologia della riflessività. Come si entra nel dopo-moderno* (Bologna: il Mulino, 2011b). Cf. Margaret Archer, *Structure, Agency and the Internal Conversation* (Cambridge, UK: Cambridge University Press, 2003), and Archer, *Making Our Way*.

31. There exists what Sunstein calls, "endogeneity of embedded preferences." C. Sunstein, *Free Markets and Social Justice* (Oxford: Oxford University Press, 1997).

32. Archer, *Realist Social Theory*.

33. The need to distinguish between "agent" and "observer" lies in the fact that the same self can make observations that are not coherent in themselves and with his or her roles and/or actions.

34. These observers are necessary because (a) the social transformation process cannot be "finalized" ex ante (it is an emergent effect); (b) the black box is not trivial; and (c) the individual moral behaviors of actors in the process T^1–T^4 are not sufficient to produce an "ethical outcome" (i.e., a relational good).

35. On the notion of "moral conscience," see article 6 (moral conscience) of the *Catechism of the Catholic Church*, Part 3, section 1, chapter 1 (dignity of the human person).

36. According to this theory, agents act in a certain way even if they are aware of the harm that they cause because the environmental pressure is so strong that they would otherwise be labeled as deviant and thus would be marginalized from their social group of belonging. P. Blau, "Structural Effects," *American Sociological Review* 25.2 (1960): 178–193.

37. It is important to be aware that social relations always contain explicit or implicit normative components and can never be ethically neutral.

38. Many social evils could be avoided if agents, rather than being pushed into more or less cut-throat competition, were pushed to cooperation. Raub and Voss have analyzed the various modalities for promoting cooperation (by means of an authority, by means of iterated attempts to solve together problematic situations, by means of external incentives to cooperate) and have proposed using a model of endogenous change of preferences in which morality is "a matter of choice motivated entirely by (perhaps even purely selfish) individual

interest." W. Raub, and T. Voss, "Individual Interests and Moral Institutions: An Endogenous Approach to the Modification of Preferences," in M. Hechter, K. D. Opp, and R. Wippler (eds.), *Social Institutions: Their Emergence, Maintenance, and Effects* (New York: Aldine de Gruyter, 1990), 82.

39. On relational goods and evils, see, P. Donati and R. Solci, *I beni relazionali. Che cosa sono e quali effetti producono* (Torino: Bollati Boringhieri, 2011).

40. Donati, *Il Lavoro che emerge.*

41. G. E. M Anscombe, *Intention* (Cambridge, MA: Harvard University Press, 2000).

42. For an example, see P. Donati, "Le virtù sociali della famiglia," *Acta Philosophica*" 19.2 (2010a): 267–296. It is true that "a situation—and thus an institution, a structure, a society—is not, in and of itself, subject to moral acts; for this reason, it cannot be, in itself, good or bad. At the bottom of every situation of sin one always finds sinful people." John Paul II, *Reconciliatio et Paenitentia*, 1984, no. 16. Nevertheless, "it is not out of place to speak of 'structures of sin,' which (...) are rooted in personal sin and, thus, are always linked to the concrete acts of persons, who introduce them, consolidate them, and make them difficult to remove. And thus they grow stronger, spread, and become the source of other sins, conditioning the conduct of men" John Paul II, *Sollicitudo rei socialis* 36 (1987). So, social structures are not good or bad in themselves, but they do constrain agents in producing relational goods as opposed to evils.

43. A. Collier, *Being and Worth* New York: Routledge, 1999).

44. In fact, it is considered this way in Aristotle's philosophy and ethics and then again in the prevailing interpretation given for the thought of St. Thomas Aquinas, although prior Christian authors—and St. Thomas himself—had laid down the bases of a realistic view of relations (in particular, Gregory of Nyssa and St. Augustine).

45. An attempt in this sense was carried out by Chalmeta. G. Chalmeta, *Etica especial: El orden ideal de la vida Buena* (Pamplona: Eunsa, 1996).

46. Spoken of by Luhmann. N. Luhmann, *Paradigm Lost. Über die Etische Reflexion der Moral* (Frankfurt.: Suhrkamp, 1990).

47. R. K. Merton and R. Boudon offered many examples of this type, even if they did not see their relational character and, for this reason, confused emergent, aggregate, of composition, and perverse effects with one another as if they were all similar concepts. R. K. Merton, *Social Theory and Social Structure* (New York: Free Press, 1968), ch. 2; R. Boudon, *The Logic of Social Action: An Introduction to Sociological Analysis.* (London: Francis & Taylor, 1981).

48. Of a relational, not structuralist, type.

49. In network analysis, the broker is an intermediary agent/actor between other agents, so much so that the latter cannot communicate between them without passing through the broker.

50. I must here direct the reader to the numerous studies on network analysis. See P. Blau, "Structural Sociology and Network Analysis," in P. Marsden & N. Lin

(eds.), *Social Structure and Network Analysis* (Beverly Hills, CA: SAGE, 1982), and P. Blau, "Structures of Social Positions and Structures of Social Relations," in J. H. Turner (ed.), *Theory Building in Sociology* (London: SAGE, 1989), 43–59. See H. C. White, *Markets from Networks: Socioeconomic Models of Production* (Princeton, NJ: Princeton University Press, 2002), and H. C. White, *Identity and Control: How Social Formations Emerge,* 2nd ed. (Princeton, NJ: Princeton University Press, 2008).

51. See, P. Donati, "Engagement as a Social Relation: A Leap into Trans-Modernity," in M. S. Archer and A.M. Maccarini (eds.), *Engaging with the World: Agency, Institutions, Historical Formations* (New York: Routledge, 2012). I would like to underscore the fact that this perspective is not present in Catholic social doctrine, in which the morality of the market is made to depend on the morality of the agents of the market and on the regulations of the state or a world authority (the United Nations). The idea of the relational subject is directed, rather, to those organizations, such as the World Trade Organization, that could be configured as "relational subject" if they were to adopt the relational perspective illustrated here.

52. Donati, *Sociologia della riflessività.*

53. On the concept of immunization, See, R. Esposito, *Immunitas. Protezione e negazione della vita* (Torino: Einaudi, 2002).

54. "Social dumping" is a term used to describe the fact that an employer moves his or her enterprise from a country or area where work is more costly to a country or area in which work is less costly and in this way can save money and increase profits. In general, it is a practice involving the export of goods from a country with weak or poorly enforced labor standards, where the exporter's costs are artificially lower than its competitors in countries with higher standards, hence representing an unfair advantage in international trade. It results from differences in direct and indirect labor costs, which constitute a significant competitive advantage for enterprises in one country, with possible negative consequences for social and labor standards in other countries. In particular, it has to do with the unemployment caused in richer nations due to the transfer of jobs with low qualifications (the shift of low-skilled jobs) from regions with high salaries to regions of the world that are poor and have lower salaries.

55. Such as, for example, L. Bruni and R. Sudgen, "Fraternity: Why the Market Need Not Be a Morally Free Zone," *Economics and Philosophy* 24 (2008), and L. Bruni and S. Zamagni, *Economia Civile. Efficienza, Equità, Felicità Pubblica* (Bologna: il Mulino, 2004).

56. What is more, considering individuals as hypo-socialized agents. See Archer, *Realist Social Theory,* and Archer, *Being Human.*

57. P. Donati, *La matrice teologica della società* (Soveria Mannelli: Rubbettino, 2010b).

58. Globalization (understood as a process that brings social issues at the level of the world) and interdependence (as an emergent structural feature of social systems, both within and between them) are distinct phenomena that operate

synergistically: the more actors increase their interdependency, the more glo-balization growths, and vice versa. To my mind, only a relational ontological and epistemological matrix can see and manage this process (Donati, *La matrice*, 2010b).

REFERENCES

Anscombe, G. E. M. *Intention.* Cambridge, MA: Harvard University Press, 2000. (Originally published 1957)
Archer, M. S. *Culture and Agency.* Cambridge, UK: Cambridge University Press, 1988.
——. *Realist Social Theory: The Morphogenetic Approach.* Cambridge, UK: Cambridge University Press, 1995.
——. *Being Human: The Problem of Agency.* Cambridge, UK: Cambridge University Press, 2000.
——. *Structure, Agency and the Internal Conversation.* Cambridge, UK: Cambridge University Press, 2003.
——. *Making Our Way Through the World: Human Reflexivity and Social Mobility.* Cambridge, UK: Cambridge University Press, 2007.
Bauman, Z. *Postmodern Ethics.* Oxford: Blackwell, 1993.
Blau, P. "Structural Effects." *American Sociological Review*, 25.2 (1960): 178–193.
——. "Structural Sociology and Network Analysis." In P. Marsden & N. Lin (eds.), *Social Structure and Network Analysis.* Beverly Hills, CA: SAGE, 1982, 273–79.
——. "Structures of Social Positions and Structures of Social Relations." In J. H. Turner (ed.), *Theory Building in Sociology.* London: SAGE, 1989, 43–59.
Blau, P., and Schwartz, J. *Crosscutting Social Circle: Testing a Macrostructural Theory of Intergroup Relations.* New York: Academic Press, 1985.
Bottero, W. "Relationality and Social Interaction." *British Journal of Sociology* 60.2 (2009): 399–420.
Boudon, R. *The Logic of Social Action: An Introduction to Sociological Analysis.* London: Francis & Taylor, 1981.
——. *Effets perverse et ordre social.* Paris: Puf, 1989.
——. "I meccanismi fondamentali dell'evoluzione sociale." *Mondoperaio* 9.4–5 (2004): 56–71.
Bruni, L., and R. Sudgen. "Fraternity: Why the Market Need Not Be a Morally Free Zone." *Economics and Philosophy* 24 (2008): 35–64.
Bruni, L., and S. Zamagni. *Economia Civile: Efficienza, equità, felicità pubblica.* Bologna: il Mulino, 2004.
Chalmeta, G. *Etica especial. El orden ideal de la vida buena.* Pamplona: Eunsa, 1996.
Coleman, J. *Individual Interests and Collective Action: Selected Essays.* Cambridge, UK: Cambridge University Press, 1986.

——. *Foundations of Social Theory*. Cambridge MA.: Belknap Press of Harvard University Press, 1990.

Collier, A. *Being and Worth*. New York: Routledge, 1999.

Dahrendorf, R. "The Changing Quality of Citizenship." In B. van Steenberger (ed.), *The Condition of Citizenship*. London: SAGE, 1994, 10–19.

Donati, P. *Teoria relazionale della società*. Milano: FrancoAngeli, 1991.

——. *Il lavoro che emerge: Prospettive del lavoro come relazione sociale in una economia dopo-moderna*. Torino: Bollati Boringhieri, 2001.

——. "The Common Good as a Relational Good," In *Nova et Vetera*, English Edition, 7.3 (2009): 603–624.

——. "Le virtù sociali della famiglia." *Acta Philosophica* 19.2 (2010a): 267–296.

——. *La matrice teologica della società*. Soveria Mannelli: Rubbettino, 2010b.

——. *Relational Sociology: A New Paradigm for the Social Sciences*. New York: Routledge, 2011a.

——. *Sociologia della riflessività: Come si entra nel dopo-moderno*. Bologna: il Mulino, 2011b.

——. "Engagement as a Social Relation: A Leap into Trans-Modernity." In M. S. Archer and A. M. Maccarini (eds.), *Engaging with the World: Agency, Institutions, Historical Formations*. New York: Routledge, 2012, 129–61.

Donati, P., and I. Colozzi. (eds.). *Il paradigma relazionale nelle scienze sociali: Le prospettive sociologiche*. Bologna: il Mulino, 2006.

Donati, P., and R. Solci. *I beni relazionali: Che cosa sono e quali effetti producono*. Torino: Bollati Boringhieri, 2011.

Elder-Vass, D. "Searching for Realism, Structure and Agency in Actor Network Theory." *British Journal of Sociology*, 59.3 (2008): 455–473.

——. *Towards a Social Ontology of Market Systems*. CRESI Working Paper 2009-06. Colchester, UK: University of Essex, 2009.

——. *The Causal Power of Social Structures: Emergence, Structure and Agency*. Cambridge, UK: Cambridge University Press, 2010.

Esposito, R. *Immunitas. Protezione e negazione della vita*. Torino: Einaudi, 2002.

Garçia, J. L. A. "Double Effect." In *Encyclopedia of Bioethics*. Rev. ed. New York: Macmillan, 1995, 637.

Griswold, C. L. Jr. *Adam Smith and the Virtues of Enlightenment*. Cambridge, UK: Cambridge University Press, 1999.

Harcourt, B. E. *The Illusion of Free Markets: Punishment and the Myth of Natural Order*. Cambridge, MA: Harvard University Press, 2011.

Jensen, T. "Beyond Good and Evil: The Adiaphoric Company." *Journal of Business Ethics* 96 (2010): 425–434.

Luhmann, N. *Reflexionsprobleme im Erziehungssysteme*. Stuttgart: Ernst Klett, 1979.

——. *Paradigm Lost: Über die Etische Reflexion der Moral*. Frankfurt: Suhrkamp, 1990.

——. *Social Systems*. Palo Alto, CA: Stanford University Press, 1995.

May, W. "Double Effect." In W. T. Reich (ed.), *Encyclopedia of Bioethics*. New York: Macmillan, 1978, 316–320.

Merton, R. K. *Social Theory and Social Structure*. New York: Free Press, 1968.

Porpora, D. V. "Four Concepts of Social Structure." *Journal for the Theory of Social Behaviour* 19.2 (1989): 195–211.

Raub, W., and T. Voss. "Individual Interests and Moral Institutions: An Endogenous Approach to the Modification of Preferences." In M. Hechter, K. D. Opp, and R. Wippler (eds.), *Social Institutions: Their Emergence, Maintenance, and Effects*. New York: Aldine de Gruyter, 1990, 81–117.

Sacco, P. L., and S. Zamagni (eds.). *Teoria economica e relazioni interpersonali*. Bologna: il Mulino, 2006.

Smith, C. *What Is a Person? Rethinking Humanity, Social Life, and the Moral Good from the Person Up*. Chicago: The University of Chicago Press, 2010.

Soros, G. "Reflexivity in Financial Markets." In George Soros, *Open Society: Reforming Global Capitalism*. New York: Public Affairs, 2000, 58–90.

Sunstein, C. *Free Markets and Social Justice*. Oxford: Oxford University Press, 1997.

Teubner, G. "A Constitutional Moment. The Logics of 'Hit the Bottom.'" In Paul Kjaer and Gunther Teubner (eds.), *The Financial Crisis in Constitutional Perspective: The Dark Side of Functional Differentiation*. Oxford: Hart, 2011, 3–42.

Tumin, M. M. "Some Principles of Stratification: A Critical Analysis." *American Sociological Review* 18.4 (1953): 387–393.

White, H. C. *Markets from Networks: Socioeconomic Models of Production*. Princeton, NJ: Princeton University Press, 2002.

——. *Identity and Control: How Social Formations Emerge*. 2nd ed. Princeton, NJ: Princeton University Press, 2008.

4

Global Warming

A CASE STUDY IN STRUCTURE, AGENCY, AND
ACCOUNTABILITY

John A. Coleman, S.J.

THERE MAY BE no more vivid example of the harms markets cause to distant others than the fate of the island nation of the Maldives. Located off the southwest tip of India, the highest point in this archipelago is eight feet above sea level. Rising ocean levels caused by global warming threaten the homes and livelihoods of its 300,000 citizens and put in jeopardy the very existence of the nation.

The former president of the Maldives, Mohamed Nasheed, has appeared in a series of international meetings to plead his country's case. He pressed, unsuccessfully, for some genuine breakthrough at the 2009 Copenhagen United Nations conference on climate change. What options are open to this poor developing nation? The Netherlands is budgeting $10 billion to bolster its dykes and sea walls in anticipation of higher sea levels; Venice has a budget of more than $5 billion to prevent it from falling under the sea; and Galveston, Texas, has allocated $4 billion for a similar shoring up of its sea walls. The Maldives lacks such resources.

I have been lecturing and writing about Catholic social thought and the environment for a number of years,[1] yet this chapter looks at the morally critical threats of global warming primarily as a case study for the larger issues addressed in this volume. Central here is the relation of structure and agency, a highly contested issue among sociological theorists.

Some accounts of structure, such as structural-functionalist theories, are so rigid or deterministic in accounting for structural causality that there is little room for agency or for genuine social change. One wants to bring the person and agency back into that one-sided structuralist picture. Other accounts, variants of symbolic interactionist or social construction theories of society, do not sufficiently recognize that social structures are properties emergent from human actions with true causal impacts, even to the point of downward causal capacities to organize and direct human consciousness and action from the structural level above. As Christian Smith puts it:

> Social structures are concurrently the causes *and* outcomes of real, sustained patterned social interactions of human action.... Structures are always and everywhere entirely the dependent, emergent products of ongoing human activities.
>
> But this also means, contra reductionistically individualistic theories, that social structures exist emergently as real entities above and beyond the level of personal being and as such possess irreducible, downward causal capacities to organize and direct human consciousness and action from a level above.[2]

Smith's position, a form of critical realism in sociology that I endorse, is very similar to the sociological positions represented by the essays of Margaret Archer, Douglas Porpora, and Pierpaolo Donati in this volume.

Catholic Social Thought

One of the aims of this chapter is to relate the critical realist understanding of structure and agency to claims in Catholic social thought about structural sin and structures of injustice. The *locus classicus* for the Catholic treatment of structural sin is found in Pope John Paul II's encyclical, *Sollicitudo Rei Socialis*.

> If the present situation can be attributed to difficulties of various kinds, it is not out of place to speak of "structures of sin" which...are rooted in personal sin and thus always linked to the concrete acts of individuals who introduce these structures, consolidate them and make them difficult to remove. And thus they grow stronger, spread and become the source of other sins and so influence people's behavior.[3]

This account, however, is not entirely clear on the relation of structure and agency. To be sure, structures do not come into being except in and through interacting individual and group causation. They are not Platonic ideals. Clearly, John Paul II understands sinful structures as emerging from individual sinful behavior. But it is not completely clear how, according to the pope, sinful structures are causal in themselves, involving also a downward causality back on the agents whose interactions generate and sustain those structures. That is, such statements in Catholic social teaching leave implicit the sociological insight that structures are emergent realities that empower or constrain, channel or diminish human agency. Another difficulty is that in some Catholic calls for moral agency to transform sinful structures, the rhetoric seems to suggest that individual agents' moral choices can rather easily do so. This overlooks the durability of social structures, and it also fails to take sufficient account of reinforcing and interlocking structures that militate against structural change.[4]

Catholic social theory, on its own, lacks any developed sociological account of structure and agency. Premodern ethics, including Catholic moral theology, traditionally assigned responsibility for any harms caused to individual causal efficacy. I should be held responsible for a harm I have caused (or played a meaningful part in causing). Morality focused primarily on intention and causality. It neglected the role of persons in creating social structures and the causal impact of those structures on persons.

Just as Catholic social thought today needs a clearer account of the relation of structure to agency, it also requires a better articulation of the relation of social causality to individual moral responsibility for the harms done to distant others through social structures. Such harms (e.g., through global warming or other effects of market that cause huge, unintended losses for some) cannot always be attributed to any particular individual. Any one individual could stop participating in the market altogether without any change in the harms caused. For example, I could tomorrow personally become almost totally carbon neutral in my daily life without diminishing the threat of global warming in any perceptible way.

To attain greater clarity on these issues, this chapter focuses on global warming. It employs the insights of Archer, Porpora, and Smith on structure and agency, as well as the work of Christopher Kutz and Albino Barrera on accountability for harms done to distant others through social structural evils or failures.[5]

The Reality of Global Warming as a
Structural Harm

Scientist John Holden summarizes the ways global warming (and other related climate changes) is already a large structural threat:

> The most important conclusions about climactic disruption—that it is real, that it is accelerating, that it's already doing significant harm, that human activities are responsible for most of it, that tipping points into really catastrophic disruption likely lurk along the "business as usual" trajectory, and that there is much that could be done to reduce the danger at affordable cost if only we get started—have not been concocted by the Sierra Club or the enemies of capitalism.[6]

The International Panel on Climate Change has sifted through thousands of scientific studies to conclude that there is a discernible increase in global warming due to human intervention. There were 280 parts per million (ppm) of CO_2 in the atmosphere at the start of the Industrial Revolution. Now there are 392 ppm, and the number is growing. As James Hansen has noted, "The tragedy is that the actions needed to stabilize climate are not only feasible but provide additional benefits."[7]

The eleven hottest years since 1860, when temperatures began to be calculated by thermometers, have occurred in the past two decades. Because CO_2 remains in the atmosphere for centuries, even if we started drastically to reduce our carbon footprint today, the likelihood is that we will experience minimally a 2 degree Celsius rise in temperature and ocean rises of at least two feet, more likely five. An increase of 2 degrees Celsius annual temperature would make the world as warm as it was in the Pliocene era, 3 million years ago when the sea level actually rose 80 feet.[8] "The poorest parts of the world will be more seriously affected than the developed countries."[9] Global warming makes the idea of economic development a cruel joke.

In 2009, the Arctic ice cap was 1.1 million square miles smaller than ever before in recorded history, reduced by an area twelve times the size of Great Britain. Between 2003 and 2008, more than a trillion tons of Greenland's ice melted. The West Antarctic was losing ice 75% faster than a decade before.[10] The tropics have been expanding since 1980. A further 8.5 million square miles of the earth are now experiencing a tropical climate, which has led to reductions of wheat, corn, and barley yields of about 40 million tons a year.[11] The ocean is also warmer and more acidic than any time in the past 800,000 years.[12] A 2009 Oxfam briefing paper, "Suffering the Science," states: "Even if we adapted the smartest possible curbs on carbon emissions, the prospects are very bleak for hundreds of millions of people, most of them among the world's poorest."[13] The Center for Strategic and International Studies has estimated that, in some models, as many as 700 million climate change refugees may emerge by mid-century.[14]

The current extinction rate of species is at least 100 times greater than the average natural rate. And due to global warming, many species must migrate to new climates to survive.[15] "Conservation International currently estimates that one species is now going extinct every twenty minutes, which is a thousand times faster than the norm during much of the earth's history."[16] World population is estimated to reach 9 billion by mid-century, and agricultural land is everywhere encroached upon. As a result, where there were 2.5 acres of land for each person on earth fifty years ago, there will soon be only half an acre of farmland per person. [17]

There are three main carbon sinks (which absorb CO_2 from the atmosphere): (a) the ocean; (b) trees, especially tropical forests; and (c) permafrost, which buries methane underground. All are under assault. The ocean has become warmer and more acidic. Many argue that hurricanes have become more forceful because of the warming of the ocean. Acidic oceans are killing coral reefs; most estimate that coral reefs will not survive if the carbon dioxide level reaches 360 ppm (it is now at 392). Acidic oceans also threaten shellfish by impeding the formation of their shells. Finally, warmer oceans have less capacity to absorb new levels of CO_2.

Tropical forests are also being laid waste. Indonesia and Brazil rank after China and the United States; their contribution to global warming arises from widespread devastation of their tropical forest lands. Deforestation currently accounts for more of the annual CO_2 increase than "all the world's cars, trucks, planes, ships and trains combined."[18]

One of the most frightening threats to climate stability would be the melting of permafrost in the Arctic areas. "The permafrost traps 1,600 billion tons of carbon with a warming effect equivalent to 270 years of CO_2 emissions at current levels."[19] Already, "one estimate is the release of methane occurring from West Siberian peat bogs is already equivalent to more than the greenhouse gasses emitted by the United States in a single year."[20]

Global warming also has a twofold impact on weather pattern changes. "Global warming increases the intensity of droughts, heat waves, and forest fires but also the intensity of the other extreme: heavier rains, extreme floods, tornadoes, tropical storms."[21] Increasing population, on its own, is exacerbating the shortage of water. But the melting glaciers in the Himalayas and the Andes portend possible catastrophic water shortages for India, China, and Peru.

There are, however, options for reducing our global carbon footprint. There are non-fossil-fuel alternatives to coal and oil, such as power from wind, wave, sunshine, flowing water, and geothermal heat—and from the reuse of wastes. Sweden's greenhouse gas emissions were 9% lower in 2005 than they were in 1990. Over that period, the economy grew by 44%. Similarly, "since 1975, per capita use of electricity in California has remained constant, while growing fifty percent higher in the rest of the United States."[22] A great deal of wasted CO_2 can be attributed to poorly constructed or under-insulated buildings. People in the United States, Canada, and Australia used about twice as much energy per capita as their peers in Europe and Japan. Moreover, "70% of cumulative world emissions of greenhouse gases come from just six countries"; the twenty most polluting countries have been responsible for 88% of greenhouse gases since the start of the industrial age.[23]

Since the beginning of the Industrial Revolution, three countries have left the largest carbon footprints: the United Kingdom, the United States, and Germany. China is now the currently largest producer of CO_2 in the world; the United States is second. But five countries (including Australia and Canada) surpass the United States in per capita output of CO_2.

The issues of structure and agency loom large in addressing global warming. "The vast majority are doing very little, if anything at all, to alter their daily habits, even though those habits are the source of the dangers climate change has in store for us."[24] Many individuals have come to believe that the issue is so large and complex that nothing they can do personally can make any significant difference. "Climate change seems to be seen as a risk the responsibility for which lies with the authorities."[25] In a 2006 international survey, the citizens of the United States were the most skeptical about whether climate change is occurring.

To do nothing about climate change is highly immoral and risky behavior. As one well-known climatologist, Tim Flannery, put it, "There is now a better than even risk that despite our best efforts, in the coming two or three decades Earth's climate system will pass the point of no return."[26] Delays will mean that efforts to mitigate or adjust to the impending changes will be ever more costly. Shifting from one form of energy to another (e.g., wood to coal or coal to oil) almost always took time to build the necessary infrastructure. While there is no yellow brick road to help us walk away from fossil fuels, some things are called for. In some sense, the polluter must pay.

Given the already damaging structural harms done by global warming and the great risks (both climatological and financial) attending failure to act, why has there been so much inaction and even skepticism about global warming? It is not as if we do not know from past climate shifts in our earth's history just how devastating shifts of more than 3 degrees Celsius would be to our economies and environment.[27] Why the inertia in acting on what we know?

Skepticism and Inaction on Global Warming

There is a strong scientific consensus on global warning. No climatologist who writes an article denying that global warming is occurring, denying that it is primarily caused by humans, or denying that there are possible catastrophic tipping points if it is not reversed could ever get such an article accepted by a bona fide scientific journal. Yet there is simultaneously an active and well-financed campaign to undercut the public's confidence in this consensus by duplicitously inflating ordinary debates about the details of climatology into arguments against the existence of global warming altogether.

There are, to be sure, points of contention among climatologists about climate change patterns. Debates range over just how the more natural and the human causes impinging on our climate coexist and interact. Thus some past climate increases came from natural solar increased outputs due to changing axes of the sun vis à vis the earth. Volcano eruptions cause a planetary cooling for a short period, and aerosol use (which had such a devastating impact on the ozone hole) also can cause cooling. In point of fact, except for human activity, natural causes on balance would be cooling the earth.

Debates also rage over the precision of proxy data (tree rings, ice bores, coral formations on the ocean, and sediment in ocean and lake bottoms) to determine the temperature of the earth in earlier eras. Most scientists are puzzled to explain why in earlier periods of global warming the warming took place by means of higher levels of temperature at the poles than in the tropics. Climatologists also differ on how much carbon dioxide the earth can absorb before generating catastrophic environmental results. The consensus of many is 350 ppm of CO_2. Other estimates have been as high as 450 to 560 ppm. There are also differences in estimates of how high the sea will rise in the current century. Similarly, differences have arisen about the likelihood of various tipping points to cascade climate warming out of control.

Such disagreements about the details of planetary warming are ordinary ingredients in all science, not evidence to support the denial of it. But "deniers use normal scientific uncertainties to undermine the status of actual scientific knowledge."[28] Science is always about probabilities. Few would avoid doing something if the probability of its being harmful was 90%. Deniers take the slim absence of 100% probabilities as evidence of "junk" science.[29]

Many of the scientists who have engaged in denial or systematic skepticism are not climatologists. Almost all such scientist skeptics have received funds for their research or interventions from foundations funded by fossil-fuel money (i.e., financial support from the oil, gas, or coal industries). Patrick Michael, for example, from the University of Virginia, publishes a "World Climate Report" full of skepticism. His work is funded by the Western Fuel Association.[30] S. Fred Singer, a notorious denier and founder of the Science and Environmental Policy Project (again fossil fuel funded), earlier took stands of denial against the harmful effects of secondhand smoke and against the reality of acid rain.[31] Another denier, Frederick Seitz, founder of the George Marshall Institute, also funded by fossil-fuel money, tried to force the Academy of Science to raise questions about Michael Mann's research leading to the hockey stick image of climate change over a 1,000-year period (little change for a long period followed by a rapid rise in recent years). However, this is a tiny minority of all scientists. In 2010, 250 members of the National Academy of Science, including eleven Nobel laureates, signed a letter saying it was good science to see global warming as human caused and noting, "For a problem as potentially catastrophic as climate change, taking no action poses a dangerous risk for our planet."[32]

Still other sources of climate denial follow the advice of Frank Luntz, a Republican Party consultant who, in a leaked memo of 2002, urged candidates to double down efforts to deny the scientific consensus on global warming. "You need to continue to make the lack of scientific certainty a primary issue in the debate," Luntz remarked in that memo.[33] Other organized sources of disinformation about global warming science include Richard Lindzen (a physicist, not a climatologist, who has received funding from fossil-fuel foundations) and the Global Climate Coalition (a consortium of fifty chemical, mining, fossil fuel, and automotive companies bent on fighting any new governmental regulations about global warming). The Koch brothers and the Scaife Foundation (both based on fossil-fuel wealth) also gave money to the American Enterprise Institute, the Heritage Foundation, and the Heartland Institute. The Heartland Institute has recently been shown to have plans to introduce climate skepticism into public school curricula. Besides fueling pseudo-scientific doubt, fossil-fuel money also feeds into skepticism fostered through talk radio. Mark Morano, who had worked for Rush Limbaugh (and later worked for Exxon Mobil), received money to form his skeptic's web page, Climatedepot.com.

As Michael Mann notes: "It was increasingly unclear that any amount of evidence or additional work would satisfy the critics. The attacks...were part and parcel of a proxy war against the science and its icons being fought by, or at the least often funded by, powerful vested interests who found the scientific evidence for climate change inconvenient for political, financial, or philosophic reasons."[34] Mann notes, almost in despair: "The scientific community and those seeking to communicate its message are greatly outmatched by a massive disinformation campaign funded by powerful vested interests driven by a single goal. That goal is to thwart efforts to regulate carbon emissions—a necessary step if we are to stabilize greenhouse gas concentrations below dangerous levels.[35] There are currently 2,340 registered lobbyists in the United States working on behalf of fossil-fuel companies.[36]

Basically, there are six stages of denial in the arguments of climate change contrarians: (1) CO_2 is not actually increasing; (2) even if it is, the increase has no impact on the climate since there is no convincing evidence of warming; (3) even if there is warming, it is due to natural causes; (4) even if the warming cannot be explained by natural causes, the human impact is small, and the impact of continued greenhouse gas emissions will be minor; (5) even if the current and projected future human effects on the earth's climate are not negligible, the changes are generally going to be good for us; and (6) whether or not the changes are going to be good for us, humans are very adept at adapting to changes; besides, it's too late to do anything about it and/or a technological fix is bound to come along when we really need it.[37]

So one finds a similar pattern of disinformation as was found earlier by those who denied the medical effects of tobacco, the harm from and costs of reducing acid rain, or the hole in the ozone layer. Now it's applied to the science of global warming. There is also some harm in the so-called "fairness doctrine" followed by journalists. They may be inclined to think the fairness doctrine means giving equal weight to the scientists and the skeptics (which feeds into the skepticism). The fairness doctrine may make sense in politics, but science is about evidence, not opinion.

The United States, which represents 5% of the world's population, "accounts for 4% of the greenhouse gas emissions from the industrial (OCED) countries as a whole. If the states of the US were separate countries, 25 would be in the top 60 nations in terms of emissions. Texas emits more greenhouse gases than France, but has only about a third of its population."[38] Yet the United States and China (the two largest emitters of CO_2) have torpedoed efforts to work out an international treaty to address global climate change and set targets for reductions in CO_2. Some of this inaction flows from the fossil-fuel interests and their lobbyists in Washington. Some stems from a libertarian objection to any further governmental regulations. Chris Mooney has argued that Republican opposition to plans to curb greenhouse gas emissions stems heavily from their distaste for regulation.[39] Some of it also stems from a free and unregulated market ideology.

Clearly, some actors are more culpable for the damage being done by global warming than others. The most blame-worthy are those industries and wealthy individuals who fund scientists willing to manufacture skepticism. But part of the problem is also societal. In democratic nations with their periodic elections and competing party interests, it is difficult to take on longer range concerns. Ordinary people who may discount their contribution to global warming or doubt that their actions could make much difference are "confronted with daily social pressure to conform to a high fossil fuel consuming lifestyle, so personal behavioral change in reality requires a lot of courage."[40]

By any account, addressing the threat of global warming will require fundamental change, and we humans resist such change.

The Structural Politics of Addressing the Harm of Global Warming

To adequately address global warming, we will need positive models of a low carbon future. Simple calls for sacrifice or scare tactics will not be sufficient to nudge along the project of lower carbon outputs. Global warming is also closely connected to a cognate national and international issue: energy security. It is remarkable that four countries that have drastically reduced their carbon output did so starting in the 1970s when the oil crisis led them to alternative forms of energy. These changes predated much public concern about global warming. France turned toward nuclear power to protect against costly and unreliable imported oil. Denmark focused on windmills, which now provide close to a third of its energy needs. Sweden turned to reusing waste (turning it into a fuel to generate electricity) and improving the energy efficiency of its buildings. Brazil opted for ethanol made from sugar cane. This last approach, however, may not be a wise alternative to oil and coal, since it creates biofuel farms on large swathes of agricultural land needed to grow food.

Thomas Friedman emphasizes that "going green" will reduce the dependency of the United States on foreign oil, which bolsters dictatorships and will create many new jobs. For his part, Anthony Giddens insists that we need to become "smarter about how we design buildings, packages, vehicles, refrigerators, air conditioning and lighting systems and constantly insisting on higher and tighter standards of efficiency for each of them."[41]

We do need some hard-headed planning and choices if we are going to reduce global warming. There is no one magic fix or miracle energy cure. As Mark Lynas notes: "The reality is that only a combination of serious energy efficiency and a wide variety of new technologies offers any hope of a way out of the crisis."[42]

Two Princeton University social scientists, Robert Socolow and Steve Pacala, came up with the idea of considering each form of technology or energy reduction possibility as a potential "wedge," one of a number of wedges that together would make the difference between an upward spiraling carbon footprint or a stabilizing one. Each of their proposed wedges represents the reduction of annual emissions by 1 billion tons of carbon by the year 2055. Implementing seven of these wedges would allow the world to achieve the goal of a CO_2 level in 2055, no larger than the one today. Socolow and Pacala urge that people not be "beguiled by the possibility of revolutionary technology," such as nuclear fusion, artificial photosynthesis, or space-based solar technology. They emphasize instead that "humanity can solve the carbon and climate problem in the first half of this century simply by scaling up what we already know how to do."[43]

While there is no silver bullet, this approach proposes a series of steps that can gain the desired lowering of our carbon footprint yet still allow economic growth. Each of the following steps would result in a reduction of 1 billion tons of carbon: (a) increase the world's fleet fuel economy from 30 to 60 miles per gallon; (b) halve the average distance traveled per car from 10,000 miles per year to 5,000; (c) build more efficient buildings; (d) initiate more efficient electricity generation with less waste; (e) displace coal with natural gas in electricity generation and quadruple the number of gas-fueled power stations; (f) add 700 one-megawatt nuclear power stations; (g) introduce carbon capture and storage (i.e., pumping CO_2 into underground geological reservoirs) at 800 megawatt coal plants; (h) increase the use of wind power (2 million one-megawatt turbines, a fifty-fold increase from today's deployment); (i) depend more on direct solar energy (a wedge would require a 700-fold increase from today's total, covering 5 million acres of land); and (j) stop the deforestation of tropical forests (since deforestation represents about 20% of human-generated greenhouse gas emissions).

There is, indeed, some good news in all these projections. First, the solutions for energy profligacy are already known (at least in germ). Second, as two of the foremost independent institutions working on sustainable development (the German Wuppertal Institute and the U.S. Rocky Mountain Institute) show in their joint book, *Factor Four: Doubling Wealth, Halving Resource Use*, sustainability will not be achieved by any one "big ticket" change but by multiple smaller changes that build on one another. Each smaller improvement (e.g., waterless toilets, low-volume showerheads, or energy-efficient grass blowers) has a multiplier effect in the reduction of greenhouse gas emissions while both livability and economic productivity also gain.[44]

This literature on achieving both the creation of wealth and reduction in resource use evokes principles highly consonant with Catholic social teaching (and often gives those Catholic principles a sociological foundation). Thus something akin to the Catholic notion of subsidiarity, for example, is named in *Agenda 21*—the detailed action agenda that emerged from the 1992 United Nations Conference on Environment and Development in Rio de Janeiro. Chapter 28 of the *Agenda 21* document states: "Because so many of the problems and solutions have their roots in local activities, the participation and cooperation of local authorities will be a determining factor in fulfilling *Agenda 21*'s objectives. As the level of governance closest to the people, they play a vital role in education, mobilizing, and responding to the public to promote sustainable development."[45] One thinks of ways in which mayors of cities or local state governments have pushed ahead the agenda for better climate change more than has the national government of the United States. One also can see here another possible wedge, to add to Pacala and Socolow's wedges: a dramatic reduction in eating foreign-grown fruits, vegetables, and other foodstuffs, thereby reducing energy use for transporting them.

Another section of *Agenda 21* resonates with the Catholic insistence on justice as participation. It mandates public hearings and a wide consultation process among the citizenry "to achieve consensus on sustainable development goals."[46] The literature about green cities is replete with references to solidarity (another value in Catholic social thought), for example, treating sister-city transfers of energy-saving technology or planting trees in the developing world. The notion of public goods (public transportation, green space) gets endorsed by *Agenda 21*, much as it does in Catholic notions of the common good.

Finally, something akin to the Catholic preferential option for the poor and the insistence that human dignity involves the satisfaction of "basic human needs" appears in *The Natural Step,* an ambitious set of sustainability goals and a process for implementing them proposed for and adapted by many companies and cities. Step 4 in its protocol reads: "Fair and efficient use of resources with respect to meeting human needs must occur. This means: Basic needs must be met with the most resource-efficient methods possible and their satisfaction must take precedence over the provision of luxuries."[47] One hears an echo of John Paul II's statement when visiting Canada: "The needs of the poor take priority over the wants of the rich."[48]

Reckoning Accountability for the Structural Evil of Global Warming

Given the urgency in reducing carbon dioxide emissions and the large structural issues involved, most commentators judge that only large actors, such as nation-states and big corporations, can possibly achieve the goals of reducing our global carbon output.

Nicholas Stern has proposed a new "global deal on climate change."[49] Stern wants to help shape negotiations for a new international global treaty, with the aim of limiting greenhouse gas concentrations. He contends that, given the level of greenhouse gases already in the atmosphere, this objective is so compelling that there is little scope for any major country or group of countries to fall behind in achieving the mandated emission cuts. "All countries must play their part. Once the basic arithmetic has been recognized, governments across the world ought to commit to credibly coordinated policies."[50]

Stern argues that carbon emissions trading will help reach global targets most efficiently. He recognizes that markets will have to be carefully designed to prevent market distortions, perverse incentives, and protectionism. Stern proposes that a worldwide cap-and-trade system be in place by 2020 that would cover all the industrial countries but also include the more affluent developing nations. The rich countries would have to accept that emissions from the less well-off countries would still grow for some time as development proceeds. Therefore, the developed countries would have to cut their emissions sharply. Stern thinks that carbon markets would also likely stimulate the technological innovations needed to reduce emissions further. He also recognizes that only a handful of countries have the technological capacity to lead in such innovations.

One significant problem, however, is that there is utterly no mention of "politics" in Stern's calculations, and no analysis of power, or of rivalries and tensions in international relations. He seems to assume that his proposed "global deal" will be reached as the nations of the world come to see reason. In a sense, like much of Catholic social thought, Stern lacks a tutored theory of power. "All must play their part," Stern claims. This is, of course, true. But a further structural issue concerns who will implement this "must." Those who place an enormous amount of faith in carbon markets often forget that carbon markets will depend on prior political support. Another structural issue with cap-and-trade schemes is a reliable monitoring program, so, for example, one can actually be sure money sent to save tropical forests (to offset one's carbon output) actually gets spent for that purpose.

Nation-states, international treaty negotiations, and the few environmentally responsible corporations have yet to act forcefully. Some think that only some ecological disaster will wake the world up. I am reminded of Mohamed Nasheed's comments in *The Island President* when he was asked about the failure to achieve much breakthrough at the United Nations environment talks in Copenhagen: "I'm afraid politicians only do the things that their people tell them to!"

This is why it is so important to also put emphasis on the actions of individuals and small nongovernmental organizations. We need both deliberate, collective efforts by nations, states, and corporations, as well as smaller "spiritual" ecological practices such as recycling, reducing one's own automobile use, moving to more energy-efficient light fixtures, planting organic gardens, and so on. We need to raise consciousness and enliven a growing number of people who will "tell their politicians" what to do. I serve on the board of the California Inter-Faith Power and Light organization (one of thirty-eight such groups), which works to mobilize congregations, mosques, and synagogues to (a) reduce the energy use in their own buildings, (b) engage in education in their congregations—including through annual preach-ins on the topic of global warming and the environment, and (c) join in lobbying efforts to push state legislature to further the issue of reduction of global warming.[51] It is worth remembering that the major energy force that created the Intergovernmental Panel on Climate Change through the United Nations initially came not from governments or large corporations but from motivated individuals working through environmental nongovernmental organizations.

From this Case Study to our Overall Book Theme

The theme of this volume can be expressed in a question: What can be learned from sociology's understanding of the emergence and causal effects of social structures that would allow moral theologians in the Catholic tradition to articulate better the moral responsibilities of market participants for harms caused by markets to distant others?

Global warming is a kind of market failure. It is the result of a structure or system of production that relies on an ever-expanding use of cheap fossil fuels. For many, environmental structural failures are somehow merely "externalities" to the market mechanism. Clearly, no one wants to lose the possibility for expanding economic productivity and wealth creation and its dispersion. No one would want India or China, Indonesia or Brazil not to grow wealthier, in the sense of creating greater economic well-being for its people. But the present trajectory of economic development relies too heavily on a dramatically increased use of fossil fuels whose impact on the environment cannot be sustained. Consider the roles of nations, firms, and individuals in this process.

Nation-states and multinational firms, collectively and individually, have the most potent possible structural influence on the growing ecological damage. Nation-states, working through global institutions, are the key actors for addressing global warming as a market failure that can do harm to distant others. By any accounting, the poorer countries will suffer more from the impact of rising sea levels and/or droughts and extreme storms due to global warming. Nations have an obligation to work for a global common good, by finding a form of treaty-based regulation that will curb excessive energy use. Cap-and-trade schemes to limit CO_2 emissions represent one such mechanism (as would a carbon tax). But early adopters of such approaches (Australia, for example) will be penalized due to higher cost of production of its products compared to the United States, China, or other nations not doing the same. So, nation-states have an obligation to find a viable international cooperative scheme—with some teeth—to curb worldwide carbon emissions.

The nation-state, through its parliament or legislature and its politicians and citizen-voters, also has a prima facie obligation to devise mechanisms to improve its own carbon footprint at home. Those countries that are most responsible for greenhouse gases generated since the start of the industrial age clearly have special responsibilities to address this structural failure following the dictum: the polluter should pay. As we earlier saw, 70% of cumulative world emissions of greenhouse gases come from just six countries.

Corporations also have obligations here, but not all corporations bear the same moral weight when dealing with global warming. Fossil-fuel companies bear a heavier responsibility to help pioneer alternative forms of energy besides oil, gas, and coal. Those companies and institutions that have sown skeptical doubt about addressing global warming also bear greater responsibility for perpetuating harms to distant others (including to generations not yet born).

Individual persons also play a critical role in global warming, of course. Individuals do not intend the harm to distant others caused by global warming, and no one person's causal input is large enough to make much difference. But individuals remain consumers as well as citizens with responsibilities to address the harms caused to distant others. Individuals participate in a way of life from which they accrue significant benefits, in this case, participation in an environmentally destructive way of life and culture. Individuals both sustain and are shaped by the economic structures whose effects give rise to global warming.

Considerable help in understanding and persuasively articulating these responsibilities is provided by the sociological analysis in other chapters in this volume. For example, Pierpaulo Donati points out that social structures consist of social relations within increasingly complex causal networks. As a result, he argues, "The ethics of intention is no longer sufficient. It must be integrated with an ethics of responsibility that is not restricted to the direct consequences of individual acts but also takes into account the indirect consequences of relational networks."[52]

Many of the essays in this book (e.g., those by Margaret Archer, Douglas Porpora, Mary Hirschfield, and Albino Barrera) explicitly address individual accountability for structural failures that cause harm to distant others. They do so by drawing on the work of Thomas Aquinas, Christopher Kutz, and Albino Barrera. Barrera, for example, has argued: "There can be complicity even in a seemingly 'unstructured' setting such as a marketplace. All that is needed is a quasi-participatory intent whereby people contribute to, draw benefits from, and perpetuate underlying social structures and institutions through their participation in them."[53] Kutz, for his part, has argued that "I am accountable for the harm or wrong we do together, independently of the actual difference I make."[54] Kutz proposes a notion of complicity based on participation rather than on explicit intention or direct causation.

I leave to other authors in this volume a more detailed account of how moral theologians in the Catholic tradition can account for the moral complicity of individuals in structural failures that cause harm to distant others. Here I want to pay more attention to the structural reality of such harms. Any account of the moral culpability of individual persons for harms to distant others must insist that "individuals" are always relational beings embedded in social structures.

We will be helped to parse individuals' culpability for the structural harms due to global warming because of their willing participation in a carbon-wasteful and harm-inducing way of life if we pause to reflect on two key notions: one from Catholic social teaching and the other from critical realism's sociological understanding of structure and agency.

The idea from Catholic social teaching is the core notion of the common good. Remember, however, that, as Pierpaulo Donati reminds us, the common good is not merely some "total good," a product of aggregation, but a relational good (an emergent effect of accumulative actions in forming a structure).[55] The common good, then, is a structural good. It refers to the societal structures that best achieve adequate human flourishing for all participants. The failure to achieve the common good is also a structural failure, a kind of common bad. Catholic social thought, not always so explicit in considering the structural reality of the common good, does insist on the duty of individuals to work for the common good according to their means. The common good is an emergent, indeed structural, property that, as Donati argues in his chapter in this volume, like any structure, is "made *by* individuals but not made *of* individuals," inasmuch as structures consist of relationships of preexisting social positions. It is in this relational dynamic "that the problem of moral responsibility is to be found."[56] Individuals benefit from participating in and sustaining social structures that cause harm to distant others. As a result, individuals, and not only nations or corporations, are complicit in global warming. Two things need to be recognized about this complicity of individuals. "To say all are accountable is not the same as to say all are equally to blame."[57] Second, "less responsible does not mean being excused."[58]

Finally, turning to a theological view, consider Barrera's judgment that "the wanton destruction of the ecosystem as a collateral effect of economic growth and development is a sin."[59] This returns us to our earlier consideration of the notion of structure and agency and the sociological insight of the critical realists, who insist that social structures are both the causes and outcomes of patterns of social interactions of human agents. Structures are, always and everywhere, entirely the dependent, emergent properties of ongoing human agency. Thus far, Catholic social teaching can probably easily follow, even if it has not clearly taken the next step. It can learn, then, from its dialogue with the social sciences a better way to construe structure, agency, and social sin if it also concludes, with Christian Smith, that "social structures exist emergently as real entities above and beyond the level of personal being and, as such, possess irreducible downward capacities to organize and direct human consciousness and action from a level above."[60]

In as much as structures emerge from and are sustained by the outcomes of human interaction, the individuals who sustain such structures (by their participation in them) are morally responsible for the harms and benefits structures generate. That is, market participants are complicit in the harms markets cause. Addressing structural or social sin requires market participants to press for changes in that social structure called the market.

To be sure, not all the change need be negative. In point of fact, the future of some forms of fossil fuel are problematic anyway. Peak oil (the time after which total world production falls) suggests that getting more oil and doing so relatively inexpensively and safely may be more difficult to achieve.[61] There is probably enough natural gas to last through this century, enough coal to last for several centuries—although coal is the worst offender in emitting CO_2. Nuclear power is carbon friendly, but we may not have sufficient time before tipping points to build enough of plants to make up for a switch from coal and oil. Moreover, there remain problems of disposing with nuclear waste. A number of global warming experts (such as Mark Lynas and Anthony Giddens) have recently, if reluctantly, come to support building more nuclear plants. How much time it will take to harness wind, solar, and wave power and connect it to a sophisticated energy grid is also not clear. Some put their faith in far-fetched schemes to hoist giant mirrors into the atmosphere to reflect back the sun's warmth or to scatter aerosol like cooling agents, despite the dangers these place on the ozone level.[62]

Although there are some parties more culpable for the structural harm of global warming than others, everyone is, in a genuine sense, implicated. Each of us has responsibilities to address this structural evil. At its heart, the issue of global warming is a species of the "tragedy of the commons" dilemma. We must find a way to prevent "free riders" who soil the commons while declining any responsibility to preserve them. Catholic social thought, of course, does see the earth as primordially a common gift to all from God, but all are also called to exercise stewardship. Nor is Catholic social thought skeptical about the reality of global warming. As Pope Benedict XVI reminded us in his 2010 World Day of Peace speech, when he spoke of

a growing crisis which it would be irresponsible not to take seriously. Can we remain indifferent before the problems associated with such realities [note the pope calls them realities, not mere hypotheses] as climate change; desertification; the deterioration and loss of productivity in vast agricultural areas; the pollution of rivers and acquifers; the loss of biodiversity; the increase of natural catastrophes; and the deforestation of equatorial and tropical regions? Can we disregard the growing phenomenon of "environmental refugees"? All these are issues with a profound impact on the exercise of human rights, such as the right to life, food, health and development.[63]

Our climate crisis requires an adequate social scientific analysis of the interaction of individuals and the social structures they create and sustain.

Only on this path can we address our moral responsibility for the harms that markets cause to distant others. The people of the Maldives—and countless others harmed in other ways by markets—await our response.

NOTES

1. John Coleman, "Environment: Catholic Vision for the Green City," *Origins*, 36.3 (2006): 33–41; John Coleman, "Globalization and Sustainability: Catholic Resources and Responses," *Origins*, 38.37 (2009): 589–595. The environment has become, recently, an integral part of Catholic social teaching, not some externality to it. This is clear in the full integration of environmental issues in Benedict XVI's social encyclical, *Caritas in veritate*, and in the revised, twentieth anniversary edition of Donal Dorr's earlier book, *Option for the Poor*, which is now titled *Option for the Poor and Caring for the Earth* (Maryknoll, NY: Orbis Press, 2012).

2. Christian Smith, *What Is a Person?* (Chicago: University of Chicago Press, 2010), 356. Smith references in this quote the work of Margaret S. Archer, *Realist Social Theory: The Morphogenetic Approach* (New York: Cambridge University Press, 1995).

3. Pope John Paul II, *Sollicitudo Rei Socialis* (Washington, DC: Office of Publishing and Promotion Services, United States Catholic Conference, 1988), 36.

4. For the durability and stability of social structures and the notion of interlocking structures, cf. Smith, *What Is a Person*, 325, 357–365, 369.

5. Christopher Kutz, *Complicity: Ethics and Law for a Collective Age* (New York: Cambridge University Press, 2000); Albino Barrera, *Market Complicity and Christian Ethics* (New York: Cambridge University Press, 2011).

6. Cited in Thomas L. Friedman, *Hot, Flat and Crowded* (New York: Farrar, Strauss and Giroux, 2008), 124.

7. James Hansen, *Storms of My Grandchildren: The Truth About the Coming Climate Catastrophe and Our Last Chance to Save Humanity* (New York: Bloomsbury, 2009), x.

8. Hansen, *Storms*, 13.

9. Anthony Giddens, *The Politics of Climate Change* (Malden, MA: Polity Press, 2009), 22.

10. As reported in "The Curse of Carbon," *The Economist*, Dec. 31, 2008.

11. Bill McKibben, *Earth: Making a Life on a Tough New Planet* (New York: Henry Holt, 2010), 6.

12. McKibben, *Earth*, 19.

13. "Suffering the Science," Oxfam Briefing Paper 130, July 6, 2009, 1.

14. Reported in "A New (Under)Class of Travelers," *The Economist*, June 27, 2009.

15. Hansen, *Storms*, 147.

16. Friedman, *Hot, Flat, and Crowded*, 141.

17. Tim Flannery, *Now or Never: Why We Must Act Now to End Climate Change and Create A Sustainable Future* (New York: Atlantic Monthly Press, 2009), 97.

18. Friedman, *Hot, Flat, and Crowded*, 34.

19. McKibben, *Earth*, 22.

20. Giddens, *The Politics*, 26.

21. Hansen, *Storms*, xv.

22. For the claim about Sweden cf. Giddens, *The Politics*, 101. For the claim about California cf. Hansen, *Storms*, 190.

23. Giddens, *The Politics*, 222.

24. Giddens, *The Politics*, 1.

25. Giddens, *The Politics*, 103.

26. Tim Flannery, *Now or Never*, 100.

27. For a careful perspective on the impact of 1 to 6 degree Celsius shifts on the earth's environment, see the careful parsing of past geological impacts of such temperature shifts in Mark Lynas, *Six Degrees: Our Future on a Hotter Planet* (Washington, DC: National Geographic, 2008). At the end of the Permian era when temperatures on Earth were 6 degrees Celsius hotter than today, 95% of all life forms went extinct. Lynas has two other good books on the topic of global warming: *High Tide: The Truth About Climate Change* (London: Picador, 2004) and *The God Planet: Saving the Planet in the Age of Humans* (New York: Fourth Estate, 2012). Other excellent treatments can be found in James Speth, *Red Sky in the Morning: America and the Crisis of the Global Environment* (New Haven, CT: Yale University Press, 2004) and *The Bridge at the End of the World: Capitalism, The Environment and Crossing from the Crisis of Sustainability* (New Haven, CT: Yale University Press, 2009).

28. Naomi Oreskes and Erik Conway, *Merchants of Doubt* (New York: Columbia University Press, 2010), 19.

29. A reliable source for understanding thee real debates about climate change can be found on the website, RealClimate.org.

30. Michael Mann, *The Hockey Stick and the Climate Wars* (New York: Columbia University Press, 2012), 106.

31. Oreskes and Conway, *Merchants of Doubt*, 129.

32. Mann, *The Hockey Stick*, 245.

33. Mann, *The Hockey Stick*, 22.

34. Mann, *The Hockey Stick*, 191.

35. Mann, *The Hockey Stick*, 254.

36. James Hansen, *Storms*, 186.

37. Mann, *The Hockey Stick*, 23.

38. Giddens, *The Politics*, 182–183. There are thirty-four OCED countries.

39. Chris Mooney, *The Republican War on Science* (New York: Basic Books, 2005).

40. Lynas, *Six Degrees*, 287.

41. Giddens, *The Politics.*, 101

42. Lynas, *Six Degrees*, 294.

43. S. Pacala and R. Socolow, "Stabilization Wedges: Solving the Climate Problem for the Next 50 Years With Current Technologies," *Science* 305 (2004): 968–972. Of course, we also need not preclude the invention of new technologies to help us address the problem. The virtue of the Pacala and Socolow article is that it shows that we can address the problem even with current technologies.

44. Ernst U. Von Weyzsacke, *Factor Four: Doubling Wealth, Halving Resource Use* (New York: Earthscan, 1998).

45. *Agenda 21: Earth Summit: The United Nations' Program of Action from Rio* (New York: United Nations, 1995), 147.

46. *Agenda 21*, 182.

47. Karl Henry Robert, *The Natural Step Story: Seeding a Quiet Revolution* (New York: New Catalyst Books, 2008), 116.

48. The previous five paragraphs are a slight revision of some paragraphs in my cited article, Coleman, "Environment," 41.

49. Stern, "Key Elements of a Global Deal on Climate Change," 5.

50. Stern, "Key Elements of a Global Deal on Climate Change," 10.

51. A cognate group is the Catholic Coalition on Climate Change.

52. Pierpaolo Donati, "The Morality of Action, Reflexivity, and the Relational Subject." this volume, 78.

53. Barrera, *Market Complicity*, 47.

54. Kutz, *Complicity*, 122.

55. Donati, "The Morality of Action," this volume, 68.

56. Donati "The Morality of Action," this volume, 58.

57. Kutz, *Complicity*, 189.

58. Barrera, *Market Complicity*, 62.

59. Barrera, *Market Complicity*, 149.

60. Smith, *What Is a Person*, 356.

61. Kenneth Deffeyes, *Hubbert's Peak: The Impending Oil Shortage* (Princeton, NJ: Princeton University Press, 2005).

62. For a discussion of the possibilities and dangers in engaging in geo-engineering to fix the earth's climate, see Jeff Goodell, *How to Cool the Planet: Geo-engineering and the Audacious Quest to Fix Earth's Climate* (New York: Houghton, Mifflin Harcourt, 2010.) Many see the geo-engineering fixes as only tactics to buy time to change our carbon dioxide levels.

63. Pope Benedict XVI, 2010 World Day of Prayer speech.

REFERENCES

Archer, Margaret S. *Realist Social Theory: The Morphogenetic Approach.* New York: Cambridge University Press, 1995.

Barrera, Albino. *Market Complicity and Christian Ethics.* New York: Cambridge University Press, 2011.

Coleman John. "Environment: Catholic Vision for the Green City." *Origins*, 36.3 (2006): 33–41.

———. "Globalization and Sustainability: Catholic Resources and Responses." *Origins*, 38.37 (2009): 589–595.

Deffeyes, Kenneth. *Hubbert's Peak: The Impending Oil Shortage.* Princeton, NJ: Princeton University Press, 2005.

Donati, Pierpaolo. "The Morality of Action, Reflexivity, and the Relational Subject." This volume.

Dorr, Donal. *Option for the Poor and Caring for the Earth.* Maryknoll, NY: Orbis Press, 2012.

Flannery, Tim. *Now or Never: Why We Must Act Now to End Climate Change and Create A Sustainable Future.* New York: Atlantic Monthly Press, 2009.

Friedman, Thomas L. *Hot, Flat and Crowded.* New York: Farrar, Strauss and Giroux, 2008.

Giddens, Anthony. *The Politics of Climate Change.* Malden, MA: Polity Press, 2009.

Goodell, Jeff. *How to Cool the Planet: Geo-engineering and the Audacious Quest to Fix Earth's Climate.* New York: Houghton Mifflin Harcourt, 2010.

Hansen, James. *Storms of My Grandchildren: The Truth About the Coming Climate. Catastrophe and Our Last Chance to Save Humanity.* New York: Bloomsbury, 2009.

John Paul II. *Sollicitudo Rei Socialis.* Washington, DC: Office of Publishing and Promotion Services, United States Catholic Conference, 1988.

Kutz, Christopher. *Complicity: Ethics and Law for a Collective Age.* New York: Cambridge University Press, 2000.

Lynas, Mark. *Six Degrees: Our Future on a Hotter Planet.* Washington, DC: National Geographic, 2008

———. *High Tide: The Truth About Climate Change.* London: Picador, 2004

———. *The God Planet: Saving the Planet in the Age of Humans.* New York: Fourth Estate, 2012.

Mann, Michael. *The Hockey Stick and the Climate Wars.* New York: Columbia University Press, 2012.

McKibben, Bill. *Earth: Making a Life on a Tough New Planet.* New York: Henry Holt, 2010.

Mooney, Chris. *The Republican War on Science.* New York: Basic Books, 2005.

Oreskes, Naomi, and Erik Conway. *Merchants of Doubt.* New York: Columbia University Press, 2010.

Pacala, S., and R. Socolow. "Stabilization Wedges: Solving the Climate Problem for the Next 50 Years with Current Technologies." *Science,* 305 (2004): 968–972.

Robert, Karl Henry. *The Natural Step Story: Seeding a Quiet Revolution.* New York: New Catalyst Books, 2008.

Smith, Christian. *What is a Person?* Chicago: University of Chicago Press, 2010.

Speth, James. *Red Sky in the Morning: America and the Crisis of the Global Environment.* New Haven, CT: Yale University Press, 2004.

———. *The Bridge at the End of the World: Capitalism, The Environment and Crossing from the Crisis of Sustainability.* New Haven, CT: Yale University Press, 2009.

Stern, Nicolas. *Key Elements of a Global Deal on Climate Change.* London : London School of Economics and Political Science, 2008. Accessed November 2, 2012: http://www.cccep.ac.uk/Publications/Other/Global-Deal-Climate-Change. pdf.

United Nations Conference on Environment and Development in Rio de Janeiro. *Agenda 21: Earth Summit: The United Nations' Program of Action from Rio.* New York: United Nations, 1995.

Von Weyzsacke, Ernst U. *Factor Four: Doubling Wealth, Halving Resource Use.* New York: Earthscan, 1998.

PART TWO

Historical Resources

5

Early Christian Philanthropy as a "Marketplace" and the Moral Responsibility of Market Participants

Brian J. Matz

THE THEME OF this volume is social causality and the moral responsibility of market participants toward distant others. This chapter investigates resources available in the writings of the early Church that can be helpful in addressing this issue.

Of course, the early Church did not have the benefit of many social scientific and even theological developments that occurred centuries later. Nonetheless, we can helpfully understand this chapter on the teachings of the early Christian writers as being situated in relation to the rest of the book, somewhere between Douglas Porpora's chapter on relational structures, Pierpaolo Donati's on moral responsibility as located in relational dynamics, and Mary Hirschfeld's on Thomas Aquinas' decoupling of individual action from economic benefits. Although the early Christian writers were insufficiently interrogative (as Christina Traina's chapter suggests from the perspective of feminist thought) and insufficiently reflexive (as Margaret Archer's suggests in what's needed for structural change), they nevertheless managed to promote an alternative vision for a just society. This they accomplished by creating within the Roman Empire a parallel, relational structure of wealth management.

This parallel structure was the *philanthropia* system, constructed by Christian churches in late antiquity. Rather than being a market in which the aim was profit-taking, and advantages for some were gained at the expense of "distant others," the *philanthropia* system was constructed with a quite different purpose in mind, precisely to aid the distant others. It was, essentially, a welfare system, a safety net for the poor and the sick.

The situation for the poor in late antiquity was depressing. About 90% of the population lived at or below subsistence wages.[1] Among this vast majority are three rough income groups. First, some research suggests 28% were definitively below subsistence level. Serious disease and early death were ever-present realities for this group, including widows, orphans, prisoners, unskilled day laborers, and some farm families. Second, a staggering 40% lived at subsistence level, with their situation so precarious that they often fell below it. This included skilled and unskilled laborers, employed artisans, as well as most merchants and small shop owners. Third, another 22% also lived at subsistence level but less precariously so. This typically included some merchants, traders, artisans, regularly employed workers, and large shop owners. That left a mere 10% of the population with surplus resources that allowed them to ride out temporary financial setbacks. This group included, not surprisingly, members of the senatorial and decurial classes, whose land wealth was substantial. It also included those merchants, traders, and artisans whose businesses were sufficiently large as to employ others.

Why was poverty so rampant and economic inequality so pronounced? Although neither the early Christians nor their secular peers were especially interested in questions of social causality, clearly some were aware that Roman society was set up in such a way that injustice was inevitable. Indeed, the earliest Christian literature points the finger at systemic injustice. In an article surveying the New Testament literature on this question, Steven Friesen recalls the explanation in the Book of Revelation (Rev. 13 and 18) that injustice reigns so long as Satan rules the world through the (Roman?) imperium. "Local aristocracies," as agents of the oppressive regime, "implement the exploitation and ensure that commerce benefits the wealthy."[2] Friesen also recalls James 5, which is a critique of rich landowners who accumulate all the available capital and subsequently oppress tenant farmers with low wages. Yet, according to Friesen, the call for justice for the poor was eventually transformed into appeals for charity for the poor in other literature. Friesen observes that the famous story of goods being shared within a community in Acts 2 is best understood as a text self-consciously substituting that method of caring for the poor in place of a forceful call for redistribution.[3] It reveals that the Acts community was not interested in social change, that it accepted the status quo, and, thus, that it did not see poverty as any particular problem that needed to be solved. Friesen reports something similar was going on in another famous early Christian text, *Shepherd of Hermas*. Charity, rather than justice for the poor, is the responsibility of the comparatively more wealthy as a means to avoid damnation.[4]

This attitude that wealth and poverty are facts of life, and that God has planned for the wealthy to share their excess with the poor as a means of exchanging temporal wealth for eternal bliss, begins to reveal some of what might be called the *philanthropia* "marketplace" in late antiquity. To be sure, the attitudes of writers such as John, in Revelation, and James did not disappear entirely from the Christian record. Their critique of poverty as a consequence of injustice is found in the anonymous Pelagian text, *On Riches*,[5] which castigates the wealthy for hoarding scarce resources. It argues that there are poor people *because* there are rich people.[6] Less acerbic, Gregory of Nazianzus lists several causes of poverty that suggest it most often stems from injustice, or at least befalls the poor through no fault of their own: "widowhood, orphanhood, exile from homeland, savagery of tyrants, callousness of magistrates, ruthlessness of tax-collectors, brutality of bandits, rapacity of thieves, confiscation or shipwreck."[7] Yet, Gregory then adds, "All alike deserve our pity and look to our hands just as we look to the hands of God whenever we are in need of something."[8] The solution to injustice that creates poverty is not to stand up against the injustice but to be charitable. Indeed, the call for charity instead of justice best describes the surprisingly large volume of literature from the Church Fathers on the matter of wealth and poverty.[9]

Having said that, it would be unfair to blame the Fathers for their lack of greater attention to issues of injustice. The Fathers were principally concerned with the cultivation of moral virtue, and this meant they could speak of righteous and unrighteous wealthy people as readily as they could righteous and unrighteous poor people.[10] Moreover, their concern with charity yielded some surprisingly positive institutions associated with a *philanthropia* market that this chapter describes in more detail below. Yet they lived in a period of history bereft of concern with entrepreneurship. It was a period also in which the early Christians could not imagine fundamentally altering the political system. Markets were especially local phenomena. A family member, friend, or patron would have been one's bank. Trade between cities, between regions, and even between empires (e.g., Roman and Persian) was limited to specialized goods. There simply did not exist many examples of broad-scale markets where one's actions could affect distant others. Unless you were among the decurial or senatorial classes, your market choices were limited to your own locality, buying and selling among your neighbors.

So even though the extant resources of Christians in late antiquity do not address the book's theme precisely, a study of the *philanthropia* system does, in fact, yield some surprisingly helpful ideas about the moral responsibility of market participants in precisely those types of markets addressed by that theme. This is because the *philanthropia* "marketplace" functioned in at least one way that is fundamentally similar to markets today. The *philanthropia* marketplace was a centralized system that offered a means by which individuals could mutually profit by exchanging their respective "goods." Resources from individual contributors (rich and poor alike) were brought together into a central location. That central location, usually a *diakonia*, facilitated the exchange of goods between the contributors (wealth from the rich to the poor; prayer and aid to enter heaven from the poor to the rich). Everyone, presumably, felt they mutually benefited from the exchange. The rich were assured of God's pleasure and, thus, a greater claim on the right to enter heaven; the poor, who already possessed a special place in God's heart, were relieved of temporal suffering. This chapter explains the contribution of the *philanthropia* marketplace to the book's theme in three stages. First, it explains the constitutive elements of the *philanthropia* marketplace. Second, it summarizes key rhetorical features in early Christian literature that greased the wheels, as it were, of the *philanthropia* marketplace, ensuring it remained a going concern. Third and finally, the chapter proposes several elements of moral responsibility for market participants that emerged from the *philanthropia* marketplace that seem equally suited to markets today.

Structures of the Philanthropia Marketplace

First, the elements of the *philanthropia* marketplace included collections for the poor and tithes or offerings to the church, the *diakonia* in churches and monasteries, the *xenodocheia*, and the large building complexes that incorporated more than one of these elements. In order to explore these elements, it is important to begin with a consideration of the New Testament references to collections by local individuals for the aid and care of those in far-off cities.

The New Testament recounts in several places one particular story that foreshadowed the later, *philanthropia* marketplace: Acts 11:29–30 recounts a particularly devastating earthquake in Judaea that impoverished many

Christians in the area. It further records that Paul and Barnabas had collected funds from Christians in Asia Minor and delivered those funds to Jerusalem church leaders to aid in the relief efforts. Later, in Galatians 2:10, Paul refers to having been asked by the Jerusalem church leaders that he remember the poor in that city, and it seems he did precisely that.[11] Paul reports in Romans 15:26–32 that he collected funds in Macedonia and Achaia. It is most likely he also received funds from Corinth after devoting two chapters of 2 Corinthians (i.e., chs. 8–9) to a request for such funds. There is reason to suspect he collected money from other cities as well.[12]

Especially relevant in this record of Paul's two collections for the poor in Jerusalem is that, both at Romans 15:25 and 2 Corinthians 9:1, Paul calls this work of his a *diakonia*, a service. To be clear, across the New Testament and in other Greek literature of the first and second centuries, the term is more predominantly associated with the message or the service of a particular individual, generally of God to humans or of emissaries between churches.[13] Yet, by the third through fifth centuries, Christian texts use the term to refer to a broad range of Christian service. Increasingly, it was associated with service to the poor, which harkens back to Paul's usage of the term at least in these two passages.[14]

The very term *deacon* became, in the early Christian era, synonymous with care for the needy. As servants to the bishops, deacons, among other duties, administered the funds of the church (the alms, tithes, and collections) to care for the needs of the poor, widows, and orphans. The collections for the poor were a regular feature of early Christian worship and are documented in second- and early-third-century texts by Justin Martyr, Tertullian, and Minucius Felix.[15] Two third-century texts—Hippolytus of Rome's *Apostolic Traditions*, the pseudo-Hippolytus *Canons*, and the *Order of the Church of the Apostles*—and the fourth-century *Apostolic Constitutions* identify the office of deacon with the distribution of these funds for poor relief.[16]

The use of the term *diakonia* for relief of the needs of the poor (as in the New Testament) and the use of the related term *deacon* for the official charged with distributing the church's collections to the needy (especially in second- and third-century Christian texts) led eventually to a physical space, a store room, within a monastery or church building being designated as the *diakonia*, within which was stored food, money, and supplies for care for the poor, widows, and orphans.

The predominant evidence for the existence of these storerooms in monasteries is found in lower Egypt, where the development of monastic communities had a nearly two-century head start on Europe and Asia Minor. In a study of Egyptian papyri and two silver objects that have *diaconia* inscribed upon them, Jean Maspero had concluded that, in the fourth through sixth centuries, the term *diaconia* referred to the material possessions of the monastery.[17] However, H.-I. Marrou, in response to Maspero's study, argued that to the papyri evidence must be added evidence from patristic literature, including two passing comments from the *Sayings of the Desert Fathers (Apophthegmata patrum)* and a passage from John Cassian's *Conferences*.[18] That evidence more convincingly proves the term *diaconia* in the papyri points not to the material goods of the monastery but to the goods of the monastery destined for the poor. We also know that the monks in charge of these storerooms were called *diaconite*.[19] Excavations at Christian sites in Egypt continue to turn up evidence of these *diaconia*.[20] Thus it is possible that, in time, even greater clarity as to the role played by *diaconia* in the monasteries of Egypt will be known.

Diaconia in churches of Europe and Asia Minor is also fairly well attested in the archaeological evidence. The best-studied church in this regard is S. Maria Antiqua in Rome. Its *diakonia* expressly functioned as a free medical clinic since at least the late sixth century.[21] Similarly, the *diakonia in* the Chapel of St. Febronia in the Church of St. John Prodromos in Constantinople offered medical care to the poor.[22] A fairly extensive list of other *diaconia* and institutions for poor relief in Constantinople in late antiquity has been compiled by Konstantina Mentzou-Meimari.[23] Finally, well into the early medieval period, some churches were built exclusively for the purpose of serving as distribution centers for poor relief. Another church in Rome, S. Maria in Dominica, is one well-documented example of this.[24]

We also learn about the existence of *diaconia* in churches in the letters of Pope Gregory the Great.[25] His letter, *To John, Praetorian Prefect of Italy*, incorporates an extended discussion of the *diaconia* in Naples.[26] In that letter, Gregory assails the prefect for having diverted for other purposes the money intended for distribution to the poor through the *diaconia*. According to Marrou, it appears (from Gregory's phrase *annonas et consuetudines* in reference to the funds) that it was the state, and not Christian tithes, that was the source of these funds for the *diaconia*.[27] Thus Gregory was aware of a *diaconia* system in the early seventh century that resembles what can often be found in state welfare programs today: Governments distribute block grants to local organizations that are trusted to use those funds to care for the poor.

In addition to providing food, money, and clothing to the poor through formal *diaconia* centers, monasteries and churches also sponsored or ran *xenodocheia*, which were hostels or inns for weary travelers and pilgrims. Staying at an inn along the major trade routes in the Greco-Roman world entailed nothing short of putting your life and your possessions in another person's hands. Violence and robbery committed against travelers staying at inns was not uncommon.[28] For this and other reasons, Christian churches began operating inns promising safety for travelers. Of course, it did not hurt that the inns were a marginally profitable enterprise in their own right; most important, they facilitated the growth of martyriums and other centers to encourage pilgrimage business, which bishops in the fourth and later centuries were keen to construct.

Perhaps the largest project in late antique Christendom incorporated a *xenodocheia*, a *diaconia* that offered medical care (akin to that provided by a modern-day hospice center) and a martyrium to generate income from pilgrims to maintain the facility: Basil of Caesarea's *Basileia*.[29] This was a complex of buildings constructed in either 368 or 370, following a devastating famine in the region, just beyond the city walls of Caesarea. Gregory Nazianzen, a friend of Basil's and eventually bishop of Constantinople, wrote a sermon preached in the churches in Asia Minor[30] that likely was used as a fundraising speech for constructing and maintaining the *Basileia*. No doubt Basil's *Basileia* was beneficial to the poor and leprous, but it was also of benefit to Basil's status within the region, as Gregory Nazianzen's encomium for Basil suggests.[31] Naturally, we should expect preaching about the plight of the poor was one strategy the Fathers had for ensuring their philanthropic institutions moved from the drawing board to reality, by generating the contributions needed to sustain them.

The influence of monasticism on the *Basileia* and other hostels, hospitals, and *diaconia* deserves further consideration. The fifth-century text *Lausiac History* by Palladius recalled the life and work of many desert monks, including the lengths to which several went in caring for the poor and beggars.[32] Palladius relates at least two important accounts that provide encouragement for Christians to found, to build, or to otherwise support the development of institutional structures that would alleviate the sufferings of the poor.

The first is that of Ephraem, a deacon in Edessa. Like Basil after him, Ephraem came to the rescue of his fellow citizens during an extended famine. We are told that Ephraem went to the wealthy citizens and asked, "Why do you not have pity on the people who are perishing, instead of letting your wealth rot for the condemnation of your souls?"[33] After several of the wealthy contributed to his relief efforts, Palladius tells us,

> [Ephraem] divided up the porticoes, and he put up about three hundred beds and cared for the famished ones. The dead he buried, and he took care of those who had hope of life, and as a matter of fact he daily provided nourishment and help to all those who came to him each day because of the famine; and this he did with the money allotted to him.[34]

Ephraem's decision to use the money given to him to feed and house the poor and to bury the dead had even then long been a part of Christian charity. His use of the porticoes of the church for sheltering the homeless became more common from Ephraem's day onward as Christian churches grew both in number and in size.

The second account of Palladius tells of a time when Macarius of Alexandria took some of the wealth of a woman committed to virginity for the construction of a hospital. Macarius had told the virgin she would receive jewels in exchange for the money, but the only "jewels" she was ever shown were the poor women and men being cared for in the hospital. This calls to mind the popularly known story of St. Lawrence who, in Rome, presented the poor people receiving financial support from his church to those who had demanded he turn over the church's wealth.[35] Thus, in addition to exhortations for personal contributions of alms or of labor to the poor, the Fathers of the third through seventh centuries preached the need for and implemented the construction and maintenance of institutional structures for alleviating economic injustice.

Lest this overview of the *philanthropia* marketplace lend itself to an overly optimistic assessment of early Christianity's motives with respect to care for the poor, it should be noted that the churches also had a legal duty in this regard. The churches were more than nudged in the direction of constructing a *philanthropia* marketplace by the awarding of tax-exempt status to clergy and to churches. Naturally, the fortunes of Christian clergy and churches began to change with the conversion of Constantine in the early fourth century.[36] In 313, soon after his conversion, he ordered exemption for clergy from the *munera civilia*, which would have including exemptions from taxes, the maintenance of public buildings, and the transport of goods to nearby soldiers.[37] Constantius II seemed both to renew and to expand this legislation with one of his own in 343, in which he exempted from taxes not only clergy but also their slaves and whatever business enterprise in which they were involved.[38]

When first initiated, these tax privileges were given because Christian ministers were seen as already performing a public good for the State by their prayers for its and the emperor's success.[39] They did not need to pay taxes on top of that. Yet, by 329, it became clear the tax exemption was so attractive that it was responsible for attracting disreputable individuals to the clerical office. In response, Constantine issued another law requiring clergy to utilize their tax-exempt resources for the benefit and maintenance of the poor.[40] Thus, after 329, the Christian ministers' claim to tax exemption, and thus their claim to be supporting the public good by other means, rested not on prayers but on the maintenance of welfare and charity programs. However, what is especially interesting is that this 329 code also stipulated that the clergy were to be selected from among the poor. The tax-exempt status for clergy was not to be abused by the wealthy.[41] Instead, churches were to select their clergy from among those who were paupers, a reference to those living at subsistence level rather than from the lowest strata, the begging poor. Presumably, members of this group would not abuse the tax exemption and also would be more attuned to the needs of the poor and so be best able to maintain the churches' charity and welfare efforts.[42] Thus the tax exemption of "poor" clergy was the cause of their own rise in political and social prominence during the fourth and later centuries. They began to assume the classical role of public benefactor (εὐεργήτης).[43]

In sum, this first section of the chapter reveals that the *philanthropia* marketplace comprised several important elements. The New Testament points to special collections by Paul for the poor in Jerusalem. In the post-apostolic era, this led to an understanding that tithes and offerings of Christians within their churches were specially to be reserved for service to the poor, including the payment of burial fees. This system was overseen by deacons in the churches who, eventually, were put in charge not merely of the donated money but also a physical space (*diakonia*) within churches or monasteries devoted to poor relief. These *diakonia* were, in some locations, storage spaces for food, clothing, and tools, while at other locations they may have been devoted more exclusively to provide medical care for the poor. In any case, their very existence led to the willingness on the part of some bishops, such as Basil of Caesarea, to combine several features of the *philanthropia* system into large complexes of buildings that met multiple needs in one place. In any case, the *diakonia* and similar structures stand out as the physical space in which the *philanthropia* market operated. All the while, the expansion of tax-exemption for clergy, churches, and church-owned buildings provided a legal rationale for the existence of the *philanthropia* marketplace and, in no small way, encouraged its expansion.

Preaching the Philanthropia Market

Having surveyed the physical and social structures that brought the *philanthropia* market to life and helped solidify its place in the wider society, consideration must now turn to the theology and the rhetoric that sustained it by supplying its *raison d'etre*. Because it was a market built on a scheme of redistribution of wealth, Christians with superfluous resources were taught about their need to share their excess wealth with the poor.[44] Naturally, each structural element (church collections, monasteries, hospitals, *diakonia*) required its own particular rhetorical touch. Richard Finn documented these different approaches across various genres of literature in *Almsgiving in the Later Roman Empire*.[45] Moving beyond Finn's work, this chapter surveys some common rhetorical themes of the clergy to move the wealthy to support the philanthropy marketplace.

Few texts are so explicit as to say, "Give your money to the church." More commonly, they say something like, "Give your money to God." Especially fitting to this chapter's theme that this philanthropy system operated like a marketplace, it is most common to read early Christian texts speak of wealth transfers as loan transactions. The wealthy person "loans" his or her money to God, who will repay it with much interest in heaven. The poor person is typically identified as the guarantor of the loan. Poor people were generally seen as closer to God because, unlike the rich, they bore no illusions that they "can make it on their own" without God. Though they lacked monetary resources, the poor thus tended to have a richer prayer life than the wealthy. Thus, they "guaranteed" the rich man's loan by praying for God's beneficence upon those who supported them in their need.

To grease the wheels of this loan transaction, priests employed several rhetorical devices. One was to generate empathy for the plight of the poor. Much like infomercials today for organizations like Save the Children, early Christian ministers painted word-pictures of the poor—for example, of a poor person whose problems are compounded by a crippling disease, or of a father pressed to sell one of his children into slavery in order to buy food for the rest. Many of these word-pictures were long and dramatic.

In the case of Basil of Caesarea's homily delivered during the time of a famine in Cappadocia, an especially dramatic description of the circumstances of a starving person was not beyond the pale. Hunger and starvation were particularly pernicious problems in the region of Cappadocia, where Basil lived. In the homily, he describes in graphic detail the wasting away of a human body as a result of starvation.

> Starvation, the distress of the famished, is the supreme human calamity, a more miserable end than all other deaths. For when one considers other life threatening calamities, the sword brings a quick end; fire too extinguishes life quickly; and even wild beasts, tearing the limbs apart with their teeth, inflict fatal wounds which assure that the distress will not be prolonged. But famine is a slow evil, always approaching, always holding off like a beast in its den. The heat of the body cools. The form shrivels. Little by little strength diminishes. Flesh stretches across the bones like a spider web. The skin loses its bloom, as the rosy appearance fades and blood melts away. Nor is the skin white, but rather it withers into black while the livid body, suffering pitifully, manifests a dark and pale mottling. The knees no longer support the body but drag themselves by force, the voice is powerless, the eyes are sunken as if in a casket, like dried-up nuts in their shells; the empty belly collapses, conforming itself to the shape of the backbone without any natural elasticity of the bowels. The person who rushes by such a body, how greatly worthy is he of chastisement? What excess of cruelty will he allow? Should he not be reckoned with the savagery of the beasts, accursed and murderous?[46] Whoever has it in his power to alleviate this evil but deliberately opts instead for profit, should be condemned as a murderer.[47]

Importantly here, Basil includes a condemnation of the inhumanity of hard-hearted wealthy Christians who "look the other way."

Most early Christian homilies on wealth and poverty relied on Jesus' parable of Lazarus and the rich man (Luke 16). The text offered a rich opportunity to excoriate the wealthy and to depict in troubling detail the plight of the poor. John Chrysostom, in the *Sermons on Lazarus and the Rich Man*, identifies several features of the life of poor people.[48] He says the noble poor stand by in silence; they do not pester the rich but condemn the insensitivity of the wealthy through their physical presence. "For when we [i.e., wealthy people] are pestered we often become harder; but when we see those who need help standing by in complete silence, even if we are more insensible than the very stones, we become ashamed at the excess of politeness and are moved to pity."[49] Chrysostom refers to the beds made of silver or other exquisite materials upon which the wealthy sleep. He contrasts this with the lot of the poor: "[W]hen you are sleeping on a bed, the poor man has thrown himself on a pile of straw by the door of the bath-house, wrapping the stalks around him, shivering, stiff with cold, pinched with hunger—even if you are the stoniest of all men, I am sure that you will condemn yourself for providing for yourself unnecessary luxury while not allowing him even what is necessary."[50]

Chrysostom also describes the humility and shame experienced by the poor in public spaces. He recounts the poor man's thoughts: "I lie here an example for onlookers, a source of shame and derision, wasting away with hunger." He describes the man's reaction: "The sight of another person in good fortune laid on him an extra burden of anguish not because he was envious and wicked, but because we all naturally perceive our own misfortunes more acutely by comparison with others' prosperity."[51] Chrysostom works carefully to engender a sensitivity in the wealthy by painting for them vivid pictures of the poor and comparing the unempathetic among them to stones [λίθοι].

Basil, in his oration against those who practice usury, similarly recounts the difficulties of the poor. He describes the poor man seeking a loan as "a man by necessity bent down...as a suppliant, practicing all humility, and uttering every manner of petition."[52] Basil also says such a man is bathed in tears since he loses his liberty as his poverty deepens. In another homily, an exposition of Jesus' parable of the rich man who tears down his barns to build bigger ones (Luke 12:13–21), Basil describes the anguish of a poor father who must sell one of his children in order to purchase grain in the marketplace. Basil writes, "With a myriad of tears he goes to sell his dearest child, but his suffering does not move you [i.e., the rich man], you take no account of nature...His tears do not arouse your pity, his groans do not soften your heart."[53]

Basil's friend, Gregory Nazianzen, preached similarly about the poor in his *Oration* 14, aptly titled by later editors, "On Loving the Poor."

In this homily, likely preached to raise funds for construction of the *Basileia*, Gregory left little to his audience's imagination in describing the lives of the poor who suffer from leprosy. "There lies before our eyes a dreadful and pathetic sight, one that no one would believe who has not seen it: human beings alive yet dead, disfigured in almost every part of their bodies, barely recognizable for who they once were or where they came from."[54] He described the lurid and decrepit conditions in which they lived:

> They are driven away from cities...from homes, from the marketplace, from public gatherings, from the streets, from festivities, from drinking parties, even—how they suffer!—from water itself....And so they wander about night and day, helpless, naked, homeless, exposing their sores for all to see,...leaning on each other's limbs in place of those they have lost,...begging for a crust of bread or a bit of food or some tattered rag to hide their shame.[55]

Gregory also expressed the anguish they feel when the wealthy spurn their requests for assistance. "To them, a kind benefactor is not someone who has supplied their need but anyone who has not cruelly sent them away."[56] Importantly, he not only paints a picture of the poor, but he even makes a direct appeal for support. The sickly poor would work to help themselves if they could, but they cannot. Wealthy Christians have an obligation to support the livelihoods of those who simply cannot support themselves. Gregory writes,

> The pitiful plight of other people is due to one thing alone, a lack of material resources, a condition that might be corrected by time, or hard work, or a friend, or a relative, or a change in circumstances. But for these people, what is no less pitiful, indeed, even more so, is that, in addition, they are deprived of the opportunity to work and help themselves acquire the necessaries of life.[57]

Gregory's audience intellectually understood what life was like for poor, sick people, but these passages in his sermon reveal that Gregory understood they needed an emotional connection to their lives as well.

One further example, Asterius of Amasea, the bishop of that city in the early fifth century, preached a homily titled *On Covetousness*. It connects the vice of coveting with the plight of the poor:

Covetousness is the mother of inequality, unmerciful, hating mankind, most cruel. On account of it, the life of men is full of inequality...[the poor] are in peril through extreme hunger and want...[they] have not the shelter of two boards. When they cannot live in open air, they either take refuge beside the furnaces of the baths, or, finding the attendants of the baths inhospitable, they dig into the dung like swine, and so contrive to get for themselves the needful warmth....The poor man has not on his wooden table any bread to break...[he is] aged and unable to walk, or lame by reason of some outrageous mutilation, does not possess the ass that he needs to carry him about,...[he] lacks oil to light his lamps,...[he] has only the ground for his bed.[58]

This homily, more than others in late antiquity, paints the widest picture of the extent of problems facing the poor: shelter, food, heat, clothing, access to health care, even access to resources, such as an oil lamp, that might offer hope for improving the situation. This homily, along with Asterius' *Homily on Lazarus and the Rich Man*, reveals a bishop concerned to use the superfluous wealth of Christians in Amasea for care of the local poor.

Along with dramatic descriptions of the plight of the poor, another equally popular rhetorical technique for inciting the wealthy to assist the poor was to warn the wealthy of eternal damnation for being too attached to their wealth. Again, the parable of Lazarus and the rich man was especially helpful. So, too, was Jesus' teaching in Matthew 25 on the separation of the sheep from the goats based on their compassion for the needs of others. This approach appealed to the self-serving motives of the wealthy; it taught them to give to the poor *not for the sake of the poor* but for the sake of their own eternal destiny.

Jerome, in his homily on the parable of Lazarus, dwells at great length on the pain, the suffering, and the eternal condemnation experienced by wealthy people in the afterlife.[59] He practically relishes the moment when he writes that the (comparatively) poorer Christians experience joy in watching the wealthy suffer in a celebration of God's inflexible justice. In reference to the chasm of which Jesus speaks in Luke 16:26, Jerome writes, "It cannot be bridged, removed, or leveled. We can see it, but cannot cross it. We see what we have escaped; you see what you have lost; our joy and happiness multiply your torments; your torments augment our happiness."[60] The homily of Peter Chrysologus on the same text similarly celebrates the rich man's demise.[61] He points out the two-fold experience of punishment after this life. The first is the punishment of the conscience as it comes to accept that the person led a life of greed when on the earth and that an eternal damnation awaits. The second is the punishment of the body and soul in the eternal fire of hell.

Salvian of Marseilles, in his rather unstudied *Four Books of Timothy to the Church,* not so subtly remarks that the greed of the rich has created storehouses for their goods—awaiting their owners' arrival—in hell. "Those who lay up treasures through greed and avarice know they are placing their wealth in hell, while those who lay them up through almsgiving and kindness rejoice because they are preparing heavenly treasures. Scripture named the location of treasures according to the merits of those who lay them up, for treasures are said to be there where they will be who lay them up."[62] He goes on to say the punishment of the wealthy is not merely eternal but also in the present life. He cites as evidence the dissatisfaction so many wealthy have with their children after watching them grow up spoiled from never having to work hard for their income.

In addition to the word pictures and the threats of eternal damnation, there were other rhetorical devices employed by early Christian priests. Some spoke of the poor as being nearer to God or being friends of God. The wealthy had many sins for which they needed to repent, and so money donated to help the poor would win a wealthy person the friendship of the poor. These new friendships should helped smooth out any problems the wealthy might still have with God. This usually was taught in collaboration with Jesus' exhortation for his followers to use money (the mammon of unrighteousness) to make friends who will provide true assistance. (Luke 16:1–9).[63]

Another rhetorical device was to address the wealthy as a special part of God's economic plan. God has given wealth to some and not to others in order to ensure productivity on the part of everyone. Basil of Caesarea, in his *Homily* 6, taught that God pays the wealthy with heavenly currency in return for the clothing, food, and shelter they provide for the poor.[64] In his *Homily* 21, Basil writes of the necessity for the regular flow of wealth around a community.[65] The swifter the flow, the better the economic conditions for everyone. Also using the river analogy, Gregory of Nyssa, in "On Good Works," says that the prosperity of one house can "save a crowd of the poor."[66] Somewhat more cynically, Theodoret of Cyrrus taught that were it not for the existence of poorer people, there would be no one willing to do certain types of work.[67] Thus a healthy economy thrives on diversity of employment, and diversity of employment depends on diversity of economic circumstances. In this view, the wealthy person's role is to offer employment and assistance to the poor.[68]

One further rhetorical move was to appeal to the psychological health of the wealthy. According to several early Christian texts, being wealthy came with a myriad of problems. If you are a usurer, you are perpetually fatigued with anxiety about whether the borrower will be able to repay your loan.[69] If you possess expensive objects at home, you are consumed with fears of being robbed[70]; or you are consumed with the thought that, after your death, they will end up in the hands of a relative whom you do not like![71] Also, the wealthy are constantly bothered with requests for assistance from prodigal flatterers, dishonest "friends," and their tenants.[72] Furthermore, successful merchants are regularly dismayed by reports of pirates or storms endangering the ships that carry their goods abroad.[73] Thus, for the sake of one's psychological health, those who have wealth are best served by simply giving it up to the church, to God, and to the poor.

In summary, this second part of the chapter has revealed the *philanthropia* marketplace was driven not solely by legal obligations stemming from churches' tax-exempt status but also by a conviction on the part of Christian ministers that something was seriously flawed about a society that did not recognize the inherent dignity of every person. Thus the rhetorical themes in Christian sermons and texts outlined here reveals that the clergy wanted the wealthy to support the *philanthropia* marketplace both for the sake of the poor and for the sake of the wealthy themselves. Not only was their eternal destiny at stake but so was their psychological health in this present life. By "selling" superfluous wealth to the *philanthropia* marketplace for the price of the poor's prayer life and the love they have from God, the rich could walk away from the exchange more wealthy than before. Thus these rhetorical themes suggest that wealth is to be defined in other than monetary ways.

Elements of Moral Responsibility

Returning to the theme of this volume, we now inquire about the moral responsibilities of the *philanthropia* market participants vis-à-vis "distant others." The construction, maintenance, and exhortations to participate in the *philanthropia* "marketplace" suggests there were several such responsibilities.

Chief among the moral responsibilities of market participants was the obligation to think of themselves as being dependent on God and on the labors of others long ago. This awareness of real relationships over time foreshadows the relational structures analyzed in Douglas Porpora's chapter in this book, and it anticipates somewhat the argument about private property eventually found in Thomas Aquinas, as articulated in Mary Hirschfeld's chapter. Essential elements for producing goods in an agrarian economy—land, climate, access to water sources—are almost entirely outside one's own control. The ability of an individual to labor and to produce goods at a profit is due in no small measure, then, to God's granting of ideal climate conditions, to his provision of ready access to arable land, and even to His gift of breath and life to the worker. Besides all of that, a worker's knowledge of a craft or trade and access to the appropriate tools are themselves the result of someone else's earlier labors. People in prior ages developed tools and techniques that are used by later workers. Thus, to the early Christians, it made little sense that someone should claim that all of the financial profit they have received in a transaction really belonged solely to them. Every person's labor and capacity to make a profit depended both on the labor of earlier workers and on the grace of God. Some percentage of their gain really belonged to the society at large.

Related to this, a second moral responsibility of market participants was to evaluate their motives in acquiring financial profits. In the Roman economy, where markets were local and most people lived on subsistence wages, the temptation to maximize one's monetary gain by withholding excess farm goods from the market to force prices up was especially high. So, too, was the temptation to make money with money through the use of one's occasional monetary surplus for usurious loans. Both of these practices are deplored in many texts of the early Church. Instead, the Christian person was taught to think of profits in terms of their place within a divinely sanctioned economic system. The capacity of one person to earn a profit in the markets and the incapacity of others to do so had a divine purpose, according to some early Christian writers. That purpose was to teach and test the virtue of both types of individuals. The one who earns a profit is to be taught the virtue of beneficence; the one who does not is to be taught the virtues of patience and humility. Thus the profit motive, such as it exists, has its *telos* in beneficence rather than personal or corporate enrichment.

Related to the matter of profit motive, a third moral responsibility of prosperous market participants was to not "buy time" by delaying the sales of goods. Superfluous wealth allowed the rich to time their entry into the marketplace so that the opportunity for profit was greatest, something modern economist identify with "monopoly power." Again, the early Christian writers discouraged this practice because of its aim to enrich oneself rather to meet the needs of others. The fitting place for superfluous wealth was the *philanthropia* marketplace, not the "buying" of time by withholding one's goods from the local markets until prices rose.

Still another element of moral responsibility is to understand financial gain as generating an opportunity cost of further impoverishing a "distant other." The lack of entrepreneurialism in the Roman Empire was largely responsible for Christian preachers and nearly everyone else in late antiquity thinking of markets as a zero-sum game. The profit of one person was presumed to impoverish another. The wealthy thought of the cost of spending their superfluous wealth on a particular luxury good as merely the loss of the opportunity to use that wealth to buy a different luxury good instead. Instead, the early Christians wanted the wealthy to consider that the opportunity cost was really the increased suffering of the sick and the poor. Thus Asterius could critique the wealthy in his region of Pontus for calculating the opportunity cost of buying a silk garment from India as the cost of not buying a bottle of imported wine. This is really a problem of the wealthy not wanting to acknowledge that "distant others" even exist. They only think about themselves.

In addition to acknowledging that the poor exist as "distant others" in marketplaces, another moral responsibility of market participants was to understand the needs of the poor. This was noted above in how early the Fathers brought vivid descriptions of poverty into their preaching. It is also revealed in their criticism of the wealthy that pass by the poor. Thus it was not enough merely to contribute to the *philanthropia* marketplace; empathy with the poor was equally important. Empathy changes how people relate to one another, recognizing that wealthy and poor share a common humanity.

Finally, in spite of the stress on the obligations of the wealthy, the early Christian literature reveals that the poor, too, had a moral responsibility within the *philanthropia* marketplace. Several texts reveal an awareness that there are righteous and unrighteous poor people. The righteous poor person is one who bears suffering with dignity. This generally meant a commitment to refrain from stealing to meet one's needs. However, the idea that the superfluous goods of the wealthy actually belong to the poor opened the way for a few early Christian writers, such as Augustine, to think the poor are not actually stealing when they take bread or clothing from the wealthy. It also meant not making oneself a nuisance in public; the poor were to proclaim their need without words, by their physical presence in the porticoes of church and other public buildings where begging was allowed.

In summary, this third portion of the chapter has stressed that both the poor and the wealthy had special moral responsibilities in the *philanthropia* marketplace. One group was required to bear its suffering in faith, while the other was to share from its surplus to reduce that suffering.

Conclusion

Undergirding each of these moral responsibilities is, of course, the recognition that the poor suffered tremendously in a society such as the Roman Empire, which was devoid of any meaningful social safety net. Such a state of affairs was intolerable not only because the poor bear the same humanity as the wealthy but also because of a conviction that God has made available "enough" resources for all, if only everyone would share. The problem is that, contrary to God's will, a small percentage of the population hoards a disproportionate share of those resources for their own benefit. This explains why nearly every Christian bishop warns the wealthy of the eternal consequences of their greed.

In the final analysis, since the bishops of the early Christian church more often than not hailed from the wealthy families of the empire, they were all too keenly aware that the "system," increasingly rigged as it was to benefit those with power, would not redistribute society's resources to benefit the poor. They also knew that the authorities would not use the Roman tax policy for this purpose either. Thus, over time, the Christian churches built up an independent system where that redistribution could happen by another means. Their *philanthropia* marketplace was a mechanism for two types of exchange, illuminating moral responsibilities for both parties in the exchange. The rich could exchange their wealth in this life for the pleasure of God and reward in heaven; the poor could receive temporal relief from their suffering in exchange for their living in prayer and humility (which already ensured their own heavenly reward) to lift up the generous wealthy to God. This exchange was meant to facilitate an awareness on the part of all that we share a common humanity and, as a result, a common date at the judgment seat of God for how we treat one another, not only those we associate with but distant others as well.

NOTES

1. Steven J. Friesen, "Injustice or God's Will? Early Christian Explanations of Poverty," in *Wealth and Poverty in Early Church and Society*, ed. Susan R. Holman (Grand Rapids, MI: Baker Academic, 2008), 20–21. This income scale is based on archaeological and textual evidence among the remains of the larger Roman cities.
2. Friesen, "Injustice or God's Will?" 23.
3. Friesen, "Injustice or God's Will?" 27–29. Friesen's argument is based on evidence that the author of Acts later self-consciously avoids praise of Paul's collection for the poor in Jerusalem. The collection was the reason Paul himself gives for the journey to Jerusalem in his own letters (cf. Rom. 15:25–27; 1 Cor. 16:1–4; 2 Cor. 8:10–15, 9:13), but Acts instead paints Paul's last journey to Jerusalem as one in which he aimed to celebrate Pentecost in the city. It seems to dismiss the collection by saying Paul came to "pay a vow" (21:24) or to bring a "gift" (24:17).
4. *Shepherd of Hermas*, Similitude 1 and 2.
5. Andreas Kessler, *Reichtumskritik und Pelagianismus: Die pelagianische Diatribe de divitiis: Situierung, Lesetext, Übersetzung, Kommentar*, Paradosis 43 (Freiburg: Universitätsverlag, 1999); English translation: B. R. Rees, *The Letters of Pelagius and His Followers* (Suffolk: Boydell Press, 1991), 171–211. Cf. Elizabeth Clark, *Reading Renunciation: Asceticism and Scripture in Early Christianity* (Princeton, NJ: Princeton University Press, 1999), 94–99; Carlo Scaglioni, " 'Guia a voi ricchi!' Pelagio e gli scritti pelangiani," in *Per foramen acus: Il cristianesimo antico di fronte alla pericope evangelica del "giovane ricco,"* Studia Patristica Mediolanensia 14 (Milan: Vita e Pensiero, 1986), 361–398.
6. The argument of this text is that the very existence of poverty is a sign that those with wealth behave unjustly. The author argues wealth, per se, is neutral, or not sinful, but that the acquisition of it is through sin (VII.5). Either way, one should steer clear of wealth. Moreover, it may not be argued that, since in the Hebrew Bible God is said to have made some people quite wealthy (e.g., Abraham and David), riches are justified in that they may be a gift from God (VIII–X). Here the author engages in a Christological reading of the Hebrew Bible. Very little of the ways that these men lived is validated by Christ (such as Abraham sleeping with Hagar, or David's adultery), but in a mystical sense, every story anticipates the life of Christ.
7. Gregory of Nazianzus, *Oration* 14.6 (Patrologia Graeca 35.864–865); English translation: Martha Vinson, *St. Gregory of Nazianzus: Select Orations*, Fathers of the Church Series 107 (Washington, DC: Catholic University of America Press, 2003), 42–43: εἴτε διὰ χηρείαν χρήζοιεν ταύτης, εἴτε δι' ὀρφανίαν, εἴτε ἀποξένωσιν πατρίδος, εἴτε ὠμότητα δεσποτῶν, εἴτε ἀρχόντων θράσος, εἴτε φορολόγων ἀπανθρωπίαν, εἴτε λῃστῶν, εἴτε ναυάγιον.

8. Vinson, *St. Gregory of Nazianzus*, 42–43: πάντες γάρ ὁμοίως ἐλεεινοί, καί οὕτω βλέποντες εἰς τάς ἡμετήρας, χείρας, ὡς ἡμεῖς εἰς τάς τοῦ Θεοῦ, περί ὧν ἄν δεώμεθα.

9. Interested readers are encouraged to review some of the following "source books" on texts about wealth and poverty from the Church Fathers: Charles Avila, *Ownership: Early Christian Teaching* (Maryknoll, NY: Orbis Books, 1983); R. Sierra Bravo and Florentino Del Valle, eds., *Doctrina social y economica de los padres de la Iglesia: Coleccion general de documentos y textos* (Madrid: Biblioteca Fomento Social, 1967); Paul Christophe, *Les pauvres et la pauvreté des origenes au XVe siècle. Ière partie*, Bibliothèque d'Histoire du Christianisme 7 (Paris: Desclée de Brouwer, 1985), esp. pp. 9–63; Igino Giordani, *Il messaggio sociale dei primi padri della Chiesa* (Torino: Societa Editrice Internazionale, 1939), which is available in English as *The Social Message of the Early Church Fathers*, trans. Alba I. Zizzamia (Paterson, NJ: St. Anthony Guild Press, 1944); Adalbert Gauthier Hamman, ed., *Riches et pauvres dans l'église ancienne*, Lettres Chrétiennes 6 (Paris: Grasset, 1962); Amy Oden, ed., *And You Welcomed Me: A Sourcebook on Hospitality in Early Christianity* (Nashville: Abingdon Press, 2001); Peter Phann, *Social Thought*, Message of the Fathers of the Church 20 (Wilmington, DE: Michael Glazier, 1984); Walter Shewring, *Rich and Poor in Christian Tradition* (London: Burns, Oates and Washbourne, 1948).

10. The most poignant example of this is Asterius of Amasea, *Homily* 1, titled, "On Lazarus and the Rich Man," Cornelius Datema, ed., *Asterius of Amasea: Homilies I–XIV: Text, introduction and notes* (Leiden: E. J. Brill, 1970), 7–15; English translation: Galusha Anderson and Edgar J. Goodspeed, *Ancient Sermons for Modern Times* (New York: Pilgrim Press, 1904), 17–44. I am also aware that Wendy Mayer is working on a publication that will explain this same phenomena in more detail across Chrysostom's works.

11. David J. Downs, *The Offering of the Gentiles: Paul's Collection for Jerusalem in Its Chronological, Cultural, and Cultic Contexts*, Wissenschaftliche Untersuchungen zum Neuen Testament 2.248 (Tübingen: Mohr-Siebeck, 2008), esp. in chap. 2, argues the request to remember the poor should not be confused with Paul's own initiative to later collect funds for the Jerusalem Christians. There is nothing in Galatians 2:10 that suggests Paul was obliged to do anything he had not already set his mind to doing for the poor in Jerusalem.

12. In Acts 24:17, during his trial in Jerusalem, Paul explains he had come to the city to deliver his alms to the poor. In the arrival scene, in Acts 21:17, Luke uses his familiar "we" language, which indicates Paul had not traveled alone. With him, at the very least, were Luke and Timothy. Thus it is probable Timothy had brought funds with him from Lystra or Ephesus, and Luke may have brought funds from Philippi, since that was where he was residing prior to joining Paul on the journey to Jerusalem (cf. Acts 20:6).

13. John N. Collins, *Diakonia: Reinterpreting the Ancient Sources* (New York: Oxford University Press, 1990). This argument is partially challenged, at least when the term is used of New Testament women, in Allie Ernst, *Martha from the Margins: The Authority of Martha in Early Christian Tradition*, Supplements to Vigiliae Christianae (Leiden: Brill, 2009), 179–187.

14. G. W. H. Lampe, *A Patristic Greek Lexicon* (Oxford: Clarendon Press, 1961), s.v. "διακονία" §§A-B, p. 351. Lampe's study of the term in late antique Christian literature turns up four major categories of service: service (in general), including service to the poor at A.2; service to God, also including service to the poor at B.1 and B.2.b; service of the Son of God; and service of the Holy Spirit.

15. Justin Martyr, *Apology I* 67. Cf. Patrologia Graeca 6.429; the critical editions are Justin Martyr, *Apologies*, Études Augustiniennes, 190–192; id., *Apologie pour les Chrétiens*, Paradosis 39, 122; id., *Apologiae pro Christianis*, Patristische Texte und Studien 38, 129–130. English translation: Barnard, *St. Justin Martyr. The First and Second Apologies*, Ancient Christian Writers 56, 71–72. Incidentally, this text is cited in *Deus caritas est* §22. Justin's *Apology I* is a defense of Christianity in the face of a Roman society that viewed Christianity as a danger to the welfare of the state. Justin's promotion of the charitable activity of Christian people buttresses; therefore, his claim that Christianity rather contributes to the betterment of the state and to the well-being of the state's citizens. Christian charity is not apart from or in spite of the religion's beliefs but is part and parcel with its praxis.

Tertullian, *Apology* 39. Cf. Patrologia Latina 1.470; the critical editions are Tertullian, *Opera, Pars I: Opera Catholica, Adversus Marcionem*, ed. Eligius Dekkers, Janus G. P. Borleffs, and R. Willems, Corpus Christianorum Series Latina 1 (Turnhout: Brepols, 1954), 150–153; id., *Apologeticum*, ed. Heinrich Hoppe, Corpus Scriptorum Ecclesiasticorum Latinorum 69 (Vienna: Tempsky, 1939), 91–95. English translation: Emily Joseph Daly, *Tertullian: Apologetical Works*, Fathers of the Church Series 10 (Washington, DC: Catholic University of America Press, 1950), 98–102. The larger context for the quote from Tertullian's *Apology* 39 explains the rationale for monetary offerings by Christians. The contributions are for the charitable purposes of the Christian churches. Tertullian emphasizes the gifts are voluntary, given with some sort of regularity, and that they are never an initiation fee. They are, in brief, "deposits of piety," in that the phrase both points to the piety of the giver and the pious purposes for which the money will be used. The phrase "deposits of piety" was later cited in *Rerum Novarum* 24 and in several subsequent Catholic social teaching documents.

Minucius Felix, *Octavius* 9 and 31. Cf. Patrologia Latina 3.260–63 and 335– 338; the critical edition is Minucius Felix, *Octavius*, ed. Michael Pellegrino, Corpus Scriptorum Latinorum Patrum (Turin: G. B. Paravia, 1972), 11–13, 47–48. English translation: Rudolph Arbesmann, *Minucius Felix. Octavius*, Fathers of the Church Series 10 (Washington, DC: Catholic University of America Press, 1950), 335–338, 387–389; G. W. Clarke, *The Octavius of Marcus Minucius Felix,*

Ancient Christian Writers 39 (New York: Newman Press, 1974), 82–85, 109–111. In §31, Minucius Felix argues Christians within and without the walls of their meeting places lead praiseworthy lives and are models of good character, including their giving of alms for the needs of the poor. The *Octavius* is generally considered an attempt by Minucius Felix to copy Tertullian. Whether that is so, or vice versa, or both are copies of a third, unknown source, is still debated. A helpful summary of this debate since the early nineteenth century is available in Michael E. Hardwick, *Josephus as an Historical Source in Patristic Literature through Eusebius*, Brown Judaic Studies 128 (Atlanta, GA: Scholars Press, 1989), 21–22. Examination of the interdependency is also in Clarke, *The Octavius of Marcus Minucius Felix*, 9–10 (supports priority of Tertullian).

16. Hippolytus, *Apostolic Traditions* 9; id., *Canons* 34; id., *Order of the Church of the Apostles* 22; id., *Apostolic Constitutions* 2.32, 3.7 and 3.19; F. X. Funk, *Didascalia et Constitutiones Apostolorum*, Vol. 1 (Paderborn, 1905).

17. Jean Maspero, "Sur quelques objets coptes du Musée du Caire,"*Annales du Service des antiquités d'Egypte*, 10 (1910):173–174. The papyri were published in J. Maspero, *Papyrus grecs d'époque byzantine*, Catalogue général des antiquités égyptiennes du Musée du Caire, Papyrus grecs d'époque byzantine, 4 vols. (Cairo: Institut Français d'Archéologie Orientale, 1911–1916). The silver objects (perhaps bowls for incense) were excavated from a small monastery in Luxor and are now at the Museum of Cairo. Cf. Josef Strzygowski, *Koptisch Kunst*, Catalogue général des antiquités égyptiennes du Musée du Caire (Osnabrück: Zeller, 1904), 341–344.

18. Henri-Irénée Marrou, "L'origine orientale des diaconies romaines," *Mélanges d'archéologie et d'histoire*, 57 (1940): 121–131. Although Marrou is not cited here, his conclusions are affirmed in Ewa Wipszycka, "Diaconia," in *The Coptic Encylopedia*, Vol. 3, ed. Azis S. Atiya (New York: Macmillan, 1991), 895–867. Marrou is cited in A. Kalsbach, "Diakonie," in *Reallexikon für Antike und Christentum, Lieferung 22: Deus internus (Forts.)—Diamant*, ed. Theodor Klauser et al. (Stuttgart: Anton Hiersemann, 1957), 909–917, see esp. 916.

For the *Sayings*, see Elias 3 and John the Persian 2. For the Greek text, see *Patrologia Graeca* 65.184 and 237, respectively. Only the second of these two was also preserved in the late fifth century reorganization of the *Sayings* into thematic chapters (as opposed to the earlier format of organizing the sayings alphabetically by author's name). On the dating, see Jean-Claude Guy's introductory remarks in *Les Apophthegmes des pères I-IX*, Sources Chrétiennes 387, 83. The critical edition for the thematic collection, to which one may turn for John the Persian 2, is *Les Apophthegmes des pères*, Sources Chrétiennes 387, 318–320. English translation: Benedicta Ward, *The Sayings of the Desert Fathers: The Alphabetical Collection* (London: Mowbrays, 1975), 60 and 91–92, respectively.

For Cassian, see *Conférences* XXI.1–9 in which is described Theonas' encounters with John, the distributor of alms to the poor. *Patrologia Latina* 49.1169–82;

the critical edition is John Cassian, *Collationes XXIII*, Corpus Scriptorum Ecclesiasticorum Latinorum 13, ed. Michael Petschenig, with rev. by Gottfried Kreuz (Vienna: Österreichischen Akademie der Wissenschaften, 2004), 573–584. English translation: Boniface Ramsey, *John Cassian: The Conferences*, Ancient Christian Writers 57 (New York: Newman, 1997), 719–727. Ramsey states in his introduction (cf. p. 2) that the edition by Petschenig has been reprinted almost verbatim in Pichery's 1959 edition for the Sources Chrétiennes series (cf. vol. 64).

19. Frances J. Niederer, "Early Medieval Charity," *Church History*, 21 (1952): 285.

20. Georges Descoeudres, "Kirche und Diakonia. Gemeinschaftsräume in den Ermitagen der Qusur el-Izeila," in *Explorations aux Qouçour el-Izeila lors des campagnes 1981, 1982, 1984, 1985, 1986, 1989 et 1990*, Mission Suisse d'archéologie copte de l'université de Genève; EK 8184, vol. III, ed. Philippe Bridel et al. (Louvain: Peeters, 1999), 463–517.

21. David Knipp, *The Chapel of Physicians at Santa Maria Antiqua*, Dumbarton Oaks Papers 56 (Washington, DC: Dumbarton Oaks, 2002).

22. C. Mango, "On the History of the Templon and the Martyrion of St. Artemios at Constantinople," *Zograf*, 10 (1979):40–43.

23. Konstantina Mentzou-Meimari, "Eparkhiaka evagé idrymata mekhri tou telous tés eikonomakhias" *Byzantina*, 11 (1982):243–308. For oratories and their association with hospitals and *xenodocheia*, see T. Sternberg, *Orientalium More Secutus*, Jahrbuch für Antike und Christentum, Ergänzungsband 16 (Münster, 1991), 174–77; E. Monaco, "Ricerche sotto la diaconia di S. Teodoro," *Rend-PontAcc*, 45 (1972–1973), 223–41.

24. Caroline Goodson, *The Rome of Pope Paschal I: Papal Power, Urban Renovation, Church Rebuilding and Relic Translation, 817–824*, Cambridge Studies in Medieval Life and Thought: Fourth Series (Cambridge, UK: Cambridge University Press, 2010), 100–101. Goodson records that some in the medieval period assumed, incorrectly, the church was the site where St. Lawrence had distributed goods to the poor (see later in this chapter). For that, the interested reader is directed to "Acta Laurentii ex Martyrologio Adonis," *Acta Sanctorum*, Aug. 10, pp. 518–519; "De S. Cyriaca," *Acta Sanctorum*, Aug. 21, pp. 403–406; and to Pietro Ugonio, *Historia delle stationi di Roma* (1588), folia 116v–117r.

25. Francis J. Niederer, "Early Medieval Charity," 286. Marrou, "L'origine orientale des diaconies romaines," 101–102.

26. This letter is number 21 in Register 10 of Patrologia Latina 77.1080–81. It is numbered 8 in Register 10 of the critical editions, including Gregory the Great, *Registrum epistolarum, tome II: Libri VIII–XIV*, ed. Paulus Ewald, Monumenta Germaniae Historica (Berlin: Weidmann, 1899) 242; id., *Registrum epistularum libri I–VII*, Corpus Christianorum Series Latina 140A, 833–834. No English translation of the letter has been published.

27. Marrou, "L'origine orientale des diaconies romaines," 102.

28. Tziona Grossmark, "The Inn as a Place of Violence and Danger in Rabbinic Literature," in *Violence in Late Antiquity: Perceptions and Practices*, ed. H. A. Drake (Aldershot, UK: Ashgate Press, 2006), 57–68. See also E. D. Hunt, "Travel, Tourism and Piety in the Roman Empire: A Context for the Beginning of Christian Pilgrimage," *Echos du monde classique*, 28 (1984):391–417.

29. The *Basileia* is the principal subject of Brian Daley, "Building a New City: The Cappadocian Fathers and the Rhetoric of Philanthropy," *Journal of Early Christian Studies*, 7 (1999):431–461.

30. This was Gregory's *Oration* 14, "On Loving the Poor." Having said this, I have argued elsewhere the biblical idea of loving the poor is of far greater prominence in this oration than any particular concern to buttress Basil's public works project in Caesarea. The *Basileia* certainly heightened Gregory's concern to speak about the needs of the poor, but the arguments of this oration defy an exclusive association with Basil's particular project. See my "Deciphering a Recipe for Preaching in *Oration* 14," in *Re-Reading Gregory of Nazianzus: Essays on History, Theology, and Culture*, ed. by Christopher A. Beeley, CUA Studies in Early Christianity (Washington D.C.: Catholic University of America Press, 2012), 49–66. Cf. also John McGuckin, *St. Gregory of Nazianzus: An Intellectual Biography* (Crestwood, NY: St. Vladimir's Seminary Press, 2001), 147.

31. Cf. Gregory Nazianzen, *Oration* 44.63.

32. Palladius, *Lausiac History* (Cuthbert Butler, ed., *The Lausiac History of Palladius: The Greek Text Edited with Introduction and Notes*, Texts and Studies: Contributions to Biblical and Patristic Literature, vol. 6.2 [Cambridge: Cambridge University Press, 1904]; English translation: Robert T. Meyer, *Palladius: The Lausiac History*, Ancient Christian Writers 34 [New York: Paulist, 1964]). Palladius had lived in various parts of the eastern half of the empire during the late fourth and early fifth centuries. His travels included time in Egypt, and during such times he encountered some of the monks whose stories he relates. Other stories probably came to him through his spiritual mentor, Evagrius, and still others likely came to him through written records and oral accounts.

33. Palladius, *Lausiac History* 40.2. English translation: Meyer, *Palladius*, Ancient Christian Writers 34, 116–117.

34. Ibid., 117.

35. Cf. Ambrose of Milan, *On the Work of Ministry* II.28.140–143. Patrologia Latina 16:139–141; the critical edition is Ambrose, *De officiis*, Corpus Christianorum Series Latina 15, ed. Maurice Testard (Turnhout: Brepols, 2000), 148–149. English translation: Ivor J. Davidson, *Ambrose. De officiis, Volume I: Introduction, Text, and Translation*, Oxford Early Christian Studies (Oxford: Oxford Univ. Press, 2001), 347–349.

36. For a brief history of fiscal privileges for bishops and clergy in the fourth century, see R. L. Testa, "The bishop vir venerabilis: fiscal privileges and status definition in late antiquity" *Studia Patristica* 34 (2001): 125–144.

37. *Leges saeculares* 117, in *Fontes iuris Romani antejustiniani* 2, eds. Riccobonno et al. (Firenze, 1941-1943), 794.

38. *Codex Theodosianus* 16.2.8, in C. Pharr, *The Theodosian Code and Sirmondian Constitutions* (Princeton, NJ: Princeton University Press, 1952), 442.

39. See a letter from Constantine to an African proconsul, Annullinus, recorded in Eusebius, *Ecclesiastical History* 10.5.

40. *Codex Theodosianus* 16.2.6, in C. Pharr, 441. See Angelo Di Berardino, "The poor must be supported by the wealth of the churches (Codex Theodosianus 16.2.6)," in *Prayer and Spirituality in the Early Church, Vol. 5: Poverty and Riches*, eds. Geoffrey Dunn, David Luckensmeyer and Lawrence Cross (Strathfield, NSW: St. Pauls Publications, 2009), 249–268.

41. On the lives of early Christian clergy and bishops, especially with respect to their wealth, see L. William Countryman, "Christian Equality and the Early Catholic Episcopate," *Anglican Theological Review* 63 (1981): 115–138; Testa, "The bishop *vir venerabilis*," *op. cit.*; Andrea Sterk, *Renouncing the World, Yet Leading the Church: The Monk-Bishop in Late Antiquity* (Cambridge: Harvard University Press, 2004).

42. Emperor Theodosius I repeated these ideas in a law of his own in 383 (cf. *Codex Theodosianus* 12.1.104).

43. Basil of Caearea, for instance, seemed especially keen to link his construction of the *Basileia* with a duty to provide a public benefit. Cf. Peter Brown, *Poverty and Leadership in the Later Roman Empire* (Boston: University Press of New England, 2001), 33–44. Brown provides a fresh evaluation of Basil's own actions in light of a possible re-dating of the construction of the *Basileias* (from 368 to 370) on 41–42. Basil defends his *Basileias* and its benefit to the state in his *Ep.* 94 (ed. Yves Courtonne, *Saint Basile: Lettres*, 3 vols [Paris: Belles Lettres, 1957-1966], I.204-207).

44. On superfluous wealth in early Christianity, see Brian Matz, "The Principle of Detachment from Private Property in Basil of Caesarea's *Homily* 6 and Its Context," in *Reading Patristic Texts on Social Ethics: Issues and Challenges for 21st Century Christian Social Thought*, eds. B. Matz, J. Leemans, and J. Verstraeten, CUA Studies in Early Christianity (Washington, DC: CUA Press, 2011), 159–182, esp. 165–173.

45. Richard Finn, *Almsgiving in the Later Roman Empire: Christian Promotion and Practice, 313–450*, Oxford Classical Monographs (Oxford: Oxford University Press, 2006), ch. 4.

46. I have substituted "murderous" for Holman's "a homicide" at this point in her translation. This not only is a better translation of the Greek *adrophonos*, but it makes better sense in English.

47. Basil of Caesarea, *Hom.* 8 (Patrologia Graeca 31.321; English translation: Susan Holman, *The Hungry are Dying: Beggars and Bishops in Roman Cappadocia*, Oxford Studies in Historical Theology (Oxford: Oxford University Press, 2001), 190.

48. John Chrysostom, *Conciones VII de Lazaro*, I (Patrologia Graeca 48.963–982); English translation: Catherine Roth, *John Chrysostom: On Wealth and Poverty*, Popular Patristics Series (Crestwood, NY: St. Vladimir's Seminary Press, 1984), 19–38.

49. Chrysostom, *Sermon on Lazarus* 1 (Roth, *John Chrysostom*, 22).

50. Chrysostom, *Sermon on Lazarus* 1 (Roth, *John Chrysostom*, 26).

51. Chrysostom, *Sermon on Lazarus* 1 (Roth, *John Chrysostom*, 28 and 30).

52. Basil of Caesarea, *A Psalm of David Against the Usurers, On Psalm 14*, in Agnes C. Way, *Saint Basil: Exegetic Homilies*, Fathers of the Church Series 46 (Washington, DC: Catholic University of America Press, 1963) 181.

53. Basil, *Hom.* 6.4; Basil of Caesarea, *Homélies sur la richesse*, Collection d'études anciennes, ed. Yves Courtonne (Paris: Firm-Didot, 1935), 15–37. English translation: Hieroschemamonk Janis (Berzins), "Homily on the Words of St. Luke's Gospel: 'I Will Pull Down my Barns and Build Larger Ones' and on Avarice," *Orthodox Life*, 42 (1992): 13.

54. Gregory of Nazianzus, *Or.* 14.10 (Patrologia Graeca 35.869); English translation: Vinson, *Gregory of Nazianzus*, 45.

55. Gregory of Nazianzus, *Or.* 14.12 (Patrologia Graeca 35.872–873); English translation: Vinson, *Gregory of Nazianzus*, 47.

56. Gregory of Nazianzus, *Or.* 14.12 (Patrologia Graeca 35.872–873); English translation: Vinson, *Gregory of Nazianzus*, 47.

57. Gregory of Nazianzus, *Or.* 14.9.

58. Asterius, *Hom.* 3.12; English translation: Datema, *Asterius of Amasea*, 35; English translation: Galusha Anderson and Edgar J. Goodspeed, *Ancient Sermons for Modern Times* [(New York: Pilgrim Press, 1904), 107.

59. The threat of eternal torments for the unrighteous wealthy fill many other treatises besides the three discussed here. Cf., e.g., Gregory Nazianzen, *Or.* 14; Gregory of Nyssa, *Against the Usurers*; Basil of Caesarea, *Homily* 21; id., *Homily "I Will Tear Down my Barns..."* 2; Asterius of Amasea, *Homily* 2.5–7; John Chrysostom, *Homilies on Genesis* 20.17–20.

60. Jerome, *Homilies* 86; Jerome, *Opera, Pars II: Opera homiletica*, Corpus Christianorum Series Latina 78 (Turnhout: Brepols, 1958), 510; English translation: S. Marie Ligouri Ewald, *The Homilies of Saint Jerome*, Fathers of the Church Series 57 (Washington, DC: Catholic University of America Press, 1966), 203–204.

61. Peter Chrysologus, *Hom.* 122; Sancti Petri Chrysologi, *Collectio sermonum, Pars II: Collectio sermonum a Felice episcopo parata sermonibus extravagantibus adiectis*, Corpus Christianorum Series Latina 24A, ed. Alexander Olivar (Turnhout: Brepols, 1981), 732–737; English translation: George E. Ganss, trans. *Saint Peter Chrysologus: Selected Sermons. Saint Valerian: Homilies*, Fathers of the Church Series 17 (Washington, DC: Catholic University of America Press, 1953), 208–213.

62. Salvian of Marseilles, *Four Books of Timothy to the Church* Book I.2; Salvien de Marseille, *Oeuvres I: Les Lettres. Les Livres de Timothée a l'Église*, Sources Chrétiennes, vol. 176, ed. Georges Lagarrigue (Paris: Les éditions du Cerf, 1971), 142–144; English translation: Jeremiah F. O'Sullivan, trans. *The Writings of Salvian, the Presbyter*, Fathers of the Church Series 3 (Washington, DC: Catholic University of America Press, 1947), 271.

63. Clement of Alexandria, *Quis dives salvetur*, is especially good at working this rhetorical theme. Cf. also Hermas, *Shepherd*, Similitude 2; the story of Lawrence's donation of the emperor's money to the poor in Ambrose of Milan, *On the Work of Ministry* II.28.140–143; Gregory of Nyssa, *First Homily on Loving the Poor* (aka, "On Good Works").

64. Basil of Caesarea, *Homily* 6, op. cit. Cf. also Cyprian of Carthage, *On the Lapsed*, §12.

65. Basil, *Homily* 21.5, "On Detachment from Wealth."

66. Gregory of Nyssa, *First Homily on Loving the Poor* (aka, "On Good Works").

67. Theodoret, *Orations on Providence* 6.18–28.

68. Reimund Bieringer, "Texts that Create a Future: The Function of Ancient Texts for Theology Today," in *Reading Patristic Texts on Social Ethics*, op. cit., 3–29, is appropriately critical of Theodoret's use of 1 Cor. 12:12–30 as support for this economic theory.

69. Gregory of Nyssa, *Against the Usurers*.

70. There are many examples of this, including Augustine, *Expositions on the Psalms* 131. 28; an anonymous Pelagian author's text, *On Riches* VI.4–5; John Chrysostom, *21 Homilies to the People of Antioch* II.6; Asterius, *Hom.* 1.10 (Datema, *Asterius of Amasea*, 13; English translation: Anderson and Goodspeed, *Ancient Sermons for Modern Times*, 42), says that, indeed, many who are brought before a magistrate for stealing are indeed poor and homeless.

71. John Chrysostom, *Homilies on John* 65.3; Anonymous Pelagian author of *On Riches* XIX.9, praises those who arrange their affairs so as to have nothing left at the moment of their death.

72. Asterius of Amasea, *Homilies* 3.15, "On Covetousness."

73. Asterius of Amasea, *Homilies* 3.10, "On Covetousness," actually charges the wealthy with "creating" pirates at sea and thieves on land.

REFERENCES

Anderson, Galusha, and Edgar J. Goodspeed. *Ancient Sermons for Modern Times*. New York: Pilgrim Press, 1904.

Bieringer, Reimund. "Texts that Create a Future: The Function of Ancient Texts for Theology Today." In Johan Leemans, Brian J. Matz, and Johan Verstraeten (eds.), *Reading Patristic Texts on Social Ethics*. Washington, DC: Catholic University of America Press, 2011, 3–29.

Brown, Peter. *Poverty and Leadership in the Later Roman Empire*. Boston: University Press of New England, 2001.

Clark, Elizabeth. *Reading Renunciation: Asceticism and Scripture in Early Christianity*. Princeton, NJ: Princeton University Press, 1999.

Collins, John N. *Diakonia: Reinterpreting the Ancient Sources*. New York: Oxford University Press, 1990.

Countryman, L. William. "Christian Equality and the Early Catholic Episcopate." *Anglican Theological Review*, 63 (1981):115–138.

Courtonne, Yves (ed.). *Saint Basile: Lettres*. 3 vols. Paris: Belles Lettres, 1957–1966.

Daley, Brian. "Building a New City: The Cappadocian Fathers and the Rhetoric of Philanthropy." *Journal of Early Christian Studies*, 7 (1999):431–61.

Datema, Cornelius (ed.). *Asterius of Amasea. Homilies I–XIV: Text, introduction and notes*. Leiden: E. J. Brill, 1970.

Descoeudres, Georges. "Kirche und Diakonia: Gemeinschaftsräume in den Ermitagen der Qusur el-Izeila." In Philippe Bridel et al. (eds.), *Explorations aux Qouçour el-Izeila lors des campagnes 1981, 1982, 1984, 1985, 1986, 1989 et 1990*. Mission Suisse d'archéologie copte de l'université de Genève. EK 8184, vol. III. Louvain: Peeters Press, 1999, 463–517.

Di Berardino, Angelo. "The Poor Must Be Supported by the Wealth of the Churches (Codex Theodosianus 16.2.6)." In Geoffrey Dunn, David Luckensmeyer, and Lawrence Cross (eds.), *Prayer and Spirituality in the Early Church*. Vol. 5, *Poverty and Riches*. Strathfield, NSW: St. Pauls Publications, 2009, 249–268.

Downs, David J. *The Offering of the Gentiles: Paul's Collection for Jerusalem in Its Chronological, Cultural, and Cultic Contexts*. Wissenschaftliche Untersuchungen zum Neuen Testament 2. Vol. 248. Tübingen: Mohr-Siebeck, 2008.

Ernst, Allie. *Martha from the Margins: The Authority of Martha in Early Christian Tradition*. Supplements to Vigiliae Christianae. Leiden: Brill, 2009.

Ewald, S. Marie Ligouri. *The Homilies of Saint Jerome*. Fathers of the Church Series 57. Washington, DC: Catholic University of America Press, 1966.

Finn, Richard. *Almsgiving in the Later Roman Empire: Christian Promotion and Practice, 313–450*. Oxford Classical Monographs. Oxford: Oxford University Press, 2006.

Friesen, Steven J. "Injustice or God's Will? Early Christian Explanations of Poverty." In Susan R. Holman (ed.), *Wealth and Poverty in Early Church and Society*. Grand Rapids, MI: Baker Academic, 2008, 17–36.

Funk, F. X. *Didascalia et Constitutiones Apostolorum*. Vol. 1. Paderborn: F. Schoeningh, 1905.

Goodson, Caroline. *The Rome of Pope Paschal I: Papal Power, Urban Renovation, Church Rebuilding and Relic Translation, 817–824*. Cambridge Studies in Medieval Life and Thought: Fourth Series. Cambridge, UK: Cambridge University Press, 2010.

Grossmark, Tziona. "The Inn as a Place of Violence and Danger in Rabbinic Literature." In H. A. Drake (ed.), *Violence in Late Antiquity: Perceptions and Practices*. Aldershot, UK: Ashgate Press, 2006, 57–68.

Hardwick, Michael E. *Josephus as an Historical Source in Patristic Literature through Eusebius.* Brown Judaic Studies 128. Atlanta, GA: Scholars Press, 1989.

Hieroschemamonk, Janis (Berzins). "Homily on the Words of St. Luke's Gospel: 'I Will Pull Down my Barns and Build Larger Ones' and on Avarice." *Orthodox Life,* 42 (1992):10–17.

Holman, Susan. *The Hungry Are Dying: Beggars and Bishops in Roman Cappadocia.* Oxford Studies in Historical Theology. Oxford: Oxford University Press, 2001.

Hunt, E. D. "Travel, Tourism and Piety in the Roman Empire: A Context for the Beginning of Christian Pilgrimage." *Echos du monde classique,* 28 (1984):391–417.

Kalsbach, A. "Diakonie." In Theodor Klauser et al. (eds.), *Reallexikon für Antike und Christentum, Lieferung 22: Deus internus (Forts.)—Diamant.* Stuttgart: Anton Hiersemann, 1957, 909–917.

Kessler, Andreas. *Reichtumskritik und Pelagianismus: Die pelagianische Diatribe de divitiis: Situierung, Lesetext, Übersetzung, Kommentar.* Paradosis 43. Freiburg: U niversitätsverlag, 1999.

Knipp, David. *The Chapel of Physicians at Santa Maria Antiqua.* Dumbarton Oaks Papers 56. Washington, DC: Dumbarton Oaks, 2002.

Mango, Cyril. "On the History of the Templon and the Martyrion of St. Artemios at Constantinople." *Zograf,* 10 (1979):40–43.

Marrou, Henri-Irénée. "L'origine orientale des diaconies romaines." *Mélanges d'archéologie et d'histoire,* 57 (1940):95–142.

Maspero, Jean. *Papyrus grecs d'époque byzantine.* Catalogue général des antiquités égyptiennes du Musée du Caire, Papyrus grecs d'époque byzantine. 4 vols. Cairo: Institut Français d'Archéologie Orientale, 1911–1916.

——."Sur quelques objets coptes du Musée du Caire." *Annales du Service des antiquités d'Egypte,* 10 (1910):173–174.

Matz, Brian. "The Principle of Detachment from Private Property in Basil of Caesarea's *Homily* 6 and Its Context." In J. Leemans, B. Matz, and J. Verstraeten (eds.), *Reading Patristic Texts on Social Ethics: Issues and Challenges for 21st Century Christian Social Thought.* CUA Studies in Early Christianity. Washington, DC: CUA Press, 2011, 159–182.

——. "Deciphering a Recipe for Preaching in *Oration* 14." In Christopher A. Beeley (ed.), *Re-Reading Gregory of Nazianzus: Essays on History, Theology, and Culture.* CUA Studies in Early Christianity. Washington, DC: Catholic University of America Press, 2012, 49–66.

McGuckin, John. *St. Gregory of Nazianzus: An Intellectual Biography.* Crestwood, NY: St. Vladimir's Seminary Press, 2001.

Mentzou-Meimari, Konstantina. "Eparkhiaka evagé idrymata mekhri tou telous tés eikonomakhias." *Byzantina,* 11 (1982):243–308.

Monaco, E. "Ricerche sotto la diaconia di S. Teodoro." *Rend-PontAcc,* 45 (1972–1973):223–41.

Niederer, Frances J. "Early Medieval Charity." *Church History,* 21 (1952):285–295.

O'Sullivan, Jeremiah F., trans. *The Writings of Salvian, the Presbyter.* Fathers of the Church Series 3. Washington, DC: Catholic University of America Press, 1947.

Pharr, C. *The Theodosian Code and Sirmondian Constitutions.* Princeton, NJ: Princeton University Press, 1952.

Rees, B. R. *The Letters of Pelagius and his Followers.* Suffolk, UK: Boydell Press, 1991.

Riccobonno, Salvador, Giovanni Baviera, Contardo Ferrini, Giuseppe Furlani, and Vincenzo Arangio-Ruiz (eds.). *Fontes iuris Romani antejustiniani.* Vol. 2. Florence: Apud S.A.G. Barbèra, 1941–1943, 794.

Roth, Catherine. *John Chrysostom: On Wealth and Poverty.* Popular Patristics Series. Crestwood, NY: St. Vladimir's Seminary Press, 1984.

Salvien de Marseille. *Oeuvres I: Les Lettres. Les Livres de Timothée a l'Église.* Sources Chrétiennes176. Edited by Georges Lagarrigue. Paris: Les éditions du Cerf, 1971.

Scaglioni, Carlo. "'Guia a voi ricchi!' Pelagio e gli scritti pelangiani." In *Per foramen acus: Il cristianesimo antico di fronte alla pericope evangelica del "giovane ricco."* Studia Patristica Mediolanensia 14. Milan: Vita e Pensiero, 1986, 361–398.

Sterk, Andrea. *Renouncing the World, Yet Leading the Church: The Monk-Bishop in Late Antiquity.* Cambridge, MA: Harvard University Press, 2004.

Sternberg, Theodore. *Orientalium More Secutus.* Jahrbuch für Antike und Christentum, Ergänzungsband 16. Münster: Aschendorff, 1991.

Strzygowski, Josef. *Koptisch Kunst.* Catalogue général des antiquités égyptiennes du Musée du Caire. Osnabrück: Zeller, 1904.

Testa, R. L. "The Bishop vir Venerabilis: Fiscal Privileges and Status Definition in Late Antiquity." *Studia Patristica,* 34 (2001):125–144.

Vinson, Martha. *St. Gregory of Nazianzus: Select Orations.* Fathers of the Church Series 107. Washington, DC: Catholic University of America Press, 2003.

Ward, Benedicta. *The Sayings of the Desert Fathers: The Alphabetical Collection.* London: Mowbrays, 1975.

Way, Agnes C. *Saint Basil: Exegetic Homilies.* Fathers of the Church Series 46. Washington, DC: Catholic University of America Press, 1963.

Wipszycka, Ewa. "Diaconia." In Azis S. Atiya (ed.), *The Coptic Encylopedia.* Vol. 3. New York: Macmillan, 1991, 895–867.

6

How a Thomistic Moral Framework Can Take Social Causality Seriously

Mary Hirschfeld

THE QUESTION ADDRESSED in this volume is whether, because of our causal involvement in market processes, we bear responsibility for the harms caused to distant others by markets. My particular task is to investigate what a Thomistic moral framework can contribute to answering this question.

The *Prima Secundae* of the *Summa Theologiae* takes the voluntary act of a human being as a basic unit of analysis, and one could appeal to it in order to sort out Thomas's thoughts about our responsibility for the unintended impact our actions have on distant others. However, I am not sure what that effort would add to the sorts of explorations undertaken by Albino Barrera in his chapter in this volume on market complicity.[1] Instead, I turn to the *Secunda Secundae*, which has considerable material dealing with the role of the individual in the context of the institutions that structure our lives. Thomas offers an account of the connection between the individual, the market, and the government that highlights the intrinsically social aspect of our connection to markets and thus indirectly provides a vocabulary for our responsibility as social actors.

Thomas's teachings in the *Secunda Secundae* resonate in many ways with the theory of social causality developed by critical realism, as described in detail in Douglas Porpora's chapter in this volume. Like critical realism, Thomas takes the individual seriously, but also like critical realism,

Thomas sees society as an emergent reality with properties, claims, and responsibilities of its own. On this view, individuals have agency (and therefore also responsibility) as individuals, of course, but also as participants in a social structure that is more than simply an aggregation of individuals.

Thomas's two-tiered framework provides a diagnosis for why the problem we confront in this book can seem so intractable. We live in a culture that sees the market as the realm of transactions between individuals, one in which the institution of private property allows individuals to reap the reward of their own effort and their own entrepreneurship. The notion that it is our agency as workers or entrepreneurs that "entitles" us to the market returns we earn has a ready parallel in the idea that our agency as individuals also comes with a responsibility to redress harms to others that are a direct result of our own actions. But it is far more difficult to explain why an individual should take responsibility for harms to others that are not directly linked to her own activities. For example, if an individual's best effort to go green has no measurable impact on the problem of global warming, it is not obvious why the individual should feel responsible for the problem of global warming, as John Coleman's chapter in this volume argues.

What Thomas offers us instead is a two-tiered account of the economy, which suggests that individuals benefit not only as a result of their direct efforts but also from the emergent properties of the economic system as a whole. That emergent system allows individuals to enjoy a far greater standard of living than would be possible were they to attempt to produce for themselves in splendid isolation. But if we benefit not only as a result of our efforts as individuals but also simply by virtue of our participation in a larger social system, it would seem to follow that we need to exercise responsibility not only as individuals but also as participants in that social system. An individual's effort to go green might have no effect on global warming, but as a citizen an individual can operate through political and civic channels to shape our economic system as a whole in a way that does work to slow down global warming.

In order to develop these ideas, I begin with a brief discussion of C.B. MacPherson's reading of John Locke's account of private property[2] as a good representation of the modern tendency to see the market as a sphere of private activity without reference to the emergent social properties of the economy. That account grounds the right to private property in the work effort of the individual, making it difficult to explain why an individual might be responsible for harms that cannot be directly imputed to him. To develop an alternative account, I turn to Thomas Aquinas, who affirms private property on the grounds that it channels in socially productive ways our natural tendency to look after ourselves. However, unlike Locke, Thomas maintains a two-tiered understanding of private property, seeing it as ordered both to private ends and to the common good. For Thomas, one is never just a private agent in the market but also always a member of a larger community from which one benefits and to which one is responsible.

Lest that seem to rely on an anachronistic view of society, I go on to argue that Adam Smith's analysis of the enormous productivity that results from the division of labor and specialization suggests that the emergent properties of the economic order are an essential feature of markets and that Thomas's two-tiered framework is better suited to that complexity than is the single-tiered framework one might derive from the sort of possessive individualism described by MacPherson's Locke.

Finally, I argue that Thomas provides us a way of thinking about the two-fold nature of our responsibilities as individuals and as citizens in his discussion of practical reason, which mirrors his two-tiered understanding of the individual as an individual and of the individual as a member of what sociologists might call an emergent social order. The upshot of that discussion is that our primary responsibility for the harms done to distant others is not exercised in our role as private individuals but rather in our equally important role as citizens.

The chapter concludes with the argument that the two-tiered understanding of individual agency needs to have greater currency in modern discourse and that the specific framework sketched here, drawing on Thomas Aquinas and Adam Smith, has enough purchase on modern sensibilities to be a plausible vehicle for effecting that change.

A Single-Tiered View: MacPherson's Account of Locke's Possessive Individualism

The sorts of situations we are addressing—global warming or the deleterious effects globalization can have on some—share the key feature that they are consequences of how the economic system as a whole functions. As a result, an individual acting in the market as an individual can make no perceptible difference. One can decide to minimize one's carbon footprint, for example, but unless large majorities of our fellow citizens do the same, global warming will proceed apace. Hence the conundrum: How do we assign responsibility to individuals for situations over which they have no control and that they cannot meaningfully address alone no matter how well-intentioned they might be?

Part of our difficulty in thinking through this problem is that we have inherited a mode of thought that focuses on the individual, especially in relationship to economic questions. On a generally held view, individuals go into the marketplace in order to earn an income and with that income procure the goods and services they desire. The institution of private property insures that individuals will reap the benefits of their hard work and creativity. The market mediates the conflicting or competing desires of individuals in a way that not only brings about order but also channels individuals in directions that are socially useful.

The concepts and language employed within the discipline of economics can handle some but not all of the social features of our economic activities. For example, the fact that a transaction between two individuals might have unintended consequences for a third party (a phenomenon economists dub an "externality") is well understood in the economic literature. Yet because it focuses on the individual, the language of economics cannot really capture emergent social phenomenon. To give a classic example, economics cannot explain why rational individuals would bother to vote. The reasoning parallels our problem exactly. The chance that any major election would be decided by a single vote is vanishingly small.[3] Thus an individual's vote will have no direct impact on the outcome of an election. At the same time, it is costly to vote—it takes time and energy. So why would an individual voluntarily incur the cost of voting when the outcome of the election would be the same whether or not she voted?

As C.B. MacPherson has argued, the market system and the economic language we employ to describe it is rooted in deep assumptions about human nature that he describes as "possessive individualism."[4] On this view, individuals are proprietors of their own person and capacities, for which they owe nothing to society. The essence of freedom is independence from the will of others; thus the primary mode of relationship is the voluntary contract. Given these basic principles, the essential purpose of political society is the protection of the individual's property in himself and his capacities and the maintenance of orderly relations of exchange between individuals. This tradition of thought is rooted in the individual and his act. MacPherson connects those views with those of John Locke.[5]

MacPherson's reading of Locke is not uncontroversial, but for our purposes what matters is not whether MacPherson gives an accurate account of what Locke meant but rather that this reading of Locke reflects a worldview, quite popular today, that is grounded in an extreme form of individualism. MacPherson's reading runs as follows. First, Locke does begin with a more communitarian view of property. Thus, in his *Second Treatise of Government*, he undertook to explain how we could justify private property in light of the fact that God had given the earth to mankind in common (25). His argument was essentially that in view of the fact that we have ownership of ourselves, we can claim ownership of material goods by virtue of mixing our labor with those goods, because the labor of man is properly his (27). This original property right would be constrained by the stricture that we could not claim ownership of more than we could use (31). But Locke goes on to lift that restriction by arguing that through the institution of money, we have collectively agreed to unlimited accumulation of private property (37). This formulation of the origin of property rights resonates with the modern sense that the income we earn and the property we own is rightfully ours because we worked for it (or received it as a gift from those who worked for it). On this view of property, our efforts (or those of our benefactors) are the source of our claim to ownership, and once we've made that claim, we have a primary right to use our income and wealth as we see fit. The right of ownership is not absolute. After all, the government has the power to tax. But as the rallying cry "no taxation without representation" suggests, our willingness to pay taxes is rooted in the idea that we consent to be taxed, as expressed through the taxation power entrusted to the House of Representatives. Once we've paid the taxes to which we've consented through our representatives, we are free to dispose of the remainder of our income and our property as we see fit.

MacPherson's Locke emphasizes the relationship between an individual's labor and the benefits he reaps from market activities. In doing so he sets up the conundrum we are contemplating. If we think we deserve the income and property we earn as a direct result of our activities in the market, how do we articulate our responsibility for harms done to others that are but indirectly and distantly related to our own actions? It is not hard for us to see that we are as responsible for the harms we directly cause as we are for the income we directly earn. The foundational idea that the essence of human being is freedom from the interference of others entails that we are responsible when we do interfere with others. But it is harder to articulate our responsibility for harms that are not directly linked to our own actions.

The difficulty is that the Lockean view does not easily account for the social aspect of the market. It is a view that accords society no role in having given us the gift of ourselves and our capacities and obscures the social aspect of economic activity. [6] The language of both possessive and individualism and economic science eclipses the contributions from persons and social structures to the benefits we receive in markets, tempting us to think that our success is attributable simply to our own efforts and the cooperation of those with whom we directly trade. As a result, it stands to reason that there is likewise no language for describing the responsibility we bear as individuals for the harms that come to others as a result of impersonal market workings. Though Locke's view stresses the economic activity of the individual, economic life has inescapably social features. It is time to turn to an account of private property and economic life that can do justice to the social nature of economic production while retaining a sense of the importance of the efforts of the individual. In short, we need a two-tiered view of private property, such as the one offered by St. Thomas Aquinas.

A Two-Tiered View: Aquinas on Private Property

Aquinas's account of private property in the *Summa Theologiae* (*ST*) is rooted in a view of society that does not begin with self-proprietary individuals and work up to some sort of social contract.[7] On the contrary, humans are naturally inclined to live in society (*ST*, I-II, 94, 2). The social nature of our beings is taken for granted, and Thomas's account of individual agency is embedded in that social setting, giving him a two-tiered view of human nature. We can see this by a close examination of Thomas's teachings on private property.

Like Locke, Aquinas begins with the argument that God has given the earth to mankind in common (*ST*, II-II, 66, 1). But unlike MacPherson's Locke, Thomas allows for private property insofar as it is ordered to the common good. Where Locke derives the right to private property from an individual's prior ownership of himself, Thomas allows for private property not as a right but rather as an institution that arises from human agreement and that is not contrary to natural law (*ST*, II-II, 66, 2, ad. 1). In other words, most societies recognize private property because it is socially useful to do so.

Thomas begins his vindication of the licitness of private property by distinguishing between two aspects of ownership. On the one hand, there is our power to "procure and dispense," by which Thomas seems to mean the use of property (land or capital goods) to generate income and the power to determine how the resulting income will be allocated. On the other hand, there is our "use" of external goods (*ST*, II-II, 66, 2).[8] With respect to the former, private property is lawful and even useful; with respect to the latter, goods should be held "not as one's own, but as common, so that, to wit, one is ready to communicate them to others in their need" (*ST*, II-II, 66.2). In other words, Thomas sees property and external goods through a two-tiered lens—ordered both to the individual and to the community.

Beginning with the dimension of property that relates to the individual, we find that Thomas defends private property but on grounds that differ from the ones employed by Locke. Thomas offers three reasons why private property is lawful with respect to the power to procure and dispense. First, he argues that every man is more careful to procure what is for himself alone than for what is common to all; second, it creates more order to assign property, since there would be "confusion if everyone had to look after any one thing indeterminately"; and finally, it is an antidote for bickering. But for Thomas this concerns ownership only with respect to the power to procure and dispense. To repeat, with respect to use, Thomas believes we are to hold our goods as common, ready to share them with the needy (*ST*, II-II, 66, 2).

To modern ears, there seems to be a contradiction between the first reason why private property is lawful with respect to the power to procure and dispense and the claim that with respect to use we are to hold goods as common. If private property is lawful because we would be more likely to shirk if we were not working directly for our own sustenance, how could the incentive work if we turn around and consider the goods we earn as being held in common? The answer turns on what it means to hold goods as in common.

To learn more about this we need to turn to Thomas's treatise on charity. The first important idea is that, for Thomas, love of self naturally and properly takes precedence over love of neighbor (*ST*, II-II, 26, 4). The reason for this is not that we are simply selfish beings. Rather, it's because our love of God takes precedence over everything. But our access to God is rooted in our own beings. Were we to attempt to love our neighbors more than ourselves, we would be attempting to love the creature more than our own point of access to the Creator. According to Thomas, if we truly understand the primacy of our love for God, we see that we love ourselves because we partake of God. In turn, we love our neighbors as fellows in that love of God. This order of charity is reflected in Thomas's teachings on almsgiving. There we learn that we ought to tend to our needs first. Because material well-being is subordinate to spiritual well-being, this is not an absolute. We might sacrifice our material well-being for things of greater importance: the well-being of the community, a person of particular holiness, and so on. But, ordinarily, we would tend to our material needs and then minister to the needs of others with whatever is surplus to us (*ST*, II-II, 32, 6).

On this account, private property suits human nature. We properly and naturally look to ourselves first. The assignment of private property taps into that natural interest and encourages us to work more carefully (i.e., more diligently). But notice that this proper natural interest has to do with meeting our needs. For Thomas, this is a bounded desire. In his discussions on wealth in the *Prima Secundae*, Thomas observes that the desire for natural wealth is properly finite, since such wealth is desired for natural needs, which are themselves finite. It is our concupiscent desire for artificial wealth that knows no bounds, because on acquiring it we find that it does not satisfy and so we remain hungry for more (*ST*, I-II, 2, 1, ad.3). For Thomas, these natural needs include what is necessary for us socially (*ST*, II-II, 32, 6). Although these social needs vary by station, they are nonetheless bounded. Thus, for Thomas, the self-interest that is productively channeled by private property is not the common understanding of self-interest today: the desire to maximize income in the market. The reward of effort for Thomas is limited to being the first claimant to have one's needs met by the goods one procures, but this advantage is accompanied by a duty to dispense to those in need whatever income remained after one's needs were met. Note that the dispersal of surplus funds could not even properly be called a sacrifice. The fulfillment of concupiscent desire for artificial wealth is not a good in the first place, and one sacrifices nothing by foregoing such consumption in favor of helping others.

Thomas's framework thus weakly resonates with the Lockean understanding that our efforts have some link to the benefits we derive from economic activity. Private property is a useful institution because by nature we are more diligent to secure our own needs than we might be if we were to attempt to produce directly for the common good. This connection between individual actions and the benefits one derives therefrom corresponds to Thomas's extensive treatment of our duties to treat others with justice in our economic dealings (*ST*, II-II, 78 and 79, on cheating and usury, respectively). But the accent on the direct connection between an individual's actions and the consequences flowing therefrom is embedded in an account that emphasizes the social nature of our economic activities.

We can see this in three ways. First, there is nothing in Thomas's treatment that grounds an individual's claim to a piece of property in anything that the individual has done. Instead, Thomas's argument that private property is licit rests on the functionality of such institutional arrangements. The purpose or *telos* of economic arrangements is to meet genuine human needs (*ST*, I-II, 2, 1). God has, therefore, granted humans dominion over external things with respect to their use to humanity in general (*ST*, II-II, 66, 1). The further division of that dominion in the form of individual property assignments is only with respect to the power to procure and dispense (*ST*, II-II, 66, 2). The functionality of that arrangement lies in its ability to channel our diligence and to help us order our economic activities productively (*ST*, II-II, 66, 2). As Thomas argues earlier, private property is the sort of natural right that exists only through the discernment of reason rather than any natural fittingness. Thus there is not any particular reason why a given piece of land should belong to one man or another, but rather private property emerges because it is useful to make such distinctions (*ST*, II-II, 57, 3).[9]

Moreover, those distinctions are not of necessity based on an individual's acts but rather on a determination by society about what sort of arrangements are most suitable (*ST*, I-II, 95, 4). To be clear, society might find it fitting to assign property rights based on an individual's efforts. Indeed, it might well be wise to do so. The key point is that for Thomas the assignment of private property is a conventional agreement that is an application of natural law, not something rooted directly in human nature. [10] The orientation of Thomas's theory is not about what benefits we can rightfully claim as our own based on our efforts but rather about how society can best channel human proclivities in useful directions.

The second point relates to Thomas's teachings about the properly bounded nature of our consumption. Most obviously, as already discussed, we are to hold the goods we produce as in common, with surplus income due to others. That drives a wedge between our productive activities and the consumption we can rightfully enjoy. More subtly, the very notion of what is deemed "necessary" to us is not something over which we have individual control. As Stephen Marglin argues, in the modern world, our income determines our station in life, but in premodern times one's station in life was socially determined.[11] That older notion is the framework that allows us to be able to identify some income as "surplus" to us.[12] On this view, the question of whether we can achieve our proper station has some connection to our efforts, but the station itself does not. The benefits we derive from our market activities are strongly impacted by social norms.

Finally, our sense of ownership is never to be felt as absolute. With respect to use, we are to hold our goods as if in common. As already noted, Thomas argues that God gave the earth to mankind in common for the support of our material needs. The allowance for private property is ordered to that higher end. Indeed, the claims of others to material support is such that a person who is in dire need may take what "belongs" to another as a matter of right (*ST*, II-II, 66.7.c and ad.2). Indeed, to consume more than is one's due in the face of the dire need of others might well be called a form of theft (*ST*, II-II, 66.2. ad.3).

Thomas's account of private property thus gives us an interweaving of the individual and the community, affirming our tendency to work for ourselves while not forgetting that we are members of a society with duties to others. He is neither an individualist nor a socialist. Instead, we are to have a two-tiered understanding of humans as individuals but also as members of a society.

Thomas's account of private property brings in the social aspect of economic life both with respect to the community's role in assigning property rights and with respect to the ultimate social end of our economic activities. Elsewhere in his writings, Thomas gives us a glimpse of other ways the economy should be regarded as what sociologists would call an emergent system. For starters, Thomas argues in his treatise on law that "each man, in all that he is and has, belongs to the community" (*ST*, I-II, 96.4). We could not exist apart from the community. We get a little more insight into what Thomas might mean by that in his treatment of the practice of voluntary poverty in the *Summa Contra Gentiles* (*SG*). There he takes up the objection that religious who renounce wealth are thereby unable to contribute to the good of society (*SG*, III, 131, 2). In reply, Aquinas points out that we are by nature interdependent: Some are farmers, others are builders, and so forth. The voluntary poor have not withdrawn their support from society but rather make their contribution in the form of spiritual goods (*SG*, III, 134, 2). Thomas's answer reveals a core view of society as a band of essentially interdependent individuals who have specialized, and who therefore need one another, in order to enjoy the full human good—both materially and spiritually. We cannot survive without the economic activities of others and therefore can never be understood as economically independent. Thomas himself does not develop the nature of this interdependence further, but his insight that our economic lives are essentially ordered around specialization and trade resonates with the insights of Adam Smith, who gives us a strong reason to see the economy as an emergent system, with properties that appear only at the social level.

Adam Smith and the Emergent Properties of the Economic Order

Thus far, the argument is that Thomas's framework drives a wedge between the benefits one receives from one's market activity and one's actions. If the benefits we receive are socially mediated through cultural and governmental norms and institutions, then it would follow that the market harms others experience through their participation entail that we bear social responsibility for them. If our membership in a society is foundational for all that we are and have, then as responsible members of society, we must be concerned about whether the social systems are just and about the welfare of those who are harmed by those systems. Thomas does provide an account of the connection between our market actions and our direct benefits in the form of arguing that private property rewards diligence; as stewards of private property, we are allowed to privilege our own needs when we consider how to allocate the goods produced by the property we own. He offers a corresponding account of the demands of justice in our economic dealings with others as individuals. But that discussion is set within a framework that reminds us that our economic lives are inherently social, with the corresponding claim that we have responsibilities as social actors.

Yet it might seem that Locke's account is better suited to our modern economy. It is one thing to consider ourselves as stewards of particular parcels of land rather than as owners in the modern sense; the land does not come into being as a result of human effort. The thought that we might have social obligations with respect to the fruit of the land originally given by God to us all follows rather naturally. But as Locke observed, even with land, the greater portion of its productivity is due to human cultivation. Surely that's even truer when human and physical capital replaces land as the primary productive asset. If the productive assets exist because of our own individual effort, then it is less obvious why we should feel a social obligation in the use of the fruits of those assets.

My argument here is that, to the contrary, the complex market economy reveals even more clearly the gains we all derive from the emergent properties of the economic system. In making this claim, I appeal to Adam Smith. In the opening line of *The Wealth of Nations*, Smith tells us that the greatest improvement in the productive power of labor lies in the division of labor.[13] By specializing in one particular task, we are able to enhance our proficiency at that task, economize on the time it takes to move from task to task, and are more apt to be innovative about how to perform that one task better. For an illustration of this point, Smith discusses his now-famous pin factory in which ten people working together could produce 48,000 pins whereas each working individually could probably produce no more than twenty pins a day.[14] Economic historians emphasize accumulation of capital, technological improvement, and institutional factors when trying to explain economic development over time,[15] but those factors would have little impact if it were not for the foundational truth that specialization and trade allows us to be far more productive than we would be were we to attempt to produce for ourselves in isolation.

To give a more modern example, simply consider the shirt you are wearing right now. Let's say it's a nice shirt that cost you $50. To see the value to you of living in a society where economic production is inherently social in the way Smith described, ask yourself how many hours you had to work in order to earn the $50 you used to buy the shirt. If you earn $25 per hour, that shirt cost you two hours of labor time. Next, ask yourself how long it would have taken for you to make the shirt yourself from scratch. It is very likely that it would take you considerably more than two hours to make the shirt. You would have to gather the cotton, spin it into thread, dye it, weave it into fabric, design the pattern, cut the fabric, and sew it together. If we insisted that you truly do this in isolated splendor, you would also have to make the tools involved. And if you were truly doing all of this in isolated splendor, you would have to figure out how to do all of this on your own without reference to how-to manuals. And that's just your shirt. The extra hours it would take you to produce your shirt on your own, rather than work at your job and go to the store and buy it, is a measure of the value of social economic production.

A second example to illustrate the point would be to think about the single most productive person you can think of. Let's use Bill Gates as an example and assume that he has generated the billions of dollars in economic value that he's been rewarded with by the market. Is it conceivable that Bill Gates could reproduce his present lifestyle if he were left on an island by himself—even if we supplied him with all possible raw materials necessary? The gap between the lifestyle Bill Gates could produce on his own and the lifestyle he can command on the basis of his market earnings is a measure of the value of social economic production.[16] Economists like to say that there is no free lunch; yet the fundamental oft-forgotten lesson from Smith is that the vast proportion of wealth produced by the market is exactly a free lunch. As Thomas said, we are by nature inherently interdependent. We depend on the butcher and the baker for our own commodious standard of living. This is truer than it was in Thomas's day. Peasant households manufactured most of the goods consumed by the household. Trade existed, to be sure; but a good deal of economic production in his time was autarkic in nature. That is no longer true, and it is the single most important explanation for our much higher standard of living. [17]

So where does this leave the role of incentives in driving both entrepreneurship and the accumulation of human and physical capital? The division of labor makes us vastly more productive than we would be were we producing in isolation, but entrepreneurship, innovation, and accumulation are also important sources of our material prosperity. The social nature of economic production makes any individual more productive than he would be were he to produce in isolation, but it is also the case that some individuals are more productive than others. Although the role of incentives can be overstated,[18] a valuable feature of the market economy is that it offers rewards to those who contribute the most. Yet, as we've already seen, Thomas allows societies to structure private property claims in a way that contributes to the common good. Thus structuring incentives appropriately is consistent with Thomas's framework.

Thomas's two-tiered framework thus can embrace both the economic insight into the role of incentives in spurring productivity and Adam Smith's insight about the social dividend that results from specialization and the division of labor. In doing so, the framework loosens our sense that an individual benefits *only* as a result of her own efforts in the marketplace. Instead, we see that the individual benefits both as a result of individual effort and as a result of the social aspect of economic production. By the same token, it would seem that an individual should be responsible for the direct effects of her actions but also has a responsibility as a member of society for the impact the system as a whole might have on other.

What is needed is a two-tiered language of responsibility, which a Lockean individualism cannot supply. Not surprisingly, Thomas's discussion of prudence or practical reason delivers exactly that.

Prudence in Two Keys: Taking Responsibility for the Deleterious Effects of Market Activity

Thomas's two-tiered understanding of humans as individuals who are also members of society is too complex to fully detail here.[19] But we can begin to get at it by noting that Thomas thinks that individuals are oriented to both a private good and a public good. The subject first appears in the *prima pars*, where Thomas argues that even if we had not fallen there would still be some sort of government, since there needs to be some direction toward the common good. At the same time, individuals pursue their diverse ends (*ST*, I, 96.4). In other words, we live lives as individuals but also as members of a society. That requires two forms of practical reason: one with respect to our pursuit of our private ends and one with respect to our pursuit of the common good.

Prudence is the virtue of practical reason, directing our actions toward an end. Insofar as we have two ends, there should be two species of prudence. The bulk of Thomas's discussion of prudence relates to prudence as "governing" an individual's affairs, that is, the practical reason we exercise as individuals (*ST*, II-II, 47–49). But he immediately goes on to argue that there is a distinct species of prudence relating to the governance of multitudes (*ST*, II-II, 50, introduction). Two of these forms of prudence related to the governance of a community: regnative prudence (*ST*, II–II, 50.1) and political prudence (*ST*, II-II, 50.2).[20]

Regnative prudence is the practical reason exercised by a king, directing the kingdom toward its own good. Although Thomas thinks that monarchy is, in fact, the best form of government, he goes on to argue that regnative prudence applies as well to other forms of government—either aristocracies or polities, by which he means democracies in their rightful form (i.e. not mobocracies; *ST*, II-II, 50.2. ad.2). If we consider the case of the king in a monarchy, Thomas clearly argues that the king exercises both prudence with respect to the pursuit of his own goals and prudence with respect to the common good. The king can act as a private individual but also as king. Insofar as Thomas has also said that regnative prudence can also apply to democratic forms of government, by analogy, individuals in a democratic society also have dual roles, as private individuals and also as citizens.

Thomas himself does not explore what regnative prudence would look like in a citizen in a democracy, but we can sketch out an account of it. Insofar as we are citizens in a democracy, we share a responsibility for how society is governed. On that view, an individual exercises regnative prudence as a citizen not by voting with regard to her own private interests but rather with regard to her views of how the common good should be pursued. In addition, she can exercise her responsibilities as a citizen through political action and conversation aimed at persuading others about how best to pursue the common good. The key is that the individual exercises her citizenship with regard to the common good rather than her own private good.

With the distinction between private prudence and regnative prudence in place, we are in a position to ask: What are our obligations as individuals in response to the injustices and harms that result from the market system in which we all participate? As I've mentioned in passing, Thomas has quite a bit to say about the demands of commutative justice—what we owe to those with whom we make direct exchanges. Some of his particular teachings, for example those on usury, are not easily applied to a market economy. But leaving aside the fact that we might well take issue with the particular application of the idea, Thomas's basic framework on this is quite sound. In our exchanges with others, we should aim to be equitable. There is much to say about these sorts of exchanges, but our primary interest in this volume is in what Thomas has to say about our responsibility for harms to others with whom we do not have direct exchanges. Because the market is an inherently social institution, our responsibility for the market takes social form. If the concern is that the market system generates unintended consequences that harm some, the appropriate response is at the social level, not the individual level. It therefore calls for a response through the exercise of our powers as citizens.

Beginning with political action, the basic observation is quite simple. We live in a representative democracy. We thus have a responsibility to act in the political arena in a way so as to promote policies that mitigate the harms done to some by market activities and to insure that the market functions in a way that is just. An essential insight in Daniel Finn's book *The Moral Ecology of Markets* is that everyone agrees that the market is bounded by cultural and governmental restraints—our disputes lie in how to draw those boundaries.[21] People often look at the morality of the market without considering its political context, but on this view, the two really aren't separable. The regulation of the markets falls naturally to the government, and as individuals we are obligated to be responsible citizens and advocate for market regulation that promotes justice and mitigates the adverse effects of market activity. In some sense, this is simply an argument for the system that we already have.

The government routinely acts so as to offset adverse market outcomes. For example, we have unemployment insurance and job-training programs to assist people who are harmed by both the cyclical swings of the market and the process of creative destruction, which is an essential component of the dynamics of capitalism. A great deal of economic analysis is policy analysis—assessing the efficacy of various governmental programs or regulations in offsetting inefficient or unjust outcomes that happen as a result of the workings of the market system.

The Thomistic framework would simply stress that as individuals we are obligated as citizens to vote and campaign for regimes that are genuinely dedicated to creating and implementing policy that is in service of the common good. That position is at odds with the view embedded in the subfield of modern economics known as political economy, which assumes that individuals enter into the political arena in order to pursue self-interested goals. For Thomas, we can and should distinguish between the arenas where it is appropriate to act as individuals and arenas where it is appropriate to act as citizens. Insofar as the culture is losing sight of the notion of civic responsibility in favor of the sort of view that suggests that much political activity is or even should be a matter of pursuing private goals by public means, the argument I have developed here could be helpful. Thomas's framework reminds us of the social character of economic activity and thereby undercuts the excessive individualism reflected in the idea that we are and should be nothing but self-interested agents both in the market and in the public square.

That said, Thomas's framework does not necessarily cash out in a set of policies entailing greater government *action*. What sorts of policies are genuinely useful in promoting the goal of a just market system is an empirical question. People of good will can and do disagree about the most effective means of making sure potable water is available to all, or whether it is best to combat the externalities of pollution through regulation or through market mechanisms like the sale of pollution vouchers. As Partha Dasgupta argues, many noneconomists mistake economic disagreements as arguments about values, when they are in fact arguments about facts.[22] Even if we secured perfect agreement that the government should regulate the economy with an eye toward insuring the system as a whole was just, it would remain unclear what particular policies should be adopted.

The complexity of the market system can make it difficult to discern what policies would best combat the evils we associate with the market. For example, it might seem that the best way to stop child labor practices in poor countries would be to outlaw child labor. But if it turns out that the children are being put to work because their families are desperately poor, such laws might have the unintended consequence of causing the family to starve, or having the family respond to the loss of income by sending their children out to work as prostitutes. It is possible that the more effective way of combating the practice of child labor would be to implement policies designed to promote general economic development on the grounds that families that are not starving are not likely to choose to send their children into factories or sweatshops. These sorts of questions can only be settled by serious empirical inquiry.[23]

The Thomistic framework should be seen as establishing that we should be concerned about these issues and that we have a responsibility as citizens to exercise that concern in the public square. It is silent about what policies are the most effective means of achieving those ends.[24] To put it another way, Thomas does not tell us whether "conservative" or "liberal" approaches to regulating the economy are best, but he does tell us that our goal as citizens should be to make our best judgments about the sorts of regulations that would ameliorate the harms done to some by the market system and to secure justice. Ignoring those harms out of a simple confidence in free markets is not an option.

The second arena in which we should act as responsible citizens is in taking seriously our role in shaping the cultural context in which our economic actions take place. As discussed, cultural norms shape our sense of what we "need" and thus correlatively our sense of what constitutes abundance that is properly due to others. Our modern tendency to allow income to be the primary determinant of social standing allows market logic to determine the distribution of the rewards of the market and thus bypass any reasoned discussion of whether the distribution of goods in the market reflects our cultural values. More deeply, cultural norms shape our view of private property in the more Lockean direction that creates the problem we are attempting to address. To the degree that we collectively interpret an individual's standard of living as a direct result of his own hard work, it is difficult to articulate why an individual should bear responsibility for harms done to distant others through the general workings of the market. A cultural shift toward the Thomistic understanding of property rights I have described here would make it much easier to see that we all benefit from the social nature of the economy system and that we therefore bear responsibility for the harms done to others by that same economic system.

Thomas does not directly talk about a citizen's responsibility to participate in the conversations that shape a culture. However, he clearly is aware of the fact that cultural norms shape our moral possibilities. Although human law plainly reflects an act of the will regulated by reason, Thomas argues that custom can obtain the force of law insofar as the repeated actions of individuals can be understood as reflecting an inward movement of the will (ST, I-II, 97, 3). Although Thomas grants much weight to custom (ST, I-II, 97, 2), he also recognizes that custom can sometimes corrupt moral judgment. Thus he mentions the Germans, who, according to Julius Caesar, failed to recognize that theft is a violation of natural law (ST, I-II, 94, 4). It would seem that we have a collective responsibility to shape our cultural norms and customs in a way that is consistent with good reason.

We can see that Thomas recognizes that individuals can have an impact on social norms if we consider his teachings on whether it is fitting to put heretics to death. Thomas argues that insofar as heretics can corrupt the faith of others, society can properly put a stubborn heretic to death. Were it not for the social impact of the heretic, the Church's command to be merciful would take precedence (ST, II-II, 11, 3). Without in anyway condoning Thomas's conclusion about the permissibility of killing heretics, we can at least observe that Thomas is aware that individuals have a hand in shaping cultural norms. It would thus seem that just as we have responsibilities to shape the political economy in a way that expresses concern for those harmed by the workings of the market, so too do we have responsibilities to shape the culture. Our political responsibility is exercised through our votes but also through our conversations. Our cultural responsibility is exercised through our actions and also through our conversations. In neither case can an individual have a decisive impact on the institutional and cultural forces that shape our economic lives. But, in both cases, we are obligated as citizens to do our part. My hope is that the argument in this chapter can serve as just that sort of exercise.

Conclusion

Our economic and political discourse tends to prioritize the individual in a way that makes it difficult to articulate why individuals should take responsibility for the effects that the economic system, taken as a whole, can have on others. If an individual acting as an individual cannot redress such harms, why should he change his behavior? The perspective of critical realism—articulated in the chapters by Margaret Archer, Pierpaolo Donati, and Douglas Porpora in this volume—can help us to see that we need to take into account not only our actions as individuals but also our actions as members of society, which is an emergent system with properties of its own. In this chapter, I've argued that St. Thomas Aquinas likewise sees individuals as agents in their own right but also as members of the society for which they are responsible and from which they benefit.

But Aquinas is useful not simply as an echo of critical realism. By providing us with a two-tiered account of property rights, Thomas allows us to replace the single-tiered view of property rights we have inherited from John Locke. Thomas has purchase on modern discourse because his view of property respects our modern intuition that it is proper for individuals to work for their own benefit through markets. However, he also makes clear the inadequacy of a view of economic life that focuses only on the individual.

Moreover, a Thomistic framework can potentially draw on insights from Adam Smith that are available in our culture, even if they are not often deployed today, to remind us of the social character of our work. If people can come to see more clearly that they benefit both by virtue of their own effort and by virtue of the social dividends of the division of labor, it is possible that they could come to see that they are responsible as individuals for the direct consequences of their economic activities and as citizens for the systemic consequences of their economic activities. Without such a shift in vision, pleas to individuals to change their behavior in view of problems like global warming or the damaging consequences globalization can have on many are likely to continue to fall on deaf ears.

NOTES

1. Albino Barrera, *Market Complicity and Christian Ethics* (Cambridge, UK: Cambridge University Press, 2011).

2. C. B. MacPherson, *The Political Theory of Possessive Individualism: Hobbes to Locke.* (Oxford: Oxford University Press, 1962).

3. Even in the classic case of the 2000 presidential election, the pivotal state of Florida was not decided by a single vote. Indeed, what we learned there is that the measurement errors in counting votes are sufficiently large that a single vote could never be decisive in an election with thousands or millions of participants.

4. MacPherson, *Political Theory*, 263–264.

5. John Locke, *Second Treatise of Government*, edited by C. B Macpherson (Indianapolis, IN: Hackett, 1980 [1690]), ch. 5. Citations to particular paragraphs are made in the text. My discussion here follows MacPherson, whose own interpretation is not uncontroversial. B. Andrew Lustig, "Natural Law, Property, and Justice: The General Justification of Property in John Locke," *Journal of Religious Ethics*, 19 (1991):119–148, canvasses the controversy on the subject and argues that, like Thomas, Locke grounds the right to private property in a prior conception of property as in common. For my purposes, what matters is not so much which reading does best justice to Locke's actual thought as it is that this particular reading has purchase in the culture and is therefore the one we need to deal with.

6. Locke does discuss the benefits to society of labor, arguing that improved land is far more productive than is unimproved land (40), but he nowhere discusses the social nature of labor itself—namely the fact that we are vastly more productive working together than we are working separately.

7. See Christopher A. Franks, *He Became Poor: The Poverty of Christ and Aquinas's Economic Teachings* (Grand Rapids, MI: William B. Eerdmans, 2009), 53–66 for a parallel account of the crucial differences between Aquinas and Locke.

8. Thomas's teachings on wealth-getting, especially in his discussion of whether wealth can serve as the ultimate goal of human striving (*ST*, I-II, 2.1), follows the distinction made by Aristotle between natural wealth (the goods and services we need to sustain life) and artificial wealth (money, or the means of exchange). In Book I of Aristotle, *Politics*, translated by Ernest Barker (Oxford: Oxford University Press, 1995), 21–30 (1256a–1258a), Aristotle distinguishes between acquisition of the goods needed to maintain the household and the use of those goods and services within the household (see especially 1256aI-39, pp. 21–22). I assume that Aquinas follows that distinction here in distinguishing between the procurement of goods and the use of goods. The phrase "power to procure and dispense" would refer to the entire range of activity in the market: producing goods, selling them, and using the resulting income to acquire the goods for use in the household.

9. Elsewhere Thomas writes that the distinction of possessions was not brought in by nature but devised by human reason for the benefit of human life (*ST*, I-II, 94, 5, ad. 3).

10. The tradition of Catholic social thought has at least one strand, most nota-
bly found in *Rerum Novarum* (7) and repeated in *Laborem Exercens* (12) and
Centesimus Annus (31), which does argue that the property right originates in our
labor. The right to property so-grounded is still subordinated to the common
destination of all goods. As we read in *Populorum Progressio*, "Private property,
in fact, regardless of the concrete forms of the regulations and juridical norms
relative to it, is in its essence only an instrument for respecting the principle
of the universal destination of goods; in the final analysis, therefore, it is not
an end but a means" (59). Thomas's doctrine is distinct from modern Catholic
social thought in this regard. As Manfred Spieker, "The Universal Destination
of Goods: The Ethics of Property in the Theory of a Christian Society," *Journal
of Markets and Morality*, 8.2 (2005), writes, "work as the principle of legitimacy
of individual property is not found in Thomas" (335).

11. Stephen A. Marglin, *The Dismal Science: How Thinking Like an Economist
Undermines Community* (Cambridge, MA: Harvard University Press, 2010).

12. See Mary L. Hirschfeld, "Standard of Living and Economic Virtue: Forging a
Link between St. Thomas Aquinas and the Twenty-First Century," *Journal of the
Society of Christian Ethics*, 26.1 (2006): 61–77.

13. Adam Smith, *The Wealth of Nations*, edited by Adam B. Krueger
(New York: Bantam Dell, 2003 [1776]), Book I, ch. 1, para. 1 (9).

14. Smith, *Wealth of Nations*, 11.

15. See Joel Mokyr, *The Enlightened Economy: An Economic History of Britain
1700-1850* (New Haven, CT: Yale University Press, 2009), for an excellent survey of the recent scholarship on the causes of the historic shift in growth rates
surrounding the first industrial revolution.

16. John Rawls, *A Theory of Justice*, (Cambridge, MA: Belknap Press of Harvard
University, 1971), 4, argues that this dividend we gain from the social nature
of economic life should shape how we think about distributive justice. Robert
Nozick, *Anarchy, State and Utopia*, (New York: Basic Books, 1974), 183ff., takes
issue with Rawls' conclusion that social cooperation should necessarily shape
our thinking about distributive justice. The argument between Rawls and
Nozick is of interest in its own right but has no direct bearing on the argument
being made here. How we divide up the social dividend we enjoy as a result of
the social nature of economic production is distinct from the question of what
responsibilities individuals have for the system as a whole, insofar as their own
benefits from economic life depend not only on their own efforts but also on the
social dividend.

17. The point I make here should not be confused with the widely circulated quote
by Elizabeth Warren on the social aspect of economic production. In a talk that
has circulated widely online, she says, "There is nobody in this country who got
rich on his own. Nobody. You built a factory out there—good for you! But I want
to be clear. You moved your goods to market on the roads the rest of us paid for.

You hired workers the rest of us paid to educate. You were safe in your factory because of police forces and fire forces that the rest of us paid for. You didn't have to worry that marauding bands would come and seize everything at your factory, and hire someone to protect against this, because of the work the rest of us did. Now look, you built a factory and it turned into something terrific, or a great idea—God bless. Keep a big hunk of it. But part of the underlying social contract is you take a hunk of that and pay forward for the next kid who comes along." She is rightly pointing out that the government provides institutions that enhance productivity. The point I am making here goes deeper than that—even if there were no government at all, there is still an intrinsically social aspect to economic production. That would be true whether the government intervened or not. That said, Warren is right that government spending plays a role in enhancing economic productivity.

18. Mokyr, *Enlightenment Economy*, observes that many of the innovators who made large contributions to economic growth themselves never prospered as a result. For some, at least, the social approbation for scientific and technological innovation and a genuine desire to better the lot of humanity was enough incentive.

19. For a more comprehensive treatment of the subject, see Jean Porter, "The Common Good in Thomas Aquinas," in *In Search of the Common Good*, edited by Patrick D. Miller and Dennis P. McCann (New York: T&T Clark, 2005), 94–120.

20. The other two forms are domestic economy, referring to the regulation of a household (*ST*, II-II, 50.3) and military prudence (*ST*, II-II, 50.4).

21. Daniel Finn, *The Moral Ecology of Markets: Assessing Claims about Markets and Justice* (Cambridge, UK: Cambridge University Press, 2006).

22. Partha Dasgupta, "What Do Economists Analyze and Why: Values or Facts?" *Economics and Philosophy*, 21 (2005):221–278.

23. In the past decade or so, the field of development economics has shifted away from macro-scale models in order to analyze impediments to economic development in favor of more micro-level empirical research. The result is a much more nuanced account of the lives of the poor and the sorts of policies that might help improve their daily lives. See Abhijit V. Banerjee and Esther Duflo, *Poor Economics: A Radical Rethinking of the Way to Fight Global Poverty* (New York: Public Affairs, 2011), for a highly readable account of the latest research in this area.

24. Similarly, Paul J. Weithman, "Natural Law, Property, and Redistribution," *Journal of Religious Ethics*, 21.1 (1993): 165–180, offers a strong argument that Thomas should not be read as advocating that the distribution of income should be left to the government. The alternative model is that the individual take responsibility for sharing surplus wealth with others, and there are cogent reasons for wanting to leave that in the hands of the individual.

REFERENCES

Aquinas, Thomas. *Summa Theologica*. Translated by the Fathers of the English Dominican Province. 3 vols. New York: Benzinger Brothers, 1947–1948.

Aristotle. *Politics*. Translated by Ernest Barker. Oxford: Oxford University Press, 1995.

Banerjee, Abhijit, and Esther Duflo. *Poor Economics: A Radical Rethinking of the Way to Fight Global Poverty*. New York: Public Affairs, 2011.

Barrera, Albino. *Market Complicity and Christian Ethics*. Cambridge, UK: Cambridge University Press, 2011.

Dasgupta, Partga. "What Do Economists Analyze and Why: Values or Facts?" *Economics and Philosophy*, 2 (2005):221–278.

Finn, Daniel. *The Moral Ecology of Markets: Assessing Claims about Markets and Justice*. Cambridge, UK: Cambridge University Press, 2006.

Franks, Christopher A. *He Became Poor: The Poverty of Christ and Aquinas's Economic Teachings*. Grand Rapids, MI: William B. Eerdmans, 2009.

Hirschfeld, Mary L. "Standard of Living and Economic Virtue: Forging a Link Between St. Thomas Aquinas and the Twenty-First Century," *Journal of the Society of Christian Ethics*, 26 (2006):61–77.

John Paul II. *Centesimus annus*. Vatican: Libreria Editrice Vaticana, 1991. Accessed May 7, 2013: http://www.vatican.va/holy_father/john_paul_ii/encyclicals/documents/hf_jp-ii_enc_01051991_centesimus-annus_en.html.

———. *Laborem exercens*. Vatican: Libreria Editrice Vaticana, 1981. Accessed May 7, 2013: http://www.vatican.va/holy_father/john_paul_ii/encyclicals/documents/hf_jp-ii_enc_14091981_laborem-exercens_en.html.

Leo XIII. *Rerum Novarum*. Boston: Daughters of St. Paul, 1891.

Locke, John. *Second Treatise of Government*. Edited by C. B. MacPherson. Indianapolis, IN: Hackett, 1980. (Originally published in 1690)

Lustig, B. Andrew. "Natural Law, Property, and Justice: The General Justification of Property in John Locke." *Journal of Religious Ethics*, 19 (1991):119–148.

MacPherson, C. B. *The Political Theory of Possessive Individualism: Hobbes to Locke*. Oxford: Oxford University Press, 1962.

Marglin, Stephen A. *The Dismal Science: How Thinking Like an Economist Undermines Community*. Cambridge, MA: Harvard University Press, 2010.

Mokyr, Joel. *The Enlightened Economy: An Economic History of Britain 1700–1850*. New Haven, CT: Yale University Press, 2009.

Nozick, Robert. *Anarchy, State and Utopia*. New York: Basic Books, 1974.

Porter, Jean. "The Common Good in Thomas Aquinas." In Patrick D. Miller and Dennis P. McCann (eds.), *In Search of the Common Good*. New York: T&T Clark, 2005, 92–121.

Rawls, John. *A Theory of Justice*. Cambridge, MA: Belknap Press of Harvard University, 1971.

Smith, Adam. *The Wealth of Nations.* Edited by Adam B. Krueger. New York: Bantam Dell, 2003. (Originally published in 1776).

Spieker, Manfred. "The Universal Destination of Goods: The Ethics of Property in the Theory of a Christian Society." *Journal of Markets and Morality,* 8.2 (2005): 335.

Weithman, Paul J. "Natural Law, Property, and Redistribution." *Journal of Religious Ethics,* 21.1 (1993), 165–180.

PART THREE

Analytical Resources

7

Facing Forward

FEMINIST ANALYSIS OF CARE AND AGENCY ON A
GLOBAL SCALE

*Cristina L. H. Traina**

HOW SHOULD WE think about our responsibilities for the effects that our economic activities have on others? Sometimes the relationships are clear and the solution is easy. The owner of the best dairy in my area uses his profits to support political causes I consider grossly unjust. I don't buy his ice cream, and therefore I don't support his efforts. Case closed. But most of the time the relationships are foggier, and this fogginess presents the problem put in focus by this volume: harms caused by markets to distant others.

Suppose I am buying a refrigerator, a necessary appliance. If I had the time and energy, I might be able to learn where the raw materials were mined or produced, where the parts were made and assembled, what the workers in each place earned, and whether any harmful substances were incorporated into the refrigerator or released into the environment during production. Yet even if I did make the effort to learn all these things—unlikely, if I am buying the fridge hurriedly because my old one has failed and my food is spoiling—this knowledge would leave an unsettling remainder. How do I describe the ethics of my indirect participation

* Thanks to all of the conference attendees and especially to Dan Finn for helpful advice, pointed queries, and generous ruminations. Their important observations have improved this essay greatly, although not as much as if I had managed to incorporate them all. For that deficit, I am responsible.

in international materials extraction markets, temporary labor forces, cross-country transportation systems, and habits of American life and commerce that dictate that grocery stores be large and widely spaced, necessitating infrequent car shopping and large home refrigerators?

This level of questioning moves us from simple, face-to-face relationships to questions of emergence, in which small acts, events, and habits combine on the grand scale to produce patterns of relations and distribution that seem to have a life of their own and actually drive our behavior. Emergence—as employed in other essays in this volume and described with particular clarity by Douglas Porpora—is a morally neutral, inevitable phenomenon that can lead to either flourishing or devastation. For instance, the Roman Catholic notion of the common good—in which the whole of the benefits shared by a collaborative society is greater, and of a different order, than the sum of its parts and that creates a sturdy pattern of productive relationships—can be understood as an example of emergence. But so can what is often called social sin, the cumulative effects of small actions that create unjust, self-perpetuating systems with broader, more harmful effects than a simple summation of the contributing behaviors would predict. These are all the more harmful because, once the systems are in place, actions *within* them may be ethically irreproachable individually and yet devastating cumulatively.[1]

Emergence is to moral theology what the theory of relativity is to Newtonian mechanics: It creates challenges for accounts of moral accountability because it operates on a scale at which the effects of individuals' actions and intentions can no longer be calculated arithmetically. All the essays in this volume suggest resources for addressing these challenges. Here I introduce methodological perspectives from contemporary philosophy that encourage us to phrase the problem of individual accountability slightly differently than Roman Catholic moral theology did in the past and then to explore two more focused discussions in feminist ethics that are especially productive: one that helps us reconceive our accountability to distant others and one that helps us understand ourselves as moral agents in emergent situations.

Like most authors in the volume, I embrace a perspective that is critical—that is, rational, scientific, questioning—and realist—that is, affirming the existence of things and the possibility of speaking truthfully about them. To this I add a feminist natural law conviction about the possibility and duty of pursuing flourishing justly and about the bounded infinitude of combinations of relationships and practices that can support just flourishing within the broad, flexible limits set by human biology, human psychology, and the systems of the planet on which we live.[2] But in this essay I draw self-consciously from feminist philosophers outside the Christian tradition because of their capacity to expand and complement natural law thought.[3]

Finally, in most of what follows I paint with unfairly broad brush strokes. Catholic moral theology is more nuanced, and feminist philosophical ethics is more varied, than I account for here. My aim is only to show that although feminist philosophical ethics does not always ask the accountability question in the form of "how can an agent calculate and morally evaluate her own distant effects?", the questions this perspective explores help us understand how to act responsibly in a complex, emergent global setting.

Methodological Concerns

Roman Catholic ethics of the past two centuries developed nearly indomitable strengths in two different levels of analysis. The first was casuistry: various techniques for assigning personal fault, especially useful in complex circumstances. It worked best in situations where obligations could be reduced to clear responsibilities to self or others in personal relationships (like obedience) and where intention was the central moral concern. The second was the development of prophetic criteria for measuring justice on the societal scale, with special vigor in the social justice tradition that began with *Rerum Novarum* (1891).[4]

Recent decades of theological debate over social sin have revealed, however, that Catholic moral theology has been less effective in connecting these levels. Two issues are critical: how to understand an individual's blameworthiness or praiseworthiness for the broad social effects to which her actions have contributed, and how to assess her personal liability (rather than her calling, a spiritually compelling but ethically less precise measure) for righting wrongs generated in such social processes contrary to her intentions. Emergence magnifies the complexity of the problem, warning us away from precise accountings of quantities of praise and blame and steering us toward scales, regions, and styles of responsibility. For instance, emergence implies that our efforts toward justice will almost always need to be collaborative.

Feminist philosophy's initial contributions are methodological. Feminist philosophers do not, by and large, either prejudge chains of causation or dissect percentages of blame for destructive effects (or percentages of praise for constructive ones). Rather, they focus on developing a habit of critical analysis, and multiple critical perspectives that this habit can employ, to ensure that they will recognize and describe as many strands of causation and accountability as possible. They tend to pursue several perspectives simultaneously, much as we must walk all the way around a Japanese rock garden if we wish to appreciate each of its elements.[5] They warn us away from the interests and methods that often hide important parts of the situation from us, steering us toward others that reveal what might have been hidden in full view.

Most obviously, feminist philosophers emphasize gender analyses. Historically, these arose in national settings, but they are also indispensable in matters of justice in intercultural and international economic relations. For example, how a policy affects an ethnic group or national economy on average tells us nothing about the gendered ways in which it influences people at individual, household, or communal levels. Furthermore, most feminist philosophers extend their methods beyond gender to examine agency and suffering in other oppressive situations. Feminist philosophy's particular sort of "paying attention," honed on gender issues, applies to victimization and marginalization of all kinds.[6]

Let us consider five of these methodological contributions. First, as noted above, feminist philosophers share with other liberationist thinkers a tendency to embrace standpoint theory, the conviction that our view of any given situation depends on where we stand to look at it. Many feminist philosophers adopt multiple perspectives—sometimes simultaneous, sometimes tailored to particular kinds of situations—producing rich, highly textured, partial, and plural views of reality.[7] One consequence is that thoughtful feminist philosophical analyses almost never yield neat, clear attributions of praise and blame but tend to illuminate several responsible actors serially. A second consequence is that feminists hold that the key determinants of standpoint are our interests and our experience.

Thus epistemological questions—how we know what we know about the situation—are moral questions from the start: What interests and experiences will I privilege, or use as my "lens," for viewing reality? For instance, CEO Jamie Dimon, banking regulators, stockholders, holders of variable-interest investments, and holders of no-interest accounts will have different, if overlapping, views on the 2012 JP Morgan Chase investment debacle in which more than $4 billion were lost. And yet these views do not hold equivalent moral weight. For instance, if our goal is to protect the vulnerable, we may privilege the perspectives of basic account holders most strongly, and then representatives of the public interest (the bank regulators), over the presumably less vulnerable Dimon, the interest-bearing account holders, and the stockholders. Providing a less comfortable example, Marian Eide uses standpoint theory to suggest that a gentile pacifism de facto guarded by smart bombs may really be gratuitous and untrustworthy, "a new guise for the protection of privilege accorded the powerful" whose talk is cheap because they are in little danger of suffering attacks from outside.[8]

Second, feminist ethics tend to be future-oriented.[9] This may seem obvious: Isn't the purpose of ethics to help us decide how to behave? Yet in matters of individual accountability, Roman Catholic moral reflection still bears the mark of the manuals, which—designed for confessors—tended to be retrospective and blame-oriented even when offering advice for future action. For instance, even today applications of just war theory sometimes imply the future perfect tense: If we declare war, *will we have been guilty of sin* for having done so?[10] The question is always, did I err (or will I have erred), and, if so, how gravely? In contrast, feminist philosophers usually spend less energy asking who is culpable for producing a state of affairs and more asking how various agents can now take responsibility for transforming it.

This does not mean that feminist philosophers are uninterested in analyzing the past. The past helps us interpret the present, teaches important lessons about the social consequences of actions, and identifies persons and systems that cause injustice. But it does all these things in the interest of future transformation of the present. This is as much a matter of ethical practice as it is of ethical theory: How much time and energy do ethicists devote to analysis of accountability for past actions and how much to identifying and determining responsibility for undertaking future efforts? These projects are mutually dependent, but whereas for manual moral theology the second was an afterthought to the first, by and large in feminist philosophy the first serves the second. Catholic social ethics shares this emphasis with feminism, but it typically has been less interested in describing *individual* accountability for social transformation.

Third, as feminist political philosopher Elizabeth Anderson put it, feminist ethics normally "start[s] thinking from the injustices we encounter in our non-ideal, unjust world, and think[s] about those problems from the perspective of those who are oppressed by that injustice."[11] Feminism is not idealist and shows no interest in the question, "How would perfect actors protected from historical experience construct a just society?"

This may be unsurprising, but it contrasts starkly with the early phases of modern Catholic social teaching. Despite its intention to respond to real, unjust treatment of factory workers, early Roman Catholic social teaching was at root idealist, founding its solutions on the "natural" relations between labor and owners that would exist in a perfect world and regretfully making concessions to human sinfulness.[12] This heritage is visible in recent ecclesiastical documents.[13] Perhaps counterintuitively, the pragmatism and lower expectations typical of feminist ethics may hold more promise for effectively addressing particular injustices in an increasingly interdependent and complex world without sacrifice of high ideals.

A fourth conviction, put bluntly, is that some people are stuck at the margins because others have staked out the center. That is, feminism describes honestly how the same policies, markets, laws, and systems that harm some benefit other classes of people, typically the classes of people who make policies and write ethics texts. Thus, the first questions we must ask about distant economic relations are (a) how do the privileged tend to protect systems that promote their own privilege, and, as Fischer inquires, (b) "through what processes can people of privilege mitigate these tendencies that are deeply inscribed in themselves?"[14]

One final methodological note is important: Early in its career, one of feminist philosophy's strongest suits was analyzing the overlapping oppressions that bear down on individuals. This is an unpromising approach if we want to know about the ethics of *producing* social, political, and economic forces. In the 1980s and 1990s, feminist philosophers continued to see oppressed victims as victims of injustice but no longer as nonagents. They strengthened their analyses of agents acting under significant constraints. Similarly, they refused to treat systems as actors.[15] Personifying intractable, powerful systems may be psychologically helpful and certainly accounts for the predictability and magnitude of their effects, but it is deceptive: It misleadingly bestows on them an intentional agency beyond that of the individuals that compose them. For example, after the spring 2012 European bailout of Spain's economy, a radio commentator reported that the markets had "responded" positively because they "thought" Spain was stable. Markets have force, but they do not "think." Recent feminist work incorporates moral and epistemic luck and other concepts that can be adapted for lessons on moral action within large systems, acknowledging systems' momentum but holding individuals responsible for benefitting unjustly from them, for acting with integrity within them, and for changing them.[16] This approach also implies that complete noncooperation with evil is an inappropriate moral goal, for one must change an unjust system from within and therefore remains complicit to a degree in it.[17]

We have seen that a significant group of contemporary feminist philosophers holds five common methodological criteria, factors by which we should judge the adequacy of philosophical methods: standpoint, future orientation, nonidealism, analysis of privilege, and ascription of moral agency. But methodology is not method. What specific interventions might help us with distant, complex agency? I elaborate below on two feminist approaches I judge to be promising: the ethics of care and discussions of constrained or burdened agency. I show how they converge in the "global care chains" described by philosopher Arlie Russell Hochschild and make some suggestions about extrapolating from this analysis to global economic relations.

The Ethics of Care

Acknowledging that individuals are morally complicit for their involvement in large and complex systems creates a contradiction: Suddenly persons seem to be morally accountable for absolutely everything in every network in which they participate, and yet plainly they lack the capacity to act on or even to analyze all these connections. Paralysis and depression, or else a radically laissez-faire attitude, seem the obvious responses. By taking account of the different levels of emergent systems, the ethics of care provides a way of thinking about these connections more manageably without lessening moral responsibility.

The ethics of care is typically dated back to Carol Gilligan. Her 1982 classic, *In a Different Voice,* argued that differences in the ways male and female college students described moral decisions owed not to the women's lower development on the Kohlberg moral reasoning scale but to their embrace of an alternative method of moral deliberation, caring, that emphasized preservation of relationships over adherence to impartial standards of justice. Subsequent work by Nel Noddings, Sara Ruddick, Eva Feder Kittay, and others drew moral wisdom from women's practices of mothering.[18]

Instead of impartiality and rights, these authors emphasized particularity, relationship, and the intense nurture that all small children need to become the rational, autonomous adults that liberal theories of justice take for granted. All these feminists argued that the ethics of care should be enlarged to illumine social and political issues. But in part because of enthusiasm within romantic or essentialist feminism and in part because of continuing association of social mothering roles with women (encouraged by some interpretations of Nancy Chodorow's work on gender and parenting), many continued to see the ethics of care as a private and feminine, rather than a political and feminist, undertaking.[19] Although this was a misreading of the thinkers in question, it was influential enough to marginalize their work to a degree. But since Susan Moller Okin laid the ground with *Justice, Gender, and the Family*, Joan Tronto, Virginia Held, Fiona Robinson, and others have argued that justice ethics are incomplete without substantial attention to the ethics of care.[20] Thus, over the past thirty years, care ethics has evolved from a psychologist's description of college-aged women's moral choices to a full-blown political ethic.

In its most restricted form, the ethics of care begins with human vulnerability. As Virginia Held argues, "care is needed by everyone when they are children, ill, or very old, and it is needed by some most of their lives."[21] Even under the best circumstances, human beings are *by nature* fundamentally dependent on others for long and crucial periods; this is not a flaw or an exception but a central fact—and perhaps the central fact—of human existence.[22] Typically, care ethics adds that even healthy, rational, normal adults are also interdependent, but the narrower premise is adequate to orient care politics.

The need for care is universal and has some common features, reflecting the requirements of the survival and formation of persons as persons. Without going into great detail about psychological research, we can say, for instance, that children need food, affection, social interaction, education, and health care not just to live but actually to become the sorts of adults who can function constructively.[23] But this care is not abstract or generic. Care requires consistent agents who faithfully attend to their vulnerable charges continuously, not just providing for physical needs episodically but also being sensitive to what their charges in particular require to thrive within their own contexts and histories.[24] Fischer notes,

A care perspective places relationships, rather than the autonomous individual of liberal theory, at the center of analysis. To capture the dynamics of relationships, a care perspective is particularly attentive to context, noting concrete interactions among persons within the environments in which they function. Narratives, with their ability to show the interplay between intellect, emotion, and action, are particularly appropriate for describing these contextual features.[25]

Care happens between persons, not between entities.

Thus care is both a set of practices—skilled activities with means and common goals but tailored to particular persons—and a value, as justice is also both a set of practices and a value.[26] Society depends upon, and assumes the presence of, myriad adults who have the time, energy, and security to do caring work for children, the ill, and the elderly. We value— or should value—care. And speaking in the terms of moral theology, it makes sense to call care a virtue as well, a habit of providing appropriately and responsively for persons who are dependent.

Care ethics have enormous, suggestive implications for all kinds of issues: our conceptions of gender, reason, emotion, and autonomy, just to name a few. Given the focus of this volume on harms caused to distant others, I examine the political and economic dimensions of the issues. As liberal feminists have done for decades, care ethics proponents point out that the work of caring is both essential and worthy; it requires time, energy, and expertise. As a matter of dignity, all deserve care when they need it, and society has an interest in ensuring that people who take on caring work have the resources to do it well. But, care ethicists argue, in America today, these people are among the most vulnerable socially and economically: Stay-at-home parents, single parents, child-care and eldercare workers, nurses' aides, social workers, and other key members of our system of care either function without pay or receive low wages with questionable job security. Many lack access to education, libraries, parks, health care, decent housing, respite care, recreation programs, and other resources that might help them care better.

These circumstances obviously inspire a broader concern for caretakers: How do we raise their wages, improve their security, and add to their tools? But they also provide important criteria by which to judge our market interaction within societies far distant from our own: In what way does our interaction with that society affect its caring work? Does it make that work easier, safer, and more secure? Or does it make that work harder, more dangerous, and riskier? Neither raising the gross national product nor improving the portfolio of rights upheld by government necessarily improves adults' capacity to care for vulnerable persons. Such developments can even harm it. For instance, twentieth-century British colonial interventions among the Masai "modernized" their economic and political structure, dealing with women through their husbands rather than directly. Although women's position was certainly not perfect before the change—for instance, female genital cutting was universal—British innovations destroyed a delicate system of shared economic and political authority, leaving women less supported and less able to care than before.[27]

What then is the relationship between care and justice? Does care replace justice, or complement it? If the latter, which takes precedence? Here we must step carefully, because "justice" does not have the same meaning in every setting. In the individualistic language of liberalism that feminist philosophy employs to argue for women's good, justice has entailed "equality, rights, and liberty" in a legal sense.[28] Especially since John Rawls, the political language of justice—in English-speaking authors at least—implies impersonal public structures or conditions on a national scale that facilitate fair distribution of resources of all sorts to persons.[29] Care, on this view, is universal and politically and socially essential but necessarily personal and even private in conduct. It involves affection, connection, and trust between persons. Therefore it can easily be infected, on a large scale, by injustice, masquerading either as urgency or as a legitimate response to diverse, apparently particular needs. For this reason, care ethicists affirm the necessity of justice on the social scale to keep care in line and the necessity of care to fend off the individualism and "reduction of worth to price"[30] toward which distributive theories of justice, like Rawls's, tempt us. In view of our contemporary tendency to take refuge in personal rights claims that excuse us from attention to others' needs for caring, the most politically prudent way to relate care and justice may be Virginia Held's. Discarding her own earlier attempts to set justice up as a minimum and add care to it, she argues,

> I now think that caring relations should form the wider moral framework into which justice should be fitted. Care seems the most basic moral value. As a practice, we know that without care we cannot have anything else, since life requires it.... Though justice is surely among the most important moral values, much life has gone on without it, and much of that life has had moderately good aspects.[31]

In certain domains, society may decide to give the individualistic rights considerations of liberal justice priority over the interdependency claims of care.[32] But they are ultimately compatible.

Yet here the language of Catholic social ethics and its more capacious definition of justice may be helpful to the ethics of care, reversing Held's formula. To the degree that the virtue of justice is the habit of acting rightly and fittingly toward all as their dignity demands, and care is the habit of acting rightly and fittingly toward persons who are dependent on us, care could (in addition to its other meanings) be considered a virtue and a species of justice. This also suggests that we have not fully pursued the virtue of justice if we have not cultivated the particular attentive responsiveness entailed by virtue of care and that love, the perfection of justice, is also necessary to the perfection of care. Second, because, as Held argues, all people need care some of the time, and some of them need it all of the time, care is a requisite of human dignity, as are the other elements of justice. Therefore the rest of us must provide care—personally, responsively, and affectionately—to the extent that we can, and we must also provide justly for its provision to others. Because justice in general is a social standard (or value) as well as a virtue entailing a practice, the care dimension of justice is also both a social standard (or value) and a virtue entailing a practice.

Turning now to the theme of this volume, this relation of care to justice explains why globalizing a care ethic does not imply that one must care compassionately, affectively, and directly for persons half a world away. Although we should avoid defining it naturalistically, the order of charity springs to mind: We care most directly and intensely for our nearest and dearest. The ethic certainly does not prohibit direct caring at a distance, but it is practical on a small scale for few of us and on a large scale for none. It simply is not possible to get to know very many distant others well enough to care competently for them or to be physically present for them without neglecting those whom we must care for at home. But we do not need to imagine ourselves into such intimate relations in order to embrace the ethic of care. As Claudia Card says,

> To be concerned to avoid participating in war, ecological destruction, and other cultural evils, we need not care in the encounter sense about potential victims. We need not be there for them in a way that evokes their conscious recognition of our conscious states or our conscious recognition of theirs.[33]

We simply need to take "the responsibility not to perpetuate unjust prac-tices that block opportunities for encounters that foster caring"[34] among persons in that distant place. Our job is not do the caring work ourselves but to enable just caring work, work that allows the well-being of both caretaker and cared-for, to occur.[35] Have we voted, donated, purchased, and collaborated in ways that improve the possibilities for just caring in places near and far? These are complicated decisions, never perfectly clean or clear. This leads us to our next question.

Constrained Agency

Perhaps the greatest puzzle in acting at a distance is sorting out agency and responsibility in the midst of complex networks of forces.

Four other chapters in this volume (by Margaret Archer, John Coleman, Pierpaolo Donati, and Douglas Porpora) bring the resources of sociology to bear on this vexing issue. In what follows, I summarize the views of feminist philosophers on the same topic. Trying to make good on just consumer intentions is a good example. The purchase of a pair of sneak-ers can send tendrils into a dozen nations. When demand rises, organic salad greens are factory farmed and free-range chickens stop ranging. And these are only the causal axes of agency. One of feminist philosophy's most important contributions and greatest struggles has been its effort to provide a balanced picture of the moral subject on other axes as well: both socially constructed and given, both constrained and autonomous, both compelled and responsible, both embodied and transcendent.

The most helpful of these conversations for our purposes describes coherent agency in the midst of social forces and in the face of victim-izing oppression. If the subject is socially constructed, can she also be self-governing in any meaningful sense?[36] And if she is a victim, coerced into choosing among unacceptable options, is she really autonomous?[37] Feminist philosophers create "both/and" answers to these questions about acting in imperfect situations; in each case they preserve the actor's agency and responsibility but follow the breadcrumbs back to a social dys-function that produces contradictions, dilemmas, or impossible choices.

One important tool in this strategy is the concept of moral luck, devel-oped to deal with two realizations: First, if we are responsible only for what is entirely under our control, we will end up being accountable for little or nothing; and second, like it or not, the amount of moral blame or credit we receive for an action often depends on factors beyond our control.[38] A classic example is speeding: If I am driving too fast to stop safely and hit a small child who has run into the street unexpectedly, I'm to blame for the injury; but if no child materializes, I'm to blame only for risky driving. Conversely, if I happen to have a patient, calculating disposition I might be applauded profusely for pulling off a sensitive diplomatic negotiation that would have required tremendous self-control for a more volatile personality but really required very little extra effort from me. In each case, luck—the presence or absence of a child, or my basic personality type—contributes profoundly to my moral accountability.

These various kinds of luck can affect both moral knowing and doing in such a way that I am constrained but also acting freely. Thomas Nagel developed the idea of moral luck to explain the varied culpability of similar agents in different circumstances, though he showed little interest in how the circumstances came about. Feminist philosophers who work with luck do not simply calculate the culpability or credit due the actor but also evaluate the circumstances and constraints that constitute an actor's bad luck. How do they arise? Are they unjust? Who is responsible for them?

One kind of morally relevant luck is epistemic. Heidi Grasswick argues that, because practices of knowing are socially constructed, the epistemic agency that grounds moral agency is adulterated through no fault of ours. Epistemic luck shapes practices of knowing, which are always " 'contaminated' with moral and political concerns."[39] Still, responsible epistemic agents must critically evaluate the practices they inherit to discover

> in what ways do they allow us to know, and are we willing to commit to those ways, keeping in mind the costs? What kind of knowledge do they permit us to construct, who attains it, and is it the kind *we* want, keeping in mind the need to clarify who that *we* is?[40]

We will never be fully successful in stripping ideological commitments from our epistemic practices, and we are not responsible for the immoral biases of the practices we inherit, but it is not true that the project of knowing is hopeless or that we are "off the hook" morally. We can hold ourselves accountable as responsible moral agents who reflect critically on our constructions of knowledge. And most feminist philosophers would argue that we should begin by asking whose interests those constructions protect.

Similarly, many feminist moral philosophers use moral luck, both implicitly and explicitly, to develop complex descriptions of accountability that recognize both the culpability of the constrained agent and the fault of those who create the constraints. Victoria Davion employs Claudia Card's work to develop a sobering reflection on collaboration with evil. Davion and Card take a one-two punch. First, they object to the protection that the theory of double effect provides to moral actors by exonerating them from moral responsibility for side effects of actions that cause foreseen but unavoidable harm. Collateral damage in bombing is a classic example. Surely, they retort, moral actors *are* morally responsible for undesired but foreseen harm, even when there is no apparent morally acceptable alternative; they *choose* the harm. Second, however, such harm does not always trump other harms or injustices; we cannot avoid all damage to good things, whether they are schools or civilians. But when such foreseen, possibly unavoidable harms come under the tent of moral analysis as chosen harms, rather than being brushed aside by the double effect strategy, it becomes necessary to ask a larger question: What systematic patterns produce such conflicts, such moments when the "good" thing to do inevitably causes damage?[41] Who beside the agent might be responsible for the foreseen side effect?

Lisa Tessman applies a similar both/and to virtues, arguing that injustice distorts and limits virtue.[42] Through bad moral luck, unjust situations "burden" the virtue of justice-seeking, traditionally thought of as coherent and salutary to the agent's welfare, by endangering the agent's flourishing. They cause unhappiness, objective risk, and what we are used to thinking of as vice. For example, a parent earning minimum wage may create exaggerated stories to tell on a rotating basis monthly to representatives of utilities whose bills she cannot pay. This is a voluntary action in pursuit of a good end—keeping her children warm and clean—and yet the situation of injustice in which it is set, not necessarily any moral inadequacy in her, forecloses the possibility of "pure" honesty. As Tessman remarks,

> This complex sense of having and not having moral responsibility for one's own character allows the oppressed person to preserve moral agency by retaining moral responsibility, and yet it does not blame the oppressed agent in a way that would simultaneously excuse all systemic or oppressive forces from responsibility.[43]

It is not the agent's fault that the world is unjust, but she must still make her way in it, protecting those for whom she has a covenant to care. Agents must often pursue goods "impurely" amid injustice for which they are not responsible.

Neither Tessman nor Card is naïve about the effects of injustice on agents. Although both argue that moral virtue can endure through the sorts of bad moral luck that deform character, both hold that maintaining virtue requires actively resisting the harmful forces that constrain the agent in the present or wounded her moral development in the past.[44] Card argues at length that systematic injustice typically fragments victimized persons and communities, making it difficult for them to respond constructively and to accept accountability.[45] Susan Wendell reminds us that although identifying oppression is important, a person occupying the "victim" position can too easily focus on past abuses and abdicate current moral responsibility. If this occurs, the victim becomes complicit in the evils she suffers, leaving injustice unchallenged and avoiding hard choices.[46] In both cases, the "victim" is truly accountable for the harm she does, *and* we can blame the system—that is, the persons who perpetuate unjust relations and practices—for distorting her moral character. In the Roman Catholic moral tradition, encouraging another to sin is one of the gravest forms of complicity in evil.

However, most people who find themselves acting within systems that cause harm are not victims in Wendell's sense. Does moral luck help them evaluate their own complicity? I believe that it does. In keeping with the principle of questioning privilege, we need to assume that unjust systems distort the moral agency of the privileged as deeply as they do the agency of the victimized. Tessman hints that classical Aristotelian virtues may themselves be the products of unjust distortion, as only the privileged have the leisure and security to imagine the unity and coherence of the virtues or to focus on self-cultivation, both of which are likely to entail a certain unvirtuous blindness to the suffering of others or at least to the difficult moral circumstances in which these others live.[47] In this sense we could say that the privileged too are victims of bad moral luck, for which they are no more or less responsible than are the marginalized. The oppressed in Tessman's argument suffer from "bad luck" that is apparently individual—they cannot both flourish personally and fulfill the classical virtues. The privileged suffer from and bestow bad luck in the sense that the rest of us cannot flourish either personally or communally if we adhere to their vision of virtue and their faulty conception of moral education.[48]

The bad luck of the privileged has graver consequences than that of the oppressed in two additional senses. First, because this bad moral education is shared by others in power, it is unlikely to challenge the privileged in daily life; they may never experience the kind of dissonance between their situation and their moral standards that inspires critical reflection. Second, and worse, the effect of their distorted moral framework is magnified by the power they hold. They can alter the system more easily than its victims can. As Margaret Archer might put it in her chapter in this volume, their "reflexivity" is typically more potent within the social system. If to have the capacity to contribute to the righting of injustice is to have the responsibility to do so, it is even more imperative that the privileged take responsibility for situations and standards for whose creation they are not responsible but whose benefits they enjoy complicitly.[49] An attitude of "regret or something like it" is an appropriate accompaniment to transformative action.[50] As Douglas Porpora and Pierpaolo Donati argue in this book, this responsibility for change arises mainly not from my having created a situation (although this would intensify my responsibility) but from my capacity to improve it.

In the language of Susan Wendell's roles, neither the marginalized nor the privileged is responsible for creating a system of oppression originally, but both habits of mind are ultimately self-deceptive and as a consequence epistemically and morally limiting. Both actively perpetuate oppression. People in both positions must take responsibility for change, adopting the role of the backward-looking critical analyst of oppression or the forward-looking responsible actor. Each of these roles is a journey, rather than the key to omniscience, but both, if pursued honestly, arrive at knowledge that contributes to the realization of justice and care.[51] Both privileged and marginalized are obligated to use the power they have for change, although the privileged carry the greater burden.

How does this long detour help us to understand constrained agency? It reminds us that when impossible choices arise, moral goodness requires that we spend less energy weighing the minuscule distinctions between two bad options to establish praise or blame for the constrained agent and more energy understanding and altering the forces that produced the impossible choice that the agent faces. Although feminist philosophy has focused primarily on constrained victims, people with significant social, economic, and political power are likewise constrained. This fact does not excuse them from taking responsibility for altering the constraints; rather, it warns them against avoiding constructive action out of fear of soiling themselves with complicity.[52]

Wendell, Card, Tessman, and others help us see that, in the real world, complicity in existing injustice will always be unavoidable. Anxiety over this fact is a temptation to evil: If we become distracted by our desire for moral purity, we will abdicate our responsibility to alter destructive systems. And the more power we have to effect change, the graver this moral failure becomes. Further, care ethics remind us that not all forces we feel as constraints on agency are morally problematic. Interdependence and obligations of care direct our energies and priorities. In this way they lead us toward the conflicts that produce insight into systematic evils.

Global Care Chains

A case study may help demonstrate how the discussion above affects this book's focus on the harms caused to distant others by markets. Arlie Russell Hochschild's writings on global care chains, which draw on the ethnographic work of Rhacel Parreñas, illustrate the profound, complex interdependence that follows on globalization.[53] Hochschild writes that in a typical global care chain, an educated Filipina mother looking for better wages to support her own children, and perhaps avoiding a difficult spouse, might emigrate to Los Angeles to work as a nanny for a professional couple. Meanwhile, she hires a nanny for her children in Manila at perhaps one-tenth the wage she herself is earning. Then her own nanny arranges for a grandmother, aunt, or older sibling to care for *her* children, often free of charge. As the cord unravels back, compensation and respect for child-rearing typically unravel, as well as another element central to care ethics and immeasurable in market terms: love. Migrant childcare and eldercare workers often displace their intense, affective, responsive connections with their own distant families onto the ones for whom they care, feeling closer to their "clients" than to their own kin. Hochschild argues that any adequate treatment of the phenomenon must find a way to describe and weigh this displaced love, which is at the center of all genuine care work but that does not enter into economic analyses of migration and remittances.

Hochschild judges "primordialism" (her label for the view that every woman should care for her own children) both sexist and unrealistic. But she also rejects any uncritical embrace of capitalist "marketisation," which increases inequalities not only in income but also in access to care. The problem is not that purchased care cannot be loving care; it can. The problem is that, when combined with gross inequalities of income, purchased care creates a chain of displacement at the end of which lies neglect unseen by the wealthiest purchaser.[54]

Allison Weir highlights another dimension of the phenomenon of purchased care, the fiction of free choice.[55] Weir rejects a laissez-faire vision of freedom as autonomy and independence, a vision that creates a problematic litmus test: A person chooses freely if she is offered at least two options, no matter how unattractive those options are. This definition of freedom assumes that interests conflict and must be negotiated. Instead, Weir proposes that

> from the perspective of immigrant domestic workers, real freedom would mean *not* having to choose between *either* leaving your home and family to do domestic work in another country, where you are effectively a domestic slave, vulnerable to abuse and manipulation by a wealthy family, all so that you can make enough money to support your own family, which you may never see again, *or* staying with your own family in impoverished conditions produced by the global capitalist economy. This is an impossible choice, which no one should be forced to make.[56]

Weir's agents are making choices to take responsibility for their families' care, but they are doing so under tight constraints that reveal a number of problems: They must trade relationships with their families for the relative financial security of a distant position that is low-paying and vulnerable in the best of cases. These pressures appear in individual lives and seem to be personal, but like all "impossible choices," they point back to a systematic problem: lack of adequate social and economic support for caregiving. Stated positively, then, freedom would be not independence but interdependence, in which common interests are forged and common responsibilities are demanded. Caregiving is not a "lifestyle choice" that can be either shouldered or passed on to others, as annual Mother's Day columns in American newspapers imply, but a common responsibility that deserves respect and, when paid, adequate remuneration.[57]

A realistic effort to make caregiving more just would draw from both marketization and primordialism without accepting the premises of either. It would put caretaking at the center of our values on the global scale, accept migration and paid caretaking as facts of life, and figure out how to make the choices both to accept and to seek paid care work freer and less desperate.[58] This may not be as easy as it sounds. The apparent solution to the problem is to encourage economic development in countries that are undergoing "care drain" and generally even the distribution of resources globally. Eva Feder Kittay's probing analysis of care chains, like most of Catholic social teaching and most common-sense compassionate responses to American immigration pressures, recommends exactly this.[59]

But, says Hochschild, common-sense solutions are illusory. It turns out that the economic churning of development can *increase* migration flows. Simply improving economies will not keep people at home.[60] In addition, neoliberal economic expansion is likely to increase wealth gaps within nations, exaggerating the injustices of domestic care chains. This returns us to the central conviction shared by all three authors: We must recognize the social value of caring work, the universal interdependence that it implies, and the further implications of this interdependence for our understandings of freedom and responsibility. Thus we must be realistic. We must put the cared-for and the caretakers at the center of the discussion. Like Hochschild, we should reject primordialism, but we must affirm children's need for continuity and love. We should reject marketization, but we must make caring work secure and, when paid, well-enough remunerated to be chosen without enormous risk or loss to caretakers and their families. Paid work must become more flexible. Borders must become more permeable. Then the choices paid caregivers and their clients make will be genuinely free, not coerced.

How does this brief exploration of care chains stack up against the methodological points and substantive suggestions developed in this essay? Standpoint theory is essential. The authors adopt the standpoint not of economists but of marginalized women who migrate to provide care, using their experiences as lenses for revealing larger structural problems on an international scale. They do not generally adopt the standpoint of the children, ill, and elderly who need care, who especially at the end of the chain are dangerously marginalized; the authors assume, a bit naïvely, that the interests of caregivers stand in for those of these even more vulnerable care-receivers. Yet, their analysis is future-oriented and nonidealistic: How can analysis of present and past difficulties help us to create a future that is both more just and more nurturing? It critiques privilege by showing wealthy Americans the human cost of their widely accepted care arrangements. Finally, although the critique does not move far beyond system-blaming, the authors imply that individual actors must collaborate to change policy through political processes.

Most important, these considerations place care at the center of international discussions on economy and migration, insisting both that care be delivered and that caretakers live decent lives reflecting the importance of their work. It also adds nuance to our understanding of agency and privilege. First, at every level of the care chain, women are forced into nonideal choices about employment and childcare and end up functioning as employers of other women who must make the same difficult choice with fewer resources. That is, most of the participants in the chain are simultaneously oppressors and victims, underlining the need for them to make common cause to alter the systems that pit them against each other. Second, care chain analysis criticizes definitions of freedom developed by the privileged that emphasize independence and autonomy; it points to the inadequacy of the liberal concepts of fairness and rights to support care. That is, care reveals the bad moral luck that has led the privileged to advance inadequate, socially destructive definitions of justice.

Conclusion

Because of their focus on intimate caring relations, feminist analyses of global care chains illumine dimensions of global commerce that economic and human rights analyses miss. In fact—returning to our premises—it is difficult to "see" global care chains at all without the lens of feminist ethics of care, or to interpret them without a vision of constrained agency. But similar analyses can be applied to factory farming, industrial outsourcing, call centers, and myriad other developments of the global economy. One example strikes close to home: Due to employment practices and government regulations, legal, justly paid work is nearly impossible for felons and for persons whose immigration or asylum status is being decided. The ethics of care points out their inability to care for themselves and their families legally, and feminist applications of moral luck and burdened virtue point out that such persons ought not be blamed for resorting to illegal employment to fulfill these obligations.[61]

In this case, as in others, feminist discussions of care and constrained agency do not directly help us to calculate our "portion" of causality for this situation or fine-tune our categorization of varieties of cooperation in its evils. Feminists do not deny the import of these questions, which are crucial for judging intent and for discovering the effects that practical interventions actually have. But feminists shift the focus of moral analysis from the calculation of personal guilt for past events to description of personal and corporate responsibility for future transformation of present injustices. In particular, they demand that we judge our actions toward our distant neighbors by their effects on our neighbors' ability to give and receive care.

NOTES

1. Robert Nozick is among the more well-known recent philosophers to reject this vision of human action. See Robert Nozick, *Anarchy, State, and Utopia* (New York: Basic Books, 1974).

   For a helpful discussions of theological applications of emergent evolution, see Patrick H. Byrne, "Ecology, Economy and Redemption as Dynamic: The Contributions of Jane Jacobs and Bernard Lonergan," *Worldviews: Global Religions, Culture, and Ecology,* 7.1 (2003): 5–26, accessed December 17, 2012: http://www.nd.edu/~ecoltheo/text_byrne.htm. Thanks to William George for this reference.

2. To envision bounded infinitude, think of a circle. It contains infinitely many points, and yet most imaginable points are outside the circle. Similarly, our givenness grounds an infinitude of possible just social arrangements, but there are also infinitely many unjust ones.

3. Among others, scholars who follow this general approach include Lisa Sowle Cahill, Margaret Farley, Christine Gudorf, and Patricia Beattie Jung. For excellent recent feminist natural law discussions of accountability and complicity, see, e.g., Julie Hanlon Rubio, "Moral Cooperation with Evil and Social Ethics," *Journal of the Society of Christian Ethics,* 31:1 (2011): 103–122; M. Cathleen Kaveny, "Appropriation of Evil: Cooperation's Mirror Image," *Theological Studies,* 61 (2000): 280–313; M. Cathleen Kaveny, "Intrinsic Evil and Political Responsibility," *America* (October 27, 2008), accessed December 17, 2012: http://www.america-magazine.org/content/article.cfm?article_id=11166.

4. Leo XIII, *Rerum Novarum* (Vatican: Libreria Editrice Vaticana, n.d. [1891]), accessed December 17, 2012: http://www.vatican.va/holy_father/leo_xiii/encyclicals/documents/hf_l-xiii_enc_15051891_rerum-novarum_en.html.

5. See, e.g., Lorraine Code, "Responsibility and Rhetoric," *Hypatia,* 9.1 (1994): 1–20, esp. 16.

6. See, e.g., Code, "Responsibility and Rhetoric;" Susan Sherwin, "Moral Perception and Global Visions," *Bioethics,* 15.3 (2001): 175–188, esp. 179–180; and Victoria Davion, "Feminist Perspectives on Global Warming, Genocide, and Card's Theory of Evil," *Hypatia.* 24.1 (2001): 160–177, esp. 161.

7. Susan Wendell demonstrates this richness in "Oppression and Victimization: Choice and Responsibility," *Hypatia*, 5.3 (1990): 15–46.

8. Marian Eide, "'The Stigma of Nation': Feminist Just War, Privilege, and Responsibility," *Hypatia*, 23.2 (2008): 56.

9. See Heidi E. Grasswick, "The Impurities of Epistemic Responsibility: Developing a Practice-Oriented Epistemology," in *Recognition, Responsibility, and Rights: Feminist Ethics and Social Theory*, edited by Robin Fiore and Hilde Lindemann Nelson (Lanham, MD: Rowman & Littlefield, 2003), 89–104, esp. 94–95; Jennifer Everett and Shelley Wilcox, "Moral Discourse and Social Responsibility: Comments on Machan's Critique of Jaggar," *Journal of Social Philosophy*, 29.3 (1998): 142–152, esp. 149–150; Claudia Card, *The Unnatural Lottery: Character and Moral Luck* (Philadelphia: Temple University Press, 1996); Wendell, "Oppression and Victimization"; and Joan Tronto, "Is Peacekeeping Care Work? A Feminist Reflection on the 'Responsibility to Protect,'" in *Global Feminist Ethics*, edited by Rebecca Whisnant and Peggy DesAutels (Lanham, MD: Rowman & Littlefield, 2008), 179–200.

10. The just peacemaking discussion that has burgeoned in Roman Catholic circles avoids this error. It found its genesis in Glen H. Stassen, *Just Peacemaking: Transforming Initiatives for Justice and Peace* (Louisville: Westminster/ John Knox Press, 1992).

11. Elizabeth Anderson, "Toward a Non-Ideal, Relational Methodology for Political Philosophy: Comments on Schwartzman's *Challenging Liberalism*," *Hypatia*, 24.4 (2009): 130. See also Charles Mills, "Schwartzman vs. Okin: Some Comments on *Challenging Liberalism*," *Hypatia*, 24.4 (2009): 164–177. Mills is a philosopher of race, not a feminist philosopher. Here he self-consciously employs and critiques feminist analyses because of their structural usefulness.

12. See Leo XIII, *Rerum Novarum*, and Pius XI, *Quadragesimo Anno* (Vatican: Libreria Editrice Vaticana, n.d.[1931]), accessed December 17, 2012: http://www. vatican.va/holy father/pius xi/encyclicals/documents/hf p-xi enc 19310515 quadragesimo-anno en.html.

13. In *Deus caritas est* (Vatican: Libreria Editrice Vaticana, 2005), Benedict XVI overcomes some of these tendencies. To the degree that he addresses governments, agencies, and other collectives, however, remnants of the earlier vision remain. See http://www.vatican.va/holy father/benedict xvi/encyclicals/documents/hf ben-xvi enc 20051225 deus-caritas-est en.html (accessed December 17, 2012).

14. Marilyn Fischer, "Caring Globally: Jane Addams, World War One, and International Hunger," in *Global Feminist Ethics*, edited by Rebecca Whisnant and Peggy DesAutels (Lanham, MD: Rowman & Littlefield, 2008), 75.

15. This claim is in tension with Douglas Porpora's and Pierpaolo Donati's implication in this volume that unstructured collectives can be seen as subjects. I agree in a sociological sense that they act, have effects, and have intentions. but I am

not sure it makes sense in ethics to say that unstructured collectives have *moral* intentions beyond those of the individuals who make them up, even though individuals' intentions may be uncritical and not fully conscious. In that sense, then, it is hard to call collectives *moral* subjects. Structured collectives, in which conditions of membership are explicit, can more easily be seen as moral subjects, but the holders of intentions are still the members, even when the whole they create may be emergent.

16. For more on moral and epistemic luck, see the penultimate section of this chapter.

17. Cooperation with an unjust system is often mediate, not immediate, cooperation and is sometimes considered inculpable. But feminist moral theories hold that judgments of past culpability are not the main point of moral analysis; the goal is solidarity and wisdom in the struggle to overcome the systems that make such cooperation, which is always problematic, inevitable.

18. Carol Gilligan, *In a Different Voice: Psychological Theory and Women's Development* (Cambridge, MA: Harvard University Press, 1982); Nel Noddings, *Caring, a Feminine Approach to Ethics & Moral Education* (Berkeley: University of California Press, 1984); Sara Ruddick, *Maternal Thinking: Toward a Politics of Peace* (Boston: Beacon Press, 1989); Eva Feder Kittay, *Love's Labor: Essays on Women, Equality, and Dependency* (New York: Routledge, 1999).

19. Nancy Chodorow, *The Reproduction of Mothering: Psychoanalysis and the Sociology of Gender* (Berkeley: University of California Press, 1978).

20. Susan Moller Okin, *Justice, Gender, and the Family* (New York: Basic Books, 1989); Joan Tronto, *Moral Boundaries: A Political Argument for an Ethic of Care* (New York: Routledge, 1993); Fiona Robinson, *Globalizing Care: Ethics, Feminist Theory, and International Relations* (Boulder, CO: Westview Press, 1999); Virginia Held, *The Ethics of Care: Personal, Political, and Global* (New York: Oxford, 2006).

21. Held, *Ethics of Care*, 69.

22. "Nature" is a word that requires critical definition. In this case I mean that our best historical and current descriptions of humanity involve universal physical and developmental dependency essential to our "becoming" human. Other kinds of dependency due to illness, disability, and aging might be in theory nearly eliminated through eugenics and extermination, but these practices produce a morally repugnant definition of humanity. In short, we are dependent, often profoundly.

23. Deprivation of various kinds in infancy and childhood can cause neurological and other deficits that cannot easily be overcome later in life. Some deficits make it difficult for a person ever to develop a moral sense or to become a truly responsible agent. See Cristina Traina, *Erotic Attunement: Parenthood and the Ethics of Sensuality* (Chicago: University of Chicago Press, 2011).

24. Held, *Ethics of Care*, 53.

25. Fischer, "Caring Globally," 63.

26. Held, *Ethics of Care*, 38. See, e.g., Tronto, "Peacekeeping," 189–195, for a concise account of Tronto's components of the practice of care.

27. See Theresa Tobin, "Using Rights to Counter 'Gender-Specific' Wrongs," *Human Rights Review*, 10.4 (2009): 521–530.

28. Held, *Ethics of Care*, 68.

29. John Rawls, *A Theory of Justice* (Cambridge, MA: Belknap Press, 1971).

30. William Schweiker, personal communication. See also Virginia Held, "Gender Identity and the Ethics of Care in Globalized Society," in *Global Feminist Ethics*, edited by Rebecca Whisnant and Peggy DesAutels (Lanham, MD: Rowman & Littlefield, 2008), 43–58, esp. 52–53.

31. Held, *Ethics of Care*, 71. See also Lisa Tessman, *Burdened Virtues: Virtue Ethics for Liberatory Struggles* (New York: Oxford, 2005), 167–168.

32. Held, *Ethics of Care*, 72. Postow argues that no theory spelling out these negotiations is needed. Rather, one may determine which is at stake: in Held's terms, whether individual rights or interdependency is more endangered in any given situation. See B. C. Postow, "Care Ethics and Impartial Reasons," *Hypatia*, 23.1 (2008): 1–8.

33. Card, *Unnatural Lottery*, 83.

34. Card, *Unnatural Lottery*, 85.

35. This other-concern may seem naively dependent on goodwill, but Aslaksen argues that economic models based solely on self-interest are no more realistic than those that rely at least in part on generosity (see Julie Aslaksen, "Gender Constructions and the Possibility of a Generous Economic Actor," *Hypatia*, 17.2 [2002]: 118–132). Fischer, drawing on the work of Jane Addams, suggests that narrative is useful—not in constructing a bridge to a particular distant other but in creating an "international mind" through "webs of connection" that bring the distant close ("Caring Globally," 73–74). Enabling caring work to occur often includes advocacy, which requires careful listening and deep knowledge of the context; see Christine M. Koggel, "Ecological Thinking and Epistemic Location: The Local and the Global," *Hypatia*, 23.1 (2008): 177–186. For more developed arguments on globalizing care, see Robinson, *Globalizing Care*, and Held, *Ethics of Care*, ch. 10.

36. See, e.g., Held, "Gender Identity," 47–48.

37. See Allison Weir, "Global Care Chains: Freedom, Responsibility, and Solidarity," *The Southern Journal of Philosophy*, 46 (2008): 166–175, esp. 167.

38. Thomas Nagel, "Moral Luck," in *Mortal Questions*, by Thomas Nagel (New York: Cambridge University Press, 1979), 24–38; and Dana K. Nelkin, "Moral Luck," in *Stanford Encyclopedia of Philosophy*, edited by Edward N. Zalta (Stanford, CA: Stanford University, 2008), accessed December 17, 2012: http://plato.stanford.edu/archives/fall2008/entries/moral-luck/.

39. Grasswick, "Impurities," 98. Grasswick is speaking of involuntary cultural contamination, not intentional epistemic lenses (like the preferential option for the poor).

40. Grasswick, "Impurities, 102.

41. Davion, "Feminist Perspectives on Global Warming," 175.

42. Tessman, *Burdened Virtues,* 53–80. See also Claudia Card, *The Unnatural Lottery.*

43. Tessman, *Burdened Virtues,* 38.

44. Tessman, *Burdened Virtues*; Card, *Unnatural Lottery,* 41–42. The latter can be a more challenging project than the former. In cases of extreme abuse or neglect, it may be impossible. For extraordinary practical examples of the strategy of creative resistance from a position of victimization, see the essays in Ching-In Chen, Jai Julani, and Leah Lakshmi Piepzna-Samarasinha (eds.), *The Revolution Starts at Home: Confronting Violence within Activist Communities* (Boston: South End Press, 2011).

45. Card, *Unnatural Lottery,* 41–48. Fragmentation of identity can, however, be turned to constructive transformation; see Ann Ferguson, "Moral Responsibility and Social Change: A New Theory of Self," *Hypatia,* 12.3 (1997): 116–141.

46. Wendell, "Oppression and Victimization," 26–29.

47. Tessman, *Burdened Virtues,* 159–168. Here "burdened virtue" contains a foggy point: Should we say that the classical virtues are still in force but in our situation burden us by endangering our flourishing, or should we adjust the virtues to the situation, calling this adjustment a "burden" on virtue? Both articulations seem too idealistic for a present- and future-oriented realist feminist philosophy.

48. There is not space here to discuss the distinction between Tessman's vision of flourishing and a Roman Catholic vision. Unlike Tessman's account, Roman Catholic visions of flourishing, despite their strong commitment to social justice, make room (in situations of martyrdom, for instance) for a moral flourishing that yields no other practical rewards. On the other hand, in natural law visions virtue necessarily contributes to the common good, as the good of the person is assumed to be compatible with the communal good.

49. When Wendell treats this distortion under the perspective of the oppressor ("Oppression and Victimization," 23–26), it implies conscious or intentional distortion that solidifies the oppressor's privilege and blames the victim. Although this behavior exists and is gravely unjust, I am suggesting that a pattern that resembles the blindness of whites to their own privilege is, because less intentional, less conscious, and more widespread, ultimately more harmful to society than intentional oppression; see for instance Bryan Massingale, *Racial Justice and the Catholic Church* (Maryknoll, NY: Orbis Books, 2010). This distortion is still bad moral luck because it involves the agent in creating injustice and inspiring others to evil, however odd it may seem to call moral luck that advantages its holder "bad."

50. Everett and Wilcox, "Moral Discourse and Social Responsibility," 150. See also Tessman, *Burdened Virtues,* 163.

51. Wendell, "Oppression and Victimization," 37–40.

52. Eide, "The Stigma of Nation," 56.
53. Arlie Russell Hochschild, "Global Care Chains and Emotional Surplus Value," in *On the Edge: Living with Global Capitalism*, edited by Will Hutton and Anthony Giddens (London: Jonathan Cape, 2000), 130–146; Arlie Russell Hochschild, "Love and Gold," *The Scholar and Feminist Online*, 8.1 (2009), accessed December 17, 2012: http://sfonline.barnard.edu/work/hochschild_01.htm.
54. Hochschild, "Global Care Chains," 141–142.
55. Weir, "Global Care Chains," 169.
56. Weir, "Global Care Chains," 167. Emphasis in original.
57. Weir, "Global Care Chains," 167, 171–172. Weir's formal definition of freedom— "the capacity to be in relationships that one desires: to love whom and what you choose to love, and...an expansion of self in relationship" (169, italics removed)—seem to me more voluntaristic and liberal than the rest of her argument, which assigns heavy responsibilities for care to all.
58. See Hochschild, "Global Care Chains," 141–142; and Weir, "Global Care Chains," 173.
59. Eva Feder Kittay, "The Global Heart Transplant and Caring Across National Boundaries," *The Southern Journal of Philosophy* 46 (2008): 138–165, 148–149, 158. Kittay echoes Hochschild's description of care as a resource that is being drained away from developing countries.
60. Hochschild, "Global Care Chains," 143, cites Douglas S. Massey, "March of Folly: U.S. Immigration Policy after NAFTA," *The American Prospect* (March-April, 1998): 22–33.
61. See, e g., Michelle Alexander, *The New Jim Crow: Mass Incarceration in the Age of Colorblindness* (New York: New Press, 2010).

REFERENCES

Alexander, Michelle. *The New Jim Crow: Mass Incarceration in the Age of Colorblindness.* New York: New Press, 2010.

Anderson, Elizabeth. "Toward a Non-Ideal, Relational Methodology for Political Philosophy: Comments on Schwartzman's *Challenging Liberalism.*" *Hypatia,* 24.4 (2009): 130–145.

Aslaksen, Julie. "Gender Constructions and the Possibility of a Generous Economic Actor." *Hypatia,* 17.2 (2002): 118–132.

Benedict XVI. *Deus caritas est.* Vatican: Libreria Editrice Vaticana, 2005. Accessed December 17, 2012: http://www.vatican.va/holy_father/benedict_xvi/encyclicals/documents/hf_ben-xvi_enc_20051225_deus-caritas-est_en.html.

Byrne, Patrick H. "Ecology, Economy and Redemption as Dynamic: The Contributions of Jane Jacobs and Bernard Lonergan." *Worldviews: Global Religions, Culture, and Ecology,* 7.1 (2003): 5–26. Accessed December 17, 2012: http://www.nd.edu/~ecoltheo/text_byrne.htm.

Card, Claudia. *The Unnatural Lottery: Character and Moral Luck*. Philadelphia: Temple University Press, 1996.

Chen, Ching-In, Jai Julani, and Leah Lakshmi Piepzna-Samarasinha (eds.). *The Revolution Starts at Home: Confronting Violence within Activist Communities*. Boston: South End Press, 2011.

Chodorow, Nancy. *The Reproduction of Mothering: Psychoanalysis and the Sociology of Gender*. Berkeley: University of California Press, 1978.

Code, Lorraine. "Responsibility and Rhetoric." *Hypatia*, 9.1 (1994): 1–20.

Davion, Victoria. "Feminist Perspectives on Global Warming, Genocide, and Card's Theory of Evil." *Hypatia*, 24.1 (2001): 160–177.

Eide, Marian. "'The Stigma of Nation': Feminist Just War, Privilege, and Responsibility." *Hypatia*, 23.2 (2008): 48–60.

Everett, Jennifer, and Shelley Wilcox. "Moral Discourse and Social Responsibility: Comments on Machan's Critique of Jaggar." *Journal of Social Philosophy*, 29.3 (1998): 142–152.

Feder Kittay, Eva. *Love's Labor: Essays on Women, Equality, and Dependency*. New York: Routledge, 1999.

——. "The Global Heart Transplant and Caring Across National Boundaries." *The Southern Journal of Philosophy*, 46 (2008):138–165.

Ferguson, Ann. "Moral Responsibility and Social Change: A New Theory of Self." *Hypatia*, 12.3 (1997): 116–141.

Fischer, Marilyn. "Caring Globally: Jane Addams, World War One, and International Hunger." In Rebecca Whisnant and Peggy DesAutels (eds.), *Global Feminist Ethics*. Lanham, MD: Rowman & Littlefield, 2008, 61–79.

Gilligan, Carol. *In a Different Voice: Psychological Theory and Women's Development*. Cambridge, MA: Harvard University Press, 1982.

Grasswick, Heidi E. "The Impurities of Epistemic Responsibility: Developing a Practice-Oriented Epistemology." In Robin Fiore and Hilde Lindemann Nelson (eds.), *Recognition, Responsibility, and Rights: Feminist*. Lanham, MD: Rowman & Littlefield, 2003, 89–104.

Hanlon Rubio, Julie. "Moral Cooperation with Evil and Social Ethics." *Journal of the Society of Christian Ethics*, 31.1 (2011): 103–122.

Held, Virginia. *The Ethics of Care: Personal, Political, and Global*. New York: Oxford, 2006.

——. "Gender Identity and the Ethics of Care in Globalized Society." In Rebecca Whisnant and Peggy DesAutels (eds.), *Global Feminist Ethics*. Lanham, MD: Rowman & Littlefield, 2008, 43–57.

Hochschild, Arlie Russell. "Global Care Chains and Emotional Surplus Value." In Will Hutton and Anthony Giddens (eds.), *On the Edge: Living with Global Capitalism*. London: Jonathan Cape, 2000, 130–146.

——. "Love and Gold." *The Scholar and Feminist Online*, 8.1 (2009). Accessed December 17, 2012: http://sfonline.barnard.edu/work/hochschild_01.htm.

Kaveny, Cathleen M. "Appropriation of Evil: Cooperation's Mirror Image." *Theological Studies*, 61 (2000):280–313.

———. "Intrinsic Evil and Political Responsibility." *America* (October 27, 2008). Accessed December 17, 2012: http://www.americamagazine.org/content/article.cfm?article_id=11166.

Koggel, Christine M. "Ecological Thinking and Epistemic Location: The Local and the Global." *Hypatia*, 23.1 (2008): 177–186.

Leo XIII. *Rerum Novarum*. Vatican: Libreria Editrice Vaticana, n.d. (Originally published 1891) Accessed December 17, 2012: http://www.vatican.va/holy_father/leo_xiii/encyclicals/documents/hf_l-xiii_enc_15051891_rerum-novarum_en.html.

Massey, Douglas S. "March of Folly: US Immigration Policy after NAFTA." *The American Prospect* (March-April 1998): 22–33.

Massingale, Bryan. *Racial Justice and the Catholic Church*. Maryknoll, NY: Orbis Books, 2010.

Mills, Charles. "Schwartzman vs. Okin: Some Comments on *Challenging Liberalism*." *Hypatia*, 24.4 (2009): 164–177.

Nagel, Thomas. "Moral Luck." In Thomas Nagel, *Mortal Questions*. New York: Cambridge University Press, 1979, 24–38.

Nelkin, Dana K. "Moral Luck." In Edward N. Zalta (ed.), *Stanford Encyclopedia of Philosophy*. Stanford, CA: Stanford University, 2008. Accessed December 17, 2012: http://plato.stanford.edu/archives/fall2008/entries/moral-luck/.

Noddings, Nel. *Caring, a Feminine Approach to Ethics & Moral Education*. Berkeley: University of California Press, 1984.

Nozick, Robert. *Anarchy, State, and Utopia*. New York: Basic Books, 1974.

Okin, Susan Moller. *Justice, Gender, and the Family*. New York: Basic Books, 1989.

Pius XI. *Quadragesimo Anno*. Vatican: Libreria Editrice Vaticana, n.d. (Originally published 1931) Accessed December 17, 2012: http://www.vatican.va/holy_father/pius_xi/encyclicals/documents/hf_p-xi_enc_19310515_quadragesimo-anno_en.html.

Postow, B. C. "Care Ethics and Impartial Reasons." *Hypatia*, 23.1 (2008): 1–8.

Rawls, John. *A Theory of Justice*. Cambridge, MA: Belknap Press, 1971.

Robinson, Fiona. *Globalizing Care: Ethics, Feminist Theory, and International Relations*. Boulder, CO: Westview Press, 1999.

Ruddick, Sara. *Maternal Thinking: Toward a Politics of Peace*. Boston: Beacon Press, 1989.

Sherwin, Susan. "Moral Perception and Global Visions." *Bioethics*, 15.3 (2001): 175–188.

Stassen, Glen H. *Just Peacemaking: Transforming Initiatives for Justice and Peace*. Louisville: Westminster/John Knox Press, 1992.

Tessman, Lisa. *Burdened Virtues: Virtue Ethics for Liberatory Struggles*. New York: Oxford, 2005.

Tobin, Theresa. "Using Rights to Counter 'Gender-Specific' Wrongs." *Human Rights Review,* 10.4 (2009): 521–530.

Traina, Cristina. *Erotic Attunement: Parenthood and the Ethics of Sensuality.* Chicago: University of Chicago Press, 2011.

Tronto, Joan. *Moral Boundaries: A Political Argument for an Ethic of Care.* New York: Routledge, 1993.

———. "Is Peacekeeping Care Work? A Feminist Reflection on the 'Responsibility to Protect." In Rebecca Whisnant and Peggy DesAutels (eds.), *Global Feminist Ethics.* Lanham, MD: Rowman & Littlefield, 2008, 179–200.

Weir, Allison "Global Care Chains: Freedom, Responsibility, and Solidarity." *The Southern Journal of Philosophy,* 46 (2008):166–175.

Wendell, Susan. "Oppression and Victimization: Choice and Responsibility." *Hypatia,* 5.3 (1990): 15–46.

8

The African Concept of Community and Individual in the Context of the Market

Paul Appiah Himin Asante

THE RADICAL ACCELERATION in the flow of capital, people, goods, images, and ideologies across the face of the globe has rendered even African economies deeply integrated into the world market. Many studies have been done on this integration. Some use world system and dependency theories to postulate that poor countries are impoverished and wealthy ones enriched by the way poor countries are integrated into the "world system."[1] Dependency theory, for example, is predicated on the notion that the resources flowing from the "periphery," or poor and underdeveloped states, to the "core" wealthy states enrich the latter at the expense of the former.[2]

Since independence, African governments have used either state enterprise or market economy as economic systems with the view to lifting their people from poverty and elevating their standard of living. In the 1960s, many political leaders of the continent used their concept of *community* in the African context to serve as the basis for their political and socioeconomic order. This idea provided support for public enterprise for economic development. As a result, state-owned industries were established. These leaders believed that this economic system would help reduce economic dependence by manufacturing locally what was previously imported from the industrialized nations.

In the 1980s, the Bretton Woods institutions judged that the problems that confronted developing countries were not only economic but also structural. Accordingly, they came up with the Structural Adjustment Program to change the economic structures that in their estimation perpetuated the vicious cycle of poverty in the developing world. This program pushed for more market-oriented policies, liberalization of markets, more reliance on prices, greater openness to trade, and a bigger role for the private sector.[3] This shift from the "public enterprise" economic model of the post-independence period, though designed to improve the conditions of the people, actually made life more difficult for many people.

Currently, African nations are enmeshed in the global economy but tend to fall toward the bottom of any list measuring economic activity, such as gross domestic product per capita, despite a wealth of natural resources in the continent. In 2009, twenty-two of the twenty-four nations identified as having "low human development" on the United Nations Human Development Index were located in Sub-Saharan Africa. In 2006, thirty-four of the fifty nations on the United Nations list of least developed countries were in Africa. In many nations, gross domestic product per capita is less than $200 per year, with the vast majority of the population living on much less. In addition, Africa's share of world income has been consistently dropping over the past century by any measure. Mark Tran, citing a World Bank report on African natural resources, points out that "strong economic growth in the past decade among African countries rich in oil and minerals has failed to make a significant dent on their poverty levels."[4] The report confirms the common perception that, to a large extent, the benefits of growth have not reached the poorest segments of society.

There have been many attempts by many actors in the world body to help lift Africans from poverty by using the market and macroeconomic principles, yet the gulf between the rich and the poor continues to widen and the poor become poorer. According to Joyce Appleby, the shame in the flourishing of capitalism is the stark inequality between nations and regions of the world.[5] Measures of well-being like life expectancy, family purchasing power, and children's nutrition reveal greater inequalities than fifty years ago.

This chapter takes the view that the use of the economic logic of the market to solve this problem is laudable, but the problem will continue to persist until the economics is rooted in the ethical and cultural values of the African.

Traditionally the economic activity of the African is based on the common good and the good of the individual; at its best, the emphasis is put on the former. These stem from the African notions of *community* and *individual*. A core set of ethical values—namely, common good, solidarity, love, reciprocity, generosity, and the dignity of the person—are inextricably embedded in their economic activity. In fact, it is these values that sustain and give shape to the traditional economy of the African. Any attempt to lift the African from poverty therefore should go beyond just using the economic logic of the market and incorporate the ethical values that their concept of *community* and *individual* espouses.

The Concept of Community *and* Individual

Many social scientists have contrasted two models of human societies: those based on groups and those based on the individual. Taking an evolutionary approach, they suggest that the history of mankind has been a movement in time from societies based on groups (premodern society) to those based on the individual (modern society). This contrast was part of their attempt to comprehend the massive changes that came in the wake of the French and Industrial Revolutions. It was against this background that the founding fathers of the social sciences, figures such as Karl Marx, Emile Durkheim, Max Weber, Ferdinand Tönnies, and Alexis de Tocqueville, ruminated over the new relationship between the individual and the group. Their works have given birth to two schools of thought in the social sciences: methodological individualism[6] and holism.[7]

Methodological individualists such as John Stuart Mill and Max Weber argue that all social facts must be explained wholly in terms of actions, beliefs, and desires of the individual. On the other hand, methodological holists such as Durkheim and Marx emphasize the group over the individual.

As observed above, nineteenth-century sociologists made the concept of community explicitly or implicitly the point of departure of their studies. They distinguished between preindustrial and industrial, rural and urban societies, and they used models that centered on the idea of progress as their underlying thought to buttress their contention. For example, in his distinction between *gemeinschaft*[8] and *gesellschaft*,[9] Tönnies treated communities (*gemeinschaft*) as predominantly rural, united by kinship and a sense of belonging. He depicted the change of civilization based on community to a modern society where individuals were more loosely related and only linked in associations connected by money and contracts in the market.

Henry Summer Maine argued that while the unit of an ancient society was the family, that of the modern society (*gesellschaft*) was the individual.[10] Daniel Bell in the modern era expressed the same point of view when he wrote that the fundamental assumption of modernity is that the social unit of society is not the group, the guilds, the tribe, or the city but the person.[11] E. Gellner has echoed the same view lately by attributing to the influence of modernity the belief that a new society has emerged in which single individuals could apparently carry an entire culture within themselves unaided.[12]

Many African scholars influenced by this evolutionary paradigm also make a distinction between a society based on the individual and a society based on the community. Many times they describe Africa as belonging to the latter and the West the former. However, some contemporary anthropologists have rejected these clearcut distinctions and have argued that many features of individualism are found in communities ranging from the simplest hunting and gathering societies to the most complex civilization. Thus the Western world may not be distinguished from and opposed to the rest of the world solely by the extent to which the individual or the community is emphasized.

While the notions of the individual and the community appear to be universal and cross-cultural, the ways these concepts are understood and used differ from culture to culture. The term "community" is one of the most vague and elusive terms in this globalized era. It can be used to denote many different instances of human groupings or to refer to people in a geographical area. It can also be a mental construct. Generally, "community" is a collective term referring to a group sharing a defined geographical area such as neighborhood, city, village, hamlet, and so on. Of late, however, the term has also been used to indicate a sense of identity or belonging that may or may not be tied to a geographical location.[13] In this sense, a community is formed when people have a reasonably clear idea of who has something in common with them and who doesn't. A community in this sense is a group of people sharing common traits, having a sense of belonging, and/or maintaining social ties and interactions that shape them into a distinctive social entity. This may be an ethnic, religious, academic, professional, or social entity. Accordingly, R. Warren believes that such common ties and sense of belonging may derive from beliefs in a common past or a common fate, common values, interests, kinship relations, and so on.[14]

With the improvements in technology and communication in this information age, a new type of community has emerged that Howard Rheingold terms a "virtual community."[15] This consists of a social network of individuals who interact through the Internet or other collaborative networks, potentially crossing geographical and political boundaries in order to pursue mutual interests.

There is yet another concept of community, one that is more traditionally Catholic. Here, "community" refers to the unity or communion in which the followers of Christ participate by virtue of being joined to Him through sanctifying grace. Just as the people of Israel were not a "people" until God called them out of Egypt, so the diverse gathering of believers in Christ constitutes a community precisely by virtue of Christ's reconciling grace. By this grace, Christians are joined with one another by being joined to him.

By contrast with other collectivities, a community is a collection of people with a particular social structure. In other words, unlike other collectivities, a community is a social system that includes such subsystems as government, economy, education, religion, and family. It performs such basic functions as the provision for basic economic and social needs, specialization of roles, social control, social participation, and mutual support. A community exists to further individual interest and social well-being, which are aspects of the common good.

The individual, on the other hand, is a person with a distinct identity and his or her own needs and goals. Some writers refer to the individual as the self. One notion of the individual in modern discourse draws on the Cartesian *cogito*[16] and the "self" of classical liberalism as a point of departure. The Cartesian *cogito* separates the mind from the body and classifies the individual as an autonomous rational agent capable of acting upon, but remaining unaffected by, the environment. Classical liberalism[17] accords primacy to the individual over the community.

Some contemporary social scientists argue that societies today are undergoing a process of individualization in which individuals are being taken out of their traditional ties within a family or locality and must make their own individual choices to fashion their identities and biographies. Some argue that individualism is associated with the rise of capitalism because capitalism requires people to be constructed as autonomous and enterprising economic agents who are able to relate to one another in the free market. Max Weber,[18] for example, intimated that the individualism of Protestant religions in early modern Europe was a precondition for the rise of capitalism.

The existentialists[19] Jean Sartre[20] and Frederick Nietzsche[21] suggested the individual needs to define his or her own self and circumstance. Individuals are called upon to create their own values rather than rely on external and socially imposed codes of morality. This phenomenon is a dominant feature of the culture of the contemporary West. For example, some governments have actively attempted to encourage individualism in the belief that enterprising individuals who are as free as possible from state influence and control are the best guarantors of a successful economy and enterprise culture.[22] Some scholars believe that the trend in our world today is toward heightened individualism and egotism, greater division of labor, the penetration of market values, and the spread of political concepts of equality and innate human rights, which will lead to increased individualism as de Alexis de Tocqueville[23] predicted. But others contend that we are now moving toward a global village[24] where no man is an island.

The Community and the Individual in African Society

Most Africans think of the community as composed of a large number of people, many of whom have died, a few who are living, and an infinite number who are yet to be born. The concept of community, then, brings the past, the present, and the future together into the here and now, and it also brings the spiritual and the material together. The belief is that all members of a lineage form one community, whether they are dead, born, or unborn. This concept of community is not just a borrowed idea or the product of their social relations and interactions; it is organically and inextricably linked with their anthropology and their being.

Among the Akan,[25] a matrilineal tribe in Ghana, for example, it is believed that during conception, the woman (mother) transmits her blood (*mogya*), the man (father) transmits the spirit (*sunsum or ntoro*), and God gives the soul (*okra*). The blood that the woman provides has come down by matrilineal descent from the founding ancestress of their lineage and makes them one with all who share it. In other words, the blood (*mogya*) incorporates the lineage in the child and the child in the lineage. All who share in the same blood constitute an *abusua*, a "community," located in a territory. Thus the natural environment is part of their concept of community and must always be respected. The spirit (*sunsum or ntoro*) from the man (father) grants individuality, character, and personality to the child. The soul (*okra*) from God is immortal and divine; it grants uniqueness, rationality, and transcendence to the person.

Three elements in the Akan anthropology and cosmology simultaneously make the "individual" person: the *spiritual* from God, the *community* from the woman and *individuality* from the man. Contrary to what some African scholars claim, it is not only the community, bestowed and determined by the mother through the transmission of blood, which defines the "individual." The other two elements—the *sunsum* of individuality from the father and the *okra* (soul) of uniqueness and transcendence from God—are also essential to the being of the individual, and together they define his or her identity. The individual is bound to actualize and concretize these elements in real life for his or her own survival and happiness. All these elements make it possible for the person to realize that he or she is independent and yet dependent, unique but relational.

Even though there is an element of community in the individual's being, the individual still has to learn to be a "community." Therefore, individuals are socialized and taught the core values, sometimes in the context of the performance of rituals, in order to confirm and authenticate one's membership in the community. The individual is a community, yet he or she must become a community and be an individual simultaneously. It may sound contradictory, but that is the nature and character of the Akan. Thus, for the Akan of West Africa, the separation in a person between the individual and the community is unreal. Such a separation is not true to the nature of the individual's being.

The anthropology of the Akan makes them ontologically religious,[26] as J. S. Mbiti[27] asserts of the African. It makes them relational: independent yet dependent. It gives them a worldview that is both religion centered and sociocentric. That which gives meaning to their life is their relationship and dependence on God of creation. The culture that is rooted in their anthropology encourages adaptability, flexibility, and transcendence. It honors both conformity and conflict as a way of life, thus making their culture dynamic. A core set of values that emanates from their anthropology is externalized and concretized in their culture. The values are religiosity, sacredness of life and of the environment, common good, love, unity, solidarity, togetherness, dialogue, justice, reciprocity, self-reliance, hierarchy and equality, change and continuity, independence and dependence, and dignity of the person and the community.

The "whole" in the Akan context is represented in the individual, and the individual stands for the whole community. The individual is a corporate representation of the whole. Whatever happens to the individual happens to the whole group, and whatever happens to the whole group happens to the individual. The lineage, for example, is metaphorically referred to as one person (*nipa baako*) and/or one blood (*mogya baako*) to substantiate this point. The individual in this context is unique but has a corporate personality. That is why when an individual surreptitiously or publicly perpetrates a heinous offence against a god, "mother earth,"[28] or a neighbor, the repercussions are felt by all members in the community. Further, to extirpate such a misdeed or social evil, sacrifices have to be performed to restore harmony with the deity and within the whole community. A negative act of the individual brings obloquy to the whole family.

Many taboos protect the relationship between the individual and the community, as well as between the individual and the environment. Whereas every individual, even though unique, has a corporate personality in this context, the chiefs and the *abrewa* are preeminent in this phenomenon because of their representational role. (The *abrewa* is the old woman, the source, embodiment, and symbol of the matrilineal lineage. This ancestress is also the seat of wisdom who wants peace and harmony for her children.) For example, when there is a dispute between two parties and the case is being settled by the chief and his elders in the palace, the adjudication process requires that the chief and his elders go to *egyina*, meaning "standing." The elders stand at a secluded place to deliberate on the issue. They consult the *abrewa* before they pronounce a verdict. Going to *egyina* is an act of "conjoint reflection," which N. K. Dzobo[29] calls logical demonomy: recourse to and consultation of ancestral wisdom that is attributed to the sagacity of the *abrewa*. The chief can give the verdict only by linking it to the *abrewa*; he presents it as if it is coming from the *abrewa* to make it binding and legal.[30]

When an individual succeeds in life, members of his or her community all feel they have a son or daughter who has "made it." The community is proud to associate with such individuals. As is the case with corporate personalities and corporate representations in the Old Testament, individuals represent themselves and their community at the same time. Individual Akans at certain times talk of their individuality, their own progress, achievements, rights, and interests to the exclusion of others. But often, and even when they talk about their individuality, their concept of individuality does not exclude the community.

The saying "I am because we are, and since we are, therefore I am" arises from the K*iswahili* word *"ubuntu"* and has been popularized by the writings of J. S. Mbiti and other African writers. It has sometimes been cited to magnify the role of the community in African societies to the detriment of the individual. But properly understood, this maxim means that it is in the community that the lives of individuals have meaning. It is not in living as isolated beings but in mutually interacting with other members of community that individuals realize their social aspirations. T. Okere[31] emphasized this point by stating that man is not just an individual, an island left to himself and sufficient unto himself. Man is essentially a community. K. O. Opoku[32] poignantly expresses the community-extension of the individual in traditional African society: "A man is a man because of others, and life is when you are together. Alone you are an animal."

The community and the individual are complementary in the life and existence of the African in several traditional societies. Moreover, the African concept of the community does not preclude the development of the individual or discourage personal initiatives and self-reliance. Indeed, the unity of reciprocal implication between individual and community becomes the way several African traditional societies present the pursuit of the common good. Its place is above other goods; in contrast with Western ways, the right of the community is above that of the individual.

African society manifests features of communality and individuality. Besides a strong attachment to the community, the African is individualistic, but the concept of individualism differs from Western individualism in which the individual often thinks he or she is autonomous, totally free and existentially alone in the world. Africans, on the other hand, do not see themselves as absolutely supreme in the sense that they have nothing to do with their fellows, because the individual is defined in reference to the surrounding community. Kwame Gyekye[33] corroborates this point by postulating that individuals, although originating and inextricably bound to their family community, nevertheless possess a clear concept of themselves as distinct persons of volition.

This combination of personhood and communal membership is the basis on which the family and community expect individuals to take personally meaningful and socially responsible decisions and actions. Leopold Senghor[34] agrees that traditional African society is based both on the community and on the person, and because it was founded on dialogue and reciprocity, the group has priority over the individual—but it does not crush him or her; rather the individual is allowed to blossom as a person. The proverb "Life is as you make it"[35] is interpreted in this context to mean that one cannot always depend on the group; one must be responsible for oneself as an individual.

Time and community form an interesting web of ideas. The African concept of time encompasses the past, present, and future, which are brought together here and now and simultaneously projected to the future. This sets up an interplay of sameness and change that are also at work in the community, a place of oneness, sameness, and change. Individuals can use all this as part of their cultural capital[36] to develop themselves independently as well as incorporate themselves into the community. When doing so and being creative and flexible in handling any social and economic changes, they embody the proverb *"mmere danea na woso w'adane woho bi,"* that is, "Time changes and we change with it." Even though Africans do not dichotomize being and becoming, the community always encourages individuals to become and be at the same time, to be relational and sociocentric, especially in this contemporary era.

The Market Economy and the Contemporary African

In many parts of Africa, economics is used as a modernist discourse and the market plays a very significant role in shaping this discourse. Those who have the power and the knowledge to shape this discourse are the transnational corporations, Bretton Woods Institutions, governments of developed countries, as well as governments and some elites of Africa. The discourse has its own logic and culture and is based on the premise that the market economy is the only solution to Africa's economic and social problems.

This perspective constructs in bipolar terms and disparages microstructures (such as the lineage and other aspects of African traditions) as the source of underdevelopment, while privileging the market over other cultural values. It considers indigenous knowledge, economic systems, and social structures as potential impediments to economic growth. For example, the African lineage systems are portrayed as a static and anachronistic institution with the proclivity to perpetuate the vicious cycle of poverty and underdevelopment.

The metanarrative of this discourse is based on the premise that the market economy will not only lead to economic growth and elevate the standard of living but it will also engender a modern African, one who will be free, autonomous, progressive, and self-interested. The discourse constructs illiteracy, disease, poverty, ignorance, low productivity, lack of capital, and low standard of living as emanating from the superstructures of the traditional society that need to be eradicated and jettisoned in favor of sound macroeconomic policies.

Thus the implementation of market economy heightens the sense of leaving tradition and the "local" behind in order to move to modern forms of social and economic organization and thought. It is believed that development represents a transformation of society, a movement from traditional relations, traditional ways of thinking, traditional ways of dealing with health and education, and traditional methods of production to a modern way. This discourse also defines the human being as *homo economicus,* a purely rational and materialistic being who pursues self-interest by maximizing his utility or profits, based on the availability of perfect information. This conflicts with the more adequate notion of the human being of the African who is spiritual, individual and communal, both rational and emotional.

The anthropology delineated above not only legitimizes a narrow view of individuality and social structure, but it also serves as a form of cultural capital that members utilize actively to construct both the self and society in the face of contemporary social and economic challenges. They utilize this cultural capital actively to negotiate, appropriate, contest, and interact with the social structure of the market and in the process unintentionally strengthen the primacy of market-based thinking over traditional understandings of individuality and community.

Margaret Archer, in this volume, argues that the structure and the agents are jointly responsible for each and every state of affairs. Pierpaolo Donati adds to this point by affirming that structures' causality is always mediated by agency. In the new structures created by this interaction, only a few enjoy the full benefits of the market economy, while the majority languish in penury. In other words, few people benefit from this socioeconomic order; some are lifted out of poverty, but many become poorer. Both in their own internal dynamics and their relations with the globalized world economy, this majority of the poor could be categorized as the distant other in today's globalized world. The dignity of the individual and the demands of justice require that economic choices not cause disparities in wealth to increase as they do today.[37]

Today, market structures in Africa play a critical causal role in how people come to define the "I am" and the "we are" in the maxim "I am because we are, and since we are, therefore I am." People belonging to the same household or lineage may have different interpretations of what "I am" and "we are" mean. In the context of the market, it is more likely that individuals will think of themselves as alone, be self-interested, and be preoccupied with personal success in life. But the communal elements persist deep within them and may haunt them psychologically. Thus the "I am" can be defined and practiced in the market economy by the individual egoistically but with mixed or guilty feelings, as a corporate personality, as a right and also as a "self."

"We are" in this maxim traditionally has several meanings in the African context. It is used to refer to the nuclear family, minimal lineage, maximal lineage, the clan, the tribe, and even all the members of the village to some extent. The term can also be used to refer to all the citizens of the nation, all Africans, and ultimately all children of God. Even though "we are" still can mean any of these things today, many people seem to prefer to limit it more to the nuclear family, rather than the extended family, because of socioeconomic conditions. As Anthony Cohen[38] suggests, members of a community united by shared symbols commonly differ radically on the meaning of those symbols and on their notions of a proper way of life. While the spiritual and the transcendental element are constantly within individuals, they may be in harmony or in conflict. In practice, there is always a tension within the individual. In this sense, although there is conformity on one level, the African society is saddled with conflicts, ambivalence, tension, and dynamism.

The market remains a powerful structure. African entrepreneurs and foreign investors exercise their right to seek maximum profits and contribute to the growth of the market. In the process, there is emerging a new socioeconomic order, based on progress, development, and efficiency. The emphasis here is put more on the logic of the market, including consumerism, materialism, and social inequality rather than traditional cultural and ethical values.

The market economy in Africa exhibits humans' creativity but also domination of nature and social inequality. This process is actually a liability for the long-term growth of the market, for the sociopolitical order, and, most basically, for the integral development of the human person. This will continue unless the market is grounded in ethical values of solidarity, reciprocity, subsidiarity, generosity, and the common good. It confirms what Pope Benedict XVI has taught: "Economic activity cannot solve all social problems through the simple application of commercial logic."[39] The market can be a negative force, not because it is so by nature, but because a certain ideology can make it so.

Traditionally, the economic activity of the African is based on the common good and the good of the individual. A core set of ethical values—common good, solidarity, love, reciprocity, generosity, and the dignity of the person—are inherently and inextricably embedded in their economic activity. In fact, it is these values that sustain and give shape to the traditional economy of Africa. Those actors with the power and knowledge to shape this discourse must go beyond economic and commercial logic to incorporate ethical values implicit in the African notions of community and individual. This will be necessary in order to lift many from poverty. The entrepreneur, the businessman, and the banker must come to see their work not merely as a profession but as a vocation.

One key part of the economy in many African countries, and particularly in Ghana, is actually motivated by solidarity based on kinship. This is the remittance market. For example, according to the Bank of Ghana, private remittances to Ghana rose from about $449 million in 1999 to $1.79 billion in 2009. These figures reflect only the funds sent through official channels. In addition, a sizeable number of those in the diaspora and migrants within the country use informal channels such as person-to-person and courier services to transmit their funds. These funds are usually invested in real estate or used to set up micro-enterprises, and they work to expand the domestic market. They are even used to provide social services, like clinics and schools for some communities, to complement inadequate government services.

Remittance flows to developing countries have increased substantially during the last decade to reach $325 billion in 2010. Remittances to the continent sent by 31 million Africans in diaspora reached nearly $40 billion in 2010, equivalent to 2.6% of Africa's gross domestic product.[40] Takyiwaa Manuh[41] asserts that international migration remains an important livelihood strategy for dealing with declining socioeconomic conditions. The remittance market is expanding because the Africans who are in diaspora and living in societies that are individualistic still experience the bond to their home community, even while fighting hard to achieve their individual identity. They contribute to the development of their native communities but are also active members of their unions and other groupings where they live and work.

For human and economic development, Africa as a whole and Ghana in particular need a modern economic system that is based on the values that emanate from their concepts of communality and individuality. This calls for a hybrid economy of both public and private enterprise based on African cultural and ethical values because, as Pope Benedict XVI asserts, "Authentic human social relationships of friendship, solidarity and reci-procity can also be conducted within economic activity and not only outside it or 'after it.' "[42] That is, three interdependent elements are necessary to improve the economic well-being of Africa: a vibrant market, stable govern-ments, and a culture rooted in traditional African values that animates both.

NOTES

1. Immanuel Wallerstein, *The Modern World System* (New York: Academic Press, 1974).
2. Andre Gunder Frank, *Capitalism and Underdevelopment in Latin America* (New York: Monthly Review Press, 1969).
3. .Christina Gladwin, *Structural Adjustment and African Women Farmers* (Gainesville: University of Florida Press, 1991).
4. Mark Tran "Africa's Mineral Wealth Hardly Denting Poverty Levels," *The Guardian* (October 5, 2012). Accessed October 5, 2012: http://www.theguardian.com/global-development/2012/oct/05/africa-mineral-wealth-poverty-world-bank.
5. Joyce Appleby, *The Relentless Revolution a History of Capitalism.* (New York: W. W. Norton, 2010), 363.
6. Methodological individualism is a doctrine that states that all sociological expli-cations are reducible to the characteristics of individuals. The individual is used as the unit of analysis. It was originally formed in opposition to the work of such sociologists as Emile Durkheim who argued the characteristics of individ-uals could safely be ignored in sociological explanations because "social facts" have an existence of their own and can be studied independently of individuals whose actions they determine.
7. Holism is a doctrine that says societies should be seen as wholes or as systems of interacting parts. Analysis should start from large-scale institutions and their relationships, not from the behaviour of individual action.
8. *Gemeinschaft* is usually translated as "community." In a community, relations are homogeneous and largely based on kinship and organic ties. It is character-ized by an organic solidarity, a term used by Emile Durkheim to depict tradi-tional society in which its cohesion and integration comes from homogeneity of individuals—people feel connected through similar work, educational, reli-gious training, and lifestyle.

9. *Gesellschaft*—often translated as "society," "civil society," or "association"—describes associations in which, for the individual, the larger association never takes precedence over the individual's self-interest, and these associations lack the same level of shared mores.

10. Henry Summer Maine, *Ancient Law* (London: J. M. Dent and Sons, 1861).

11. Daniel Bell, *The Cultural Contradictions of Capitalism* (New York: Basic Books, 1976).

12. E. Gellner, *Plough, Sword, and Book: The Structure of Human History* (Chicago: University of Chicago Press, 1988).

13. The whole idea of a community tied to a particular location is changing, making the concept of community very complex in modern times.

14. R. Warren, *The Community in America* (Chicago: University of Chicago Press, 1973).

15. Howard Rheingold, *The Virtual Community: Homesteading on the Electronic Frontier* (Reading, MA: Addison-Wesley, 1993).

16. Rene Descartes produced the famous dictum *"cogito ergo sum:"* I think therefore I am." His philosophy centers on the idea that the human being is a rational animal. This dictum separates the mind from the body and elevates individual consciousness to be the origin of meaning, knowledge, and action.

17. In classical liberalism, the individual is what matters for the purpose of social and political action. It holds that political organizations are justified by the contribution they make to the interests of individuals, interests that can be understood apart from the idea of society.

18. Max Weber, *The Protestant Ethics and the Spirit of Capitalism* (New York: Charles Scribner's Sons, 195).

19. Existentialists are a number of thinkers in the nineteenth and the twentieth centuries who made the concrete individual central to their thought. Existentialists start out with a detailed description of the self as the "existing individual" understood as an agent involved in a specific social and historical world.

20. Jean P. Sartre, *Being and Nothingness*, translated by Hazel Barnes (New York: Philosophical Library, 1956).

21. Frederick Nietzsche, *The Will to Power*, translated by Walter Kaufmann and R. J. Hollingdale (New York: Random House, 1967).

22. The idea is based on the premise that individualism is a feature of modernity and capitalism.

23. Alexis de Tocqueville, *L'ancien Régime*, translated by M. Patterson (Oxford: Blackwell, 1856).

24. McLuhan introduced the expression "global village" into the analysis of culture and mass media in order to depict how time and space have compressed. The world is shrinking as a result of new communication technologies.

25. The Akan tribe is to be found throughout central and southern Ghana except for the southeastern part and the western part of the Ivory Coast. Some of the tribal groups in the area are the Fante, Wassa, Asante, Nzema, Ahanta, Assin, Twifo, Sefwi, Denkyira, Bono, Akyem, Aowin, Kwahu, and Akwapim. All of them, except for some parts of the Akwapim, are matrilineal.

26. It is believed that the idea of God is innate in the African, and no one teaches the child who God is.

27. J. S. Mbiti, *African Religions and Philosophy* (London: Heinemann, 1969).

28. The earth is known by the Akan as both a "mother" and a goddess. She is a symbol of fertility and is called *Asaase Yaa* by the Asantes because they believe Thursday is her day and *Asaase Efua* by the Fantes because they believe Friday is her day.

29. N. K. Dzobo, "Logical Demonomy Among the Ewe of West Africa," *Ghana Bulletin of Theology,* 7.7 (1974).

30. In the Old Testament too, wisdom (*hokmah* in Hebrew) is used in the feminine gender.

31. T. Okere, *Philosophy, Culture and Society in Africa* (Nsukka: Afro-Orbis Publications, 2005).

32. K. O. Opoku, *West African Traditional Religion* (Accra: International Private Press, 1978), 92.

33. Kwame Gyekye, *An Essay on African Philosophical Thought: The Akan Conceptual Scheme* (Cambridge, UK: Cambridge University Press, 1988).

34. Leopold S. Senghor, *On African Socialism,* translated by Mercer Cook (New York: Praeger, 1964), 5.

35. It is a proverb about individual self-assertion and the aim of achieving something for oneself.

36. The term "cultural capital" refers to nonfinancial social assets that promote social mobility beyond economic means. Examples can include education, intellect, style of speech, dress, and even physical appearance, etc. Cultural capital (French: *le capital culturel*) is a sociological concept that was first articulated by Pierre Bourdieu. Bourdieu and Jean-Claude Passeron first used the term in *La Reproduction: Éléments pour une théorie du système d'enseignement* (Paris: Les Éditions de Minuit, 1970).

37. Paul VI, *Populorum Progressio* (Vatican: Libreria Editrice Vaticana, 1967), 33.

38. Anthony P. Cohen, *The Symbolic Construction of Community* (New York: Tavistock, 1985).

39. Benedict XVI, *Caritas in veritate* (Vatican: Libreria Editrice Vaticana, 2009), 36.

40. World Bank, *Global Economic Prospects 2006: Economic Implications of Remittances and Migration* (Washington, DC: World Bank, 2006).

41. Takyiwaa Manuh, "Ghanaian Migrants in Toronto, Canada: Care of Kin and Gender Relations," *Research Review,* 17 (2001):17–26.

42. Benedict XVI, *Caritas in veritate,* 36.

REFERENCES

"Africa Rising." *The Economist*, 3, 401.8762 (December 2011): 15.

Appleby, Joyce. *The Relentless Revolution a History of Capitalism*. New York: W. W. Norton, 2010.

Bell, Daniel. *The Cultural Contradictions of Capitalism*. New York: Basic Books, 1976.

Benedict XVI. *Caritas in Veritate*. Vatican: Libreria Editrice Vaticana, 2009.

Cohen, Anthony P. *The Symbolic Construction of Community*. New York: Tavistock, 1985.

Comaroff, J., and Simon Roberts. *Rules and Processes: The Cultural Logic of Disputes in an African Context*. Chicago: University of Chicago Press, 1981.

Descartes, Rene. *A Discourse on Method and Meditations I*. Translated by I. Lofleur. In dianapolis: Bobbs-Merrill, 1960.

Durkheim, E. *The Division of Labor in Society*. New York: Free Press, 1964.

Dzobo, N. K. "Logical Demonomy Among the Ewe of West Africa." *Ghana Bulletin of Theology*, 7.7 (1974): 329–342.

Frank, Andre Gunder. *Capitalism and Underdevelopment in Latin America*. New York: Monthly Review Press, 1969.

Gellner, E. *Plough, Sword, and Book: The Structure of Human History*. Chicago: University of Chicago Press, 1988.

Gladwin, Christina. *Structural Adjustment and African Women Farmers*. Gainesville: University of Florida Press, 1991.

Gyekye, Kwame. *An Essay on African Philosophical Thought: The Akan Conceptual Scheme*. Cambridge, UK: Cambridge University Press, 1988.

Hobbes, Thomas. *Leviathan*. Edited by Richard Tuck. Cambridge, UK: Cambridge University Press, 1996.

Maine, Henry Summer. *Ancient Law*. London: J. M. Dent and Sons, 1861.

Manuh, Takyiwaa. "Ghanaian Migrants in Toronto, Canada: Care of Kin and Gender Relations." *Research Review*, 17 (2001):17–26.

Mbiti, J. S. *African Religions and Philosophy*. London: Heinemann, 1969.

Nietzsche, Frederick. *The Will to Power*. Translated by Walter Kaufmann and R. J. Hollingdale. New York: Random House, 1967.

Okere, T. *Philosophy, Culture and Society in Africa*. Nsukka: Afro-Orbis Publications, 2005.

Opoku, K. O. *West African Traditional Religion*. Accra: International Private Press, 1978.

Paul VI. *Populorum Progressio*. Vatican: Libreria Editrice Vaticana, 1967.

Rheingold, Howard. *The Virtual Community: Homesteading on the Electronic Frontier*. Reading, MA: Addison-Wesley, 1993.

Sartre, Jean P. *Being and Nothingness*. Translated by Hazel Barnes. New York: Philosophical Library, 1956.

Senghor, Leopold S. *On African Socialism*. Translated by Mercer Cook. New York, 1967.

Tocqueville, Alexis de. *L'ancien Régime.* Translated by M. Patterson. Oxford: Blackwell, 1956.

Tonnies, F. *Community and Society.* Edited and translated by C. P. Loomis. New York: Harper Torchbook, 1957.

Tran, Mark. "Africa's Mineral Wealth Hardly Denting Poverty Levels." *The Guardian* (October 5, 2012). Accessed October 5, 2012: http://www.theguardian.com/global-development/2012/oct/05/africa-mineral-wealth-poverty-world-bank.

Warren, R. *The Community in America.* Chicago: University of Chicago Press, 1973.

Wallerstein, Immanuel. *The Modern World System.* New York: Academic Press, 1974.

Weber, Max. *The Protestant Ethic and the Spirit of Capitalism.* New York: Charles Scribner's Sons, 1958.

World Bank. *Global Economic Prospects 2006: Economic Implications of Remittances and Migration.* Washington, DC: World Bank, 2006.

9

Individuating Collective Responsibility

Albino Barrera, O.P.

CENTRAL TO THE theme of this volume is the mutual impact of social structures and individual agents. On the one hand, social structures emerge from the interaction of individual agents. On the other, social structures constrain or facilitate individuals' exercise of their agency. In other words, social causality is not only real; it is consequential.

Because of this, another point of convergence among the various authors in this book is the importance of systemic change in addressing injurious and unjust market outcomes. At the very least, harmful social structures ought to be changed. In addition—and this is the unique contribution of this chapter—we must face the critical questions of who will be held responsible for bringing about this change, why, and how we should go about identifying and justifying such obligations.

This chapter argues that it is not sufficient to talk about the potency of social structures and the resulting collective responsibility to safeguard or to change them as needed. It is just as important to carry these insights a step further and individuate such collective responsibility. This is particularly true if we are talking of our responsibility, both as individuals and as a community, for the harms our market transactions inflict on distant others. This article has a two-fold contribution. First, it argues the case for why the individual ascription of responsibility is essential, indeed unavoidable, if we are to talk of attenuating market harms to distant others. Second, it proposes a framework for weighing individual responsibility for collective harms.

Why We Should Individuate Collective Responsibility

It is important to distinguish three types of responsibility relevant for our study. The first is causal responsibility, that is, identifying the individual or collective action that brought about the outcome of interest. For example, emerging middle-class households in China and India have been in part causally responsible for the rise in food and gasoline prices, because of their increased consumption. The second is moral responsibility, that is, praiseworthiness or blameworthiness for a particular event. For example, tobacco firms are morally responsible for promoting their products despite their clearly injurious consequences for health. The third type of responsibility pertains to liability, the duty to correct or mitigate the ill effects of a particular outcome. For example, employers are liable for the misdeeds of their workers, such as an employee's theft of a customer's property.

Not all three types of responsibility are coincident. Causal responsibility is neither a necessary nor a sufficient condition for moral responsibility. Causal responsibility for a harm caused to another may, in fact, be justified, or excusable, or both and therefore not blameworthy. For example, Chinese and Indian middle classes are not morally responsible for the deleterious effects of the rise in commodity prices, even though, as economists know, they are one of the proximate causes of the increase in the prices of vital goods, such as food, minerals, and fossil fuels in recent decades.

Also, neither causal nor moral responsibility is a necessary condition for liability, as indicated in the case of employers being responsible for employee misdeeds. To take an example on a larger scale, taxpayers did not cause but were ultimately liable for the banking sector's excesses during the 2008–2009 global financial meltdown and the 2011–2012 euro crisis. Unless otherwise specified, "responsibility" refers to moral responsibility throughout this chapter.

Many of the chapters in this volume acknowledge our collective moral responsibility for correcting harmful social structures. For example, Margaret Archer argues that the reflexivity of agents incites the social change that emerges from the interaction of individual agents. Pierpaolo Donati notes a feedback effect in which agential action shapes mediating social structures in subsequent cycles and rounds of economic activity. Mary Hirschfeld calls for change at the social level, pursued through individuals' responsibility to shape their community's culture and politics. Christina Traina is emphatic that the focus should not be on the attribution of personal culpability for past wrongs but on the "future transformation of present injustices." These acknowledgments of a collective duty to effect needed systemic change means that, at a minimum, we as a collective are morally responsible for mitigating particularly severe market harms.

I argue that the acknowledgment of our collective responsibility for market structures is not good enough in dealing with the harms we inflict on distant others. We also need to individuate that collective responsibility, for both theoretical and practical reasons.

Theoretical Reasons

From a theoretical point of view, we must go beyond talk of collective responsibility, because moral agency ultimately lies with the individual.[1] It is true that the most deleterious market harms are not additive in nature, as in the case of global warming described in John Coleman's chapter. We cannot apportion in a strict arithmetic fashion causal responsibility, blameworthiness, and liability for climate change to specific individuals. To begin with, the solution requires collective action. Moreover, there is a synergistic dynamic in which the total harm is, in fact, much larger than the sum of individuals' respective contributions.

Nevertheless, despite this need for joint action, we must individuate such collective responsibility because that joint action arises from the many constituent individual contributions. Collective action is always initiated by individuals and is sustained by individuals continuing to work together. Corporations or other groups of individuals are not imbued with a moral agency separate from the moral agency of their constitutive leaders and members. Corporations incur fines and penalties for their misdeeds, but they do not go to jail. If anyone is incarcerated, it is the offending corporate officers, the key individual moral agents who plan, initiate, and direct corporate malfeasance. Similarly, from a theological viewpoint, it is not corporate groups or nations that will have to stand before God to account for the sins of economic oppression, unaddressed poverty, and a devastated ecology. It is individuals who will ultimately have to stand before God and account for their sins of commission and omission in regard to these unaddressed collective market ills.

Catholic moral theology clearly acknowledges the reality of social sin and its role in fostering personal sin. It also recognizes the need to rectify sinful social structures through collective action. Nevertheless, at the end of the day, Catholic theology holds that it is still personal conversion and action (together with grace) that ultimately hold the key to rectifying social sin. We see this even in the scriptures, especially in the repeated calls for personal conversion.

We have numerous examples of collective actions that successfully effected social change. Recall, the Nestlé boycott, the campaign against apartheid through divestment in South Africa, and the Cesar Chavez table-grape protest of an earlier generation. Even earlier, we see the abolitionist movement successfully winning over the British parliament to outlaw slave trade. More recently, we have the grassroots movement of college students that precipitated closer supervision of working conditions in apparel and electronics subcontractors. These are excellent examples of the kind of social change called for by the authors in this book. Nonetheless, it is ultimately individuals who initiated and persisted in pursuing these collective actions despite the hurdles arrayed against them.

Individuating collective responsibility is not an exercise in dividing up collective responsibility into its constituent individual components with mathematical precision. Rather, individuating collective responsibility is about sensitizing and informing individuals regarding their personal moral responsibility for discharging collective duties of which they are a part and to which they contribute.

Among the different kinds of justice described by Thomas Aquinas is general (or "legal") justice.[2] This calls on the individual to live up to his or her obligations to the common good. I propose that individuating collective responsibility would go a long way toward informing the individual of the nature and the demands of individual obligations to the common good.

A word of caution: By individuating collective responsibility, I do not mean that all requisite actions are exclusively or even necessarily performed singly—by the individual alone. It is very likely that many of the needed actions will have to occur in collaboration with others. (Recall Pope John XXIII's description of the phenomenon of socialization in *Mater et magistra*. Tasks that used to be accomplished by individuals acting on their own can no longer be done without the cooperation of ever-larger circles of people because of the increasing complexity of society.)

Individuating collective responsibility thus is also about identifying and sensitizing people to those personal duties to initiate and pursue joint action with others. In other words, far from precluding or minimizing corporate or cooperative action, individuating collective responsibility is, in fact, about improving such joint obligations by pushing individuals to think about their duties to work with others for the common good. In calling for individuating collective responsibility, I am not espousing methodological individualism. Both individuals and groups matter decisively. They are inseparable from one another, even as they are distinct, as the sociologists writing in this volume have stressed.

Practical Reasons

There are also practical reasons for individuating collective responsibility. First, globalization has greatly expanded the scope of the marketplace, from the local to literally the whole world. In an earlier age when the marketplace comprised largely neighbors and kin, market participants were bound to each other by more than just commercial relationships. In such a small local economy, there were, for example, not only bonds of mutual concern but also shaming mechanisms that prevented people from taking advantage of a weaker neighbor and from failing to live up to their share of common obligations, including mitigating harms that one may inflict on others within the same community. In that setting, free-riding, indifference, selfish behavior, and exploitation came at the risk of ruining one's noneconomic relationships with others or being made a pariah and left to fend for oneself.

Not so in the era of globalization. Economic exchange has come to be purely contractual, separate from other considerations. Moreover, it has become increasingly anonymous. When we buy a book online—even in the ecologically responsible purchase of a secondhand paperback through an Amazon-listed used book seller—we do not personally know the living and working conditions of those with whom we trade. Moreover, for many, people are simply clients or suppliers and nothing more. This turn toward impersonal exchanges has occurred at a time when we are ever more capable of inflicting harms on distant others, given the greater interdependence and the expansion in the scope of the marketplace brought about by globalization. As a result, most people do not care about the injurious ripple effects of their market transactions on distant others, nor do they have the incentive to care.

Individuating collective responsibility for market ills attenuates this problem by making people aware of both their personal causal links and their moral duties to these distant others. Ending a discussion of unjust economic relationships with a simple acknowledgment of a collective responsibility to change social structures does nothing to address this problem of indifference and impersonalism. We have to go farther and define concretely what precisely the individuals' duties are.

Second, globalization underscores our lack of a common view of morality. In a small local economy, market participants stood a better chance of sharing a common vision of the good. They were more likely to conform to some unspoken or informal rules when it came to helping one another or attenuating inadvertent market harms. Not so in a globalized economy of different cultures, ethnicities, and religions in which the most important commonality is a shared marketplace for exchanging goods and services. Given the nascent stage of this globalized marketplace, the community of nations is struggling to articulate a worldwide economic public morality—the formal and informal rules of what one should not do in the marketplace. (For example, note the unsuccessful attempts at developing legally binding global rules on cross-border financial trades in the wake of the 2008 financial debacle.)

There is as yet no fully developed global ethos concerning what the decent thing to do in the marketplace is. As a result, legal positivism fills the void. People simply conclude that what is legally permissible is morally permissible. The results are predictable, particularly in less-developed countries that have little bargaining power, that are desperate for investments and jobs, and that have weak social institutions. In many of these poor nations, we see a proliferation of sweatshops, child labor, and terribly one-sided contracts for mineral extraction generating little benefit to the host country.

Given such an underdeveloped global economic ethos, we cannot leave discourse on harm to distant others with general statements on our collective responsibility to change social structures. Given the legalistic mentality to resolving economic disputes or dilemmas, we cannot leave moral discourse at such a high level of abstraction and generality. We have to be specific when it comes to identifying market participants' causal and moral responsibilities since positivism is the default ethical reasoning in the global marketplace, given the absence of a common vision of the good. Not only will there be no action, but nations and peoples will not do their share unless required by law or shamed by the public (as in the case of the sweatshop movement). Having a clear-eyed method for individuating collective responsibility would go a long way toward understanding individual roles (whether as single consumer or citizen) in discharging our shared global economic responsibilities. The danger with undefined, "free-floating" responsibility is that whenever everyone is responsible, no one ends up being responsible, and nothing gets done.

Third, economic life is, by its nature, fraught with collective-action problems. Take the case of pollution. In an unfettered marketplace, firms have no incentive to curtail their dirty production processes because they can pass on the cost to the rest of the community by dumping their waste in the public commons—the community's rivers and air. They would not voluntarily internalize the cost of disposing these industrial by-products. Thus a common approach to this problem is for governments to intervene and force these firms to pay for such social costs either through taxation or by mandating some changes in these firms' activities.

Such a collective-action problem is also true at the individual level. Recall the prisoners' dilemma and Garrett Hardin's "Tragedy of the Commons." Optimum solutions to common problems often require individuals to sacrifice their personal interests. Unfortunately, people often free-ride on others' efforts or good will. This is the well-known problem of moral hazard in which people try to pass onto others the cost of their economic behavior. Other examples are the problem of overfishing that has depleted global fishing stocks, the overuse of antibiotics for agricultural use, and the recent bank bailouts.

Collective-action problems in economic life make it that much more urgent to individuate collective responsibility. Limiting our discourse to general discussions of collective responsibility will most likely lead to inaction. The less that is known about our personal duties regarding collective responsibility, the more abstract these obligations become and the more excuse there is for those who prefer to ignore or even deny the injurious effects of their economic activities on distant others.

Fourth, individuating collective responsibility is not an exercise in retrospective finger-pointing. It is, in fact, a forward-looking enterprise in rectifying wrongs for the sake of the next rounds of economic exchange. It is about identifying the moral agents who are in the best position to prevent future market ills. For example, identifying the origins of the problems of the 2008 global financial meltdown is not merely about imputing liability. It is also about understanding how individual market participants must behave differently to head off similar crises in the future.

Fifth, most people intuitively acknowledge that individual responsibilities vary in degree, duration, content, and warrants. Such differences are commonsensical and fair. But how do we make such differentiation unless we have a framework for taking into account individual differences? Individuating collective responsibility fills this need.

In sum, global economic integration, a pluralistic public square without a shared vision of the good, and collective-action problems are significant hurdles to acknowledging and acting on our individual and collective responsibility for the harmful ripple effects of our economic transactions on distant others. Unless we have a virtuous community, economic agents will most likely adopt lower standards and stick with what is legal, rather than what is moral. Individuating collective responsibility alerts people to their personal roles in discharging collective duties. In fact, by being rigorous in how we ascribe individual responsibility for corporate harms, we stand a better chance of moving legal positivists to take responsibility for—and action to mitigate—collective harms to distant others.

A Framework for Individuating Collective Responsibility

For all its importance, the ascription of individual responsibilities for collective harms is not an easy task. For example, legal scholars in the past century have grappled, unsuccessfully, to come up with a single set of universal rules that can adjudicate a wide variety of cases on who is liable for harms, including those collective in nature. The literature on tort jurisprudence reveals the complexity of such a task. In fact, courts have often been reduced to using prudential judgment in sorting through the maze of individual responsibilities.

Drawing from social philosophy, moral theology, and legal scholarship, I propose that there are at least five critical factors to consider in weighing individual agents' obligations for the injurious ripple effects of their market transactions, namely:

- the type and severity of harms;
- the nature of the economy;
- causality (that is, the causal chain of events);
- capabilities and knowledge of the moral agents; and
- the public ethos or the evaluator's philosophical commitments.

It is best to examine how this proposed framework works with an actual case, so let us take the controversial nature of international trade. Many former advocates of free trade have been forced to take a second look at the theoretical and practical arguments for unfettered cross-border trade. [3] In particular, developed nations have become increasingly alarmed at the collapse of their manufacturing sectors, displacing untold numbers of workers.

Type and Severity of Harms

Most people engage in economic activity in order to earn some income with which to purchase goods and services from the marketplace to satisfy their basic needs. Beyond these basic needs, they use their remaining income to satisfy their higher needs—to grow and develop body, mind, and spirit—and to save for old age or a rainy day. Economic activity serves a critical function: It allows people to secure the goods of the earth for their survival and growth. There is a fundamental utility to economic agency. In addition, one of the most important features of economic activity is that it is pursued communally. We create a division of labor; we specialize in production. We are interdependent because we can accomplish more by working together than if we were each to go solo. Thus barter or some form of market exchange is central to economic life.

Whenever people are chronically unable to satisfy even their most basic needs, not to mention their higher needs, we have a telltale sign that there are systemic problems in our shared economic life that need to be rectified. Instances of economic compulsion—when people are compelled to forego vital interests in an effort to protect other, even more vital interests—alert us that something is awry in the marketplace. In other words, most people would be disturbed to see their fellow human beings subjected to chronic,[4] involuntary economic deprivation. It is often the suffering of others that serves as an early warning of systemic market ills.

In addition to these market harms, the severity of such chronic economic deprivation is also another important indicator. It is reasonable to assume that the more severe the injury and the more widespread and persistent it is, the more grievous are the systemic flaws of the marketplace that need to be rectified.

Thus I propose that the nature and the degree of harm are the first set of factors that we have to consider in examining our obligations to distant others. A concrete benchmark we can use to detect and measure the severity of such harms is the basket of basic human needs: food, clothing, shelter, education, rest, and medical care.

In the case of international trade, such harms can be seen in both anecdotal accounts and telltale statistics on U.S. manufacturing workers who have been laid off on account of cheap imports. In many instances, erstwhile middle-class families have slipped below poverty levels, unable to secure their basic needs because of unemployment, underemployment, or low pay. Long-term unemployment has even driven some of these families to homelessness, completely dependent on assistance for food and medical care. Clearly, it is these injuries that make the community aware that there are flaws in market operations.

Nature of the Economy

The second factor that has to be weighed is the nature of the economy. Tracking down the genesis of these harms requires an understanding of the nature and the dynamics of market exchange. In the case of the distressed manufacturing workers, we want to know how they got to be where they are.

To begin with, consider how the market works. Price changes are at the heart of modern markets because they are a cost-efficient way of conveying huge amounts of information simultaneously to widely dispersed economic agents. These price changes signal to market participants how they ought to alter the disposition of their resources in response to the most recent developments in market conditions. Such signals and constant adjustments are critical because of the dynamism of the marketplace. It evolves constantly, and market participants have to react accordingly. This explains the market's much-touted strength: allocative efficiency, the ability to direct scarce resources in the timeliest manner to their most valued uses. This is the allocative function of the market's price mechanism.

Market prices perform another function—they are instrumental in distributing resources across market participants. The purchasing power of people's income is determined by the price of the goods and services they buy from the output markets. In addition, their income is a function of the price they can get from the sale of their labor, services, or capital in the input markets (i.e., wages, salaries, capital gains, dividends, and interest). In other words, price changes are a de facto redistribution of burdens and benefits across the community.

The allocative and distributive functions of price are independent of one another and are often at odds with the social goals they serve. For example, consider the issue of offshore outsourcing. Due to the global economic integration of the past three decades, many labor-intensive or low-skill goods and services can be supplied much cheaper from abroad. Thus allocative efficiency would call for outsourcing these to these foreign suppliers; and indeed, many firms have done so. Domestic consumers benefit because cheaper foreign imports are equivalent to an increase in their real incomes. In theory, displaced local manufacturing workers and firms could also benefit (after retraining and retooling) by shifting to producing higher value and higher skill goods and services. This would be a win–win proposition for everyone involved—consumers and producers both here and abroad.

Unfortunately, what is true in theory often fails in practice. Economic theory assumes that ours is a frictionless economy, goods and services are homogenous, and there is perfect information. These market features mean that displaced domestic manufacturers should be able to easily secure new skills and higher paying jobs, while firms should be able to readily pivot and produce new and more sophisticated products. These are heroic assumptions and the Achilles heel of international trade theory.

Outsourcing is not always a win–win proposition because displaced domestic manufacturing workers and firms face steep transaction costs in moving to another economic activity. This is particularly true for middle-aged and less-educated workers. Thus the distributive consequences of a more efficient disposition of global resources through offshore outsourcing are quite uneven. Many benefit (e.g., consumers and foreign suppliers) but at the expense of a relatively few who have to bear the brunt of the cost of adjustment (e.g., manufacturing workers unable to upgrade their skills). These domestic workers and firms displaced by foreign trade may be said to suffer from the adverse pecuniary externalities of regular market operations (called "externalities," because they are unintended effects on third parties and "pecuniary" because they are caused by a change in prices). Some of these effects may be severe (e.g., long-term unemployment, homelessness). In other words, price changes produce benefits and inflict losses.

Many adverse pecuniary externalities are the result of people's wrongdoing (e.g., the 2008 subprime mortgage fiasco) or flawed government policies (e.g., the U.S. ethanol program precipitating higher food prices). However, the majority of injurious pecuniary externalities are the result of normal market operations. For example, the clamor of small investors for ever-higher returns for their retirement accounts has led to new investment vehicles that speculate in commodities, including food and oil. These speculative trades have led to greater volatility in vital commodities such as food and gasoline, inflicting even further hardship and uncertainty on an already overburdened poor. People's appetite for blue-fin tuna and shark fin soup has put these two fish species at risk of extinction. Many U.S. residents' love for driving, the lack of mass transit infrastructure in the United States, and the torrid growth rate of car ownership in China have resulted in poor countries expending more of their scarce foreign exchange on ever more expensive gasoline imports.

Given their increasing wealth, consumers' greater demand for beef and biofuels has resulted in higher grain prices than should have been the case. Since the price of credit is inversely proportional to the creditworthiness of borrowers, the price of credit is regressive: The poor and the disadvantaged pay higher interest rates than the rest of the population. The demand for palm oil in many food products has led to the destruction of forests in Indonesia to make room for new palm oil plantations. Economic growth, thanks largely to globalization, has accelerated the use of fossil fuels and has exacerbated global warming. These are but a sampling of how ordinary market transactions can be injurious to distant others, particularly the poor and future generations. In other words, adverse pecuniary externalities are an expected part of market operations, including the displacement of manufacturing workers in advanced countries as part of the normal reallocation of global resources and factors of production.

In sum, understanding how and why our market transactions affect distant others is essential in any effort to examine our obligations. Thus the nature of the economy is a second important factor to consider as we seek to know how collective harms arise and what we can do about them.

Causality

A third factor to consider is causality. For most people, establishing causality is an essential step in determining their obligations to distant others for the harms they may have inadvertently inflicted. This is an intuitive insight. Most people will find it not only commonsensical but also fair.

Market participants are bound together in real relationships. We find this articulated in greater detail elsewhere in this volume, in Margaret Archer's notion of nonadditive emergents, Pierpaolo Donati's reflexivity among relational subjects, and Douglas Porpora's exposition of critical realism and its web of relationships. As a result, people's market transactions have a real impact on each other. There is an ontological foundation to economic causality.

The marketplace can be described as an emergent. Sociologists argue that social structures are the product of numerous individuals interacting with one another. These emergents are nonadditive, that is, it is best to view them as a synergy in which the resulting whole is greater than the sum of its individual parts. An excellent example is the common good. Another good example is the marketplace. Recall Mary Hirschfeld's chapter in which she rehearses Adam Smith's point on the value created by a division of labor. By working together and specializing in one facet of the operation, workers are able to produce far more pins than if they had worked independently of each other. And, of course, we could go beyond Smith's example of the pin factory and point to his oft-cited observation on the individual action of the butcher, the baker, and the brewer ultimately promoting the good of the entire community by making their goods and services readily available. People's easy access to these goods and services is another feature of the marketplace as an emergent. Readers who are mathematically inclined or familiar with economic theory can recall the phenomenon of increasing returns to scale. The increased output is not merely additive but is the result of joint action.

This mutual interaction between social structures and individuals has significant ramifications for economic policy and morality. First, it means that market participants collectively make the marketplace what it is through their individual economic transactions that reinforce market custom, law, and usage. For example, the pay disparity between the CEO and the ordinary worker is highest in the United States (anywhere from 600- to 1,000-fold), less so in Europe, and even less so in Japan. Such disparities in CEO pay across nations are partly a function of cultural norms and the formal and informal rules people tolerate or maintain. While outsized CEO compensation is acceptable and perhaps expected in business circles in the United States, it is considered bad form in Japan. The marketplace and its characteristics are ultimately the creation of its constituent market participants' practices and attitudes.

A second implication pertains to the potency of the marketplace in making life either easier or more difficult for individual market participants—the restrictions and enablements sociologists speak of. For example, in societies in which there is a high level of honesty and mutual trust, the transaction costs of conducting business are generally lower. Shopowners take consumers' word at face value and accept product returns, even for the more expensive electronic items, despite the losses incurred by retailers. In contrast, in places where fraud is commonplace, market participants are wary all the time and expend additional resources on safeguards. Shoplifting greatly adds to the price individual consumers pay for their goods. In other words, the cost of our living in a particular society is determined by its underlying institutions.

Third, the marketplace, like every social institution, is subject to change, whether for good or for ill. Social structures and institutions can change no matter how deeply entrenched they are in the custom, law, and usage undergirding them. For example, the feudal mode of production eventually gave way to the industrial factory system, just as the latter is now in its own turn giving way to the postindustrial knowledge economy. In other words, markets can and do change. They evolve over time, often due to technological breakthroughs (e.g., invention of the steam engine), organizational innovations (e.g., Fordist mass production, offshore outsourcing, Facebook), or changing public morality (e.g., nineteenth-century social legislation).

Note that such evolution is not always for the best. For example, activities that were not traditionally governed by market rules have now been commercialized. Examples are commercial surrogacy, the sale of human ova and sperm, and paid child care. This is the phenomenon of commodification. Market rules are increasingly used even in traditionally noncommercial realms.

These three features of the marketplace as an emergent reality point to the real relationships that bind market participants to one another and to the marketplace of which they are a part and to which they contribute. And because of these relationships, market participants can be held responsible (in all three senses: causally, morally, and with liability) for the injurious ripple effects of their economic decisions on distant others. In particular, these relationships lead to the following conclusions:

- Individual market transactions directly affect and effect market outcomes.
- Individual market transactions indirectly contribute to and reinforce existing market rules and practices, whether helpful or hurtful.
- Such market outcomes, rules, and practices create benefits and/or inflict injuries in the lives of market participants, both current and future.

In other words, individuals directly and indirectly affect one another, given their interdependence and the market customs, law, and usage they perpetuate as market participants. Individual market participants are linked together in a web of real relationships. As a consequence, individual market participants can be linked to distant others and to the marketplace as an emergent in a chain of causation. Individual market participants causally contribute to both beneficial and adverse pecuniary externalities.

There is much more that can be said about causality. In particular, the legal literature on torts provides a wealth of insights on how to establish causality when it comes to harms. Unfortunately, space constraints do not allow that investigation here.[5]

Applied to our case of free trade, we can say that consumers who purchase imports in lieu of local manufactures are contributory causes of the displacement of domestic workers who suddenly find themselves unemployed or underemployed due to freer cross-border trade.

Capabilities of Individual Market Participants

A fourth set of considerations pertains to the capabilities of individual market participants, though the argument is limited to a discussion only of moral responsibility and liability, that is, the duty to rectify wrongs.

Is there an obligation to attend to these adverse pecuniary externalities? If so, which ones and why? Who is morally responsible and who is liable for rectifying the ill effects of regular market operations and why? How strong are these duties, and is there a half-life to these obligations? Fulfilling our collective responsibility for market ills requires answers to these questions because, at the end of the day, it is individual moral agents, working both singly and in small groups, who will have to discharge our collective responsibility. In this regard, I propose that the capabilities of individual moral agents will be an important consideration.

In brief, everything else equal in terms of causal contribution, those who are more capable bear greater responsibilities (defined both as moral culpability and as liability) compared to those who are less capable. We can define capability in very broad terms. At the very least, such capability pertains to the person's ability to contribute toward correcting harms markets cause to distant others. Such ability includes personal skills and talents, income and wealth, social and networking capital, and sociohistorical location and role within the community. This also includes the person's knowledge. Knowledge here refers not only to what the person knows but also to what the person should have known given the resources available to that person.

Vincible ignorance, that is, ignorance that could have been easily overcome by the person given the above capabilities, does not absolve one from responsibility or liability. This is an important qualification, because some people avoid responsibility by refusing to inform or educate themselves about the ills swirling around them. The greater the degree of knowledge, the greater the degree of responsibility.

Just as with causality, most people will find it intuitive that individual responsibility is a function of individual capability (including knowledge). Many will find this commonsensical and fair. In our example of unintended consequences from price changes, mitigating the more severe effects of adverse pecuniary externalities will fall on those with the resources to ameliorate market ills, not to mention those who have benefitted enormously from such price changes. The U.S. Trade Adjustment Assistance program that provides financial assistance to workers in industries negatively affected by trade is an example. These programs are funded from general taxes and, therefore, are ultimately paid for by people who are presumed to be in a position to bear the cost of amelioration, given the progressive sliding scale of U.S. taxation. Furthermore, consumers with the necessary wherewithal or those who opt for a smaller consumption basket may choose to purchase local manufactures and agricultural produce as their own private contribution to cushioning the impact of international trade on their fellow citizens. We have already seen examples of this in the organic and local food movements. The sentiment is similar to that underlying the fair trade movement, in which consumers pay more than the market price because relationships are valuable and based on mutual respect.

Philosophical Commitments

Finally, the philosophical commitments of the evaluator and/or the general public are important factors in establishing individual and collective responsibility for harm to distant others. To begin with, people's values affect their judgment on

- whether there is a problem or a harm to begin with;
- if there is, the threshold for what constitutes injury severe enough to warrant ameliorative action;
- how to weigh causation and its contribution to the harm;
- how to weigh causation versus capability in the ascription of individual and collective responsibility;

- who is morally responsible and who is liable;
- the strength and duration of the resulting obligations; and
- which injured parties deserve assistance, how much, and for how long.

Note that these issues have to be addressed regardless of whether we are talking of individual or collective responsibility.

Consider how different philosophical approaches might address these issues. Libertarians would most likely dismiss the entire subject matter of this volume. Beyond avoiding force and fraud, there are no residual obligations outside of contracts, whether to distant others or anyone else for that matter. We are bound only by contractual obligations and have fully discharged our duties once we have lived up to the terms of our contracts. Market participants know and will pursue what is in their best interest, and they will not participate in market exchange unless they can improve their pretrade position. Thus, it is argued, manufacturing workers displaced by international trade ought to be able to find a new niche for themselves in the marketplace. After all, they should have been honing their skills to be able to move to higher value-added jobs at higher pay. Libertarians would argue that individuals ought to take care of themselves as they voluntarily participate in the marketplace. This includes distant others. Hence, they would most likely claim that there is no sense in talking about our duties for the harms we inflict on distant others. These have already been internalized by the market participants in their cost calculations.

Advocates of unfettered markets will most likely argue that the allocative function of price trumps its distributive dimension. Price changes may inflict short-term distributional adjustment costs, but in the long term, a more efficient economy will benefit all, including those who had to bear the initial adjustment cost. A rising tide will eventually lift all boats. An unfettered marketplace will be more efficient in the long run and will be able to reabsorb the manufacturing workers displaced in the short term by international trade. The displacement is merely temporary, from their point of view.

People who subscribe to John Rawls's lexical rules will argue that there are strong individual and collective duties to assist the most disadvantaged, who in all likelihood will be the ones most severely affected by adverse pecuniary externalities. Far from benefitting the most disadvantaged, the pecuniary externalities of market operations are in fact hurting the most vulnerable. In our current case, it is likely that low-skilled or less-educated workers will be most severely disadvantaged by international trade. In contrast, skeptics of a Rawlsian approach such as Robert Nozick might call such transfers and their requisite taxes "the slavery of the talented."

As is clear from Christina Traina's essay in this volume, feminists who advocate an ethics of care will most likely call for ameliorating the plight of those negatively affected by pecuniary externalities. They will also most likely vigorously call for systemic change to make such unintended consequences less injurious. They have a much lower threshold of what constitutes severe harm when it comes to identifying when and to whom assistance should be provided. They will be sympathetic to the plight of displaced manufacturing workers and call for social action to assist them with transition into a new role in the marketplace.

Catholic social thought (CST) and proponents of virtue theory will most likely acknowledge strong individual moral responsibility and liability for harm to distant others. In the first place, as we find in the parable of the Good Samaritan, there are no bounds to who is a Christian's neighbor. Distant others are neighbors and deserve assistance even if the causal contribution to the harm is minimal. The capacity to help will most likely be the most significant determinant of the strength of an individual's or group's obligation to help. Of course, such a duty to help is intensified if the causal contribution to the harm turns out to be significant. In addition, there will also be strong obligations to rectify the systemic ills going forward in order to prevent or minimize future harms. Second, both CST and virtue theory will call on individuals to redress harms and provide assistance to distant others because Christian moral life calls for such action. Recall the opening lines of the Second Vatican Council's *Gaudium et Spes* on how followers of Christ empathize with the hopes and dreams, the grief and anxieties of others, particularly of the poor. Thus, for CST and proponents of virtue theory, there is both a personal and a collective duty to assist those who have been adversely affected by international trade. In fact, the more individual agents have benefitted from such trade, the greater their obligation to share some of their gains with those who have had to bear the brunt of the costs of such trade.

This brief sketch of how different ethical approaches will most likely approach the problem of distant harm to others illustrates the importance of people's philosophical commitments in shaping their perception of reality and their views on rights and wrongs. Consequently, it is important to consider the values people bring with them into the public square of ideas. It also helps people better understand how or why they might differ from one another in their views regarding the harms they inflict on distant others.

Conclusion

The theme of this volume is our moral responsibility for harms markets cause to distant others. This chapter has argued that it is not sufficient to acknowledge that there is a collective obligation to respond. It is just as important to take this a step further and individuate that collective responsibility, to the extent possible.

This claim is not rooted in the deeply flawed position called methodological individualism, in which only individuals matter and social emergents are not real. Individuating collective responsibility does not preclude joint action by individuals. In fact, the ascription of individual responsibility also includes the individual's obligation to join with others in pursuing necessary collective action. Furthermore, even as it seeks to establish who is responsible or liable for correcting past wrongs, individuating collective responsibility is not simply an exercise in retrospective finger-pointing. It is also about establishing individual responsibility for avoiding or rectifying market ills going forward.

In a globalized marketplace that is driven primarily by contracts rather than by shared values, it is even more important to individuate collective responsibility, if only to sensitize people to their moral obligations to distant others. In the absence of a clear-eyed method for specifying this collective obligation even further, it is very likely that talk of collective responsibility for social change will not result in concrete action. Indifference and free-ridership are problems that economic globalization has exacerbated in the marketplace. As the saying goes, when everyone is responsible for a harm, no one ends up taking responsibility for correcting the injury.

As argued above, there are at least five factors that need to be considered in any reasonable account of our individual and collective responsibility for harms to distant others. These include the nature and severity of the harm; the nature of the economy; causal relations; the capabilities of agents; and the philosophical commitments of the evaluators, the general public, or both.[6] These are not the only factors that need to be considered; social philosophers, legal scholars, and policymakers will surely have more to add to this list. Yet these five considerations are the most fundamental to the necessary task of individuating the collective duty we have in correcting systemic economic harms.

NOTES

1. See, for example, Archer's argument that despite the importance of social structures, agency is ascribed to individuals alone.
2. Thomas Aquinas, *Summa Theologica* (New York: Benzinger Brothers, 1947–1948), II-II, 58.5.
3. See, for example, Paul Samuelson, "Where Ricardo and Mill Rebut and Confirm Arguments of Mainstream Economists Against Globalization," *Journal of Economic Perspectives,* 18 (2004):161–180.
4. I am not referring to natural disasters or sporadic agricultural failures. Hence, I am careful to note that these are chronic instances of deprivation.
5. For a brief survey of the literature, see Albino Barrera, *Market Complicity and Christian Ethics* (Cambridge, UK: Cambridge University Press, 2011), ch. 4. Christopher Kutz, *Complicity: Ethics and Law for a Collective Age.* (New York: Cambridge University Press, 2000) also addresses the problem posed by collective problems for the ascription of individual responsibility.
6. Coleman's contribution to this volume on global warming is another good example of the application of many of these factors in his assessment of who is morally culpable for our current ecological ills.

REFERENCES

Aquinas, Thomas. *Summa Theologica.* Translated by the Fathers of the English Dominican Province. 3 vols. New York: Benzinger Brothers, 1947–1948.
Barrera, Albino. *Market Complicity and Christian Ethics.* Cambridge, UK: Cambridge University Press, 2011.
Hardin, Garrett. "The Tragedy of the Commons." *Science,* 162 (1968):1243–1248.
John XXIII. *Mater et Magistra.* Boston: Daughters of St. Paul, 1961.
Kutz, Christopher. *Complicity: Ethics and Law for a Collective Age.* Cambridge Studies in Philosophy and Law. Cambridge, UK: Cambridge University Press, 2000.
Nozick, Robert. *Anarchy, State, and Utopia.* New York: Basic Books, 1974.
Rawls, John. *A Theory of Justice.* Cambridge, MA: Belknap Press of Harvard University Press, 1971.
Samuelson, Paul. "Where Ricardo and Mill Rebut and Confirm Arguments of Mainstream Economists Against Globalization." *Journal of Economic Perspectives,* 18 (2004):161–180.
Vatican Council II. *Gaudium et Spes.* Boston: Daughters of St. Paul, 1965.

PART FOUR

Implications

10

Social Causality and Market Complicity

SPECIFYING THE CAUSAL ROLES OF PERSONS AND STRUCTURES

Daniel K. Finn

THE SINGLE MOST intractable methodological problem facing Christian economic ethics is how to account for the causally rooted moral responsibility of market participants for harms that markets cause to distant others. Such a concern has been the focus of this volume of essays. The stitches in the shirt I am wearing were likely sewn by a woman in Asia. Her participation in the market may have increased her economic well-being, but even now she might be subject to unjust practices at her workplace. And, unbeknownst to either her or me, there may be a woman in Mexico whose economic security was swept away when the textile firm where she used to work went bankrupt due to lower-priced clothing produced by Asian seamstresses. To what extent, if any, does my purchase of this shirt make me morally complicit in the harms caused in the lives of these two women?

Christians, of course, have many warrants for the obligation to assist others in their need that are completely independent of whether the believer played any role in causing the problem. Hebrew law required that the owner of the field of grain leave the corners unharvested so that widows, orphans, and resident aliens would have access to food. Jesus taught his disciples that love of neighbor was to be their central moral commitment. And Christian teaching on individual property ownership—whether in the early Church, the Middle Ages, or the Reformation—made clear that those with a surplus were under a moral obligation to share with those unable to meet their own needs.

Yet beyond these warrants, the topic at hand is how, simply because we are market participants, we have a moral responsibility for the harms that markets cause to distant others. This is important for three reasons. First, moral arguments rooted in the Christian tradition are typically unconvincing to those who do not share Christian faith; arguments rooted in causal relationships are more persuasive in a secular world. Second, articulating the relation of social causality and moral responsibility provides an important additional reason why Christians should be concerned about their participation in markets and involved in structuring those markets in a better way. Third, because markets are truly beneficial in so many ways, without an analysis of their structural shortcomings, both ignorance and economic interest tend to focus society's moral energy on the relief of suffering without addressing its causes.

The Problems We Face

The discipline of ethics, whether in philosophy or theology, has traditionally derived moral responsibility for harms caused in the lives of others from individual causal efficacy. Putting it briefly, if I caused a problem (or played a meaningful part in causing it), I am responsible (to some degree or other) for that problem. Morality here is based in causality, among other things. A second traditional source of moral responsibility is the intention of an actor to participate in some harmful action, in many cases leaving that actor morally responsible even if he were not able to fulfill his intention. Legal philosopher Christopher Kutz illustrates this traditional approach of ethics by examining the firebombing of Dresden during World War II.[1]

From February 13–15, 1945, over 1,000 U.S. and British planes dropped thousands of tons of bombs and incendiary devices on Dresden, largely destroying some fifteen square miles surrounding the city center and killing tens of thousands of innocent civilians. Those planning and approving the attack were, of course, primarily responsible. Yet here we consider the pilots, whom we would also hold morally responsible. There were so many planes dropping so many bombs that any one pilot might be argued to have had only a very small influence on the ultimate conflagration, yet each of those pilots did indeed contribute and thus there is moral responsibility. One way to see this is to consider what would have occurred had only one pilot done the bombing. While the damage would not have been nearly as extensive, there would indeed have been a localized fire-storm with both destruction and death. Here it is clear that the individual causal efficacy of each pilot makes him complicit in the harms caused.

But any time hundreds of planes take off on a military mission, there are always a few pilots who run into engine trouble and must turn back without participating causally in the destruction. Kutz goes on to note that these pilots also bear responsibility because of their intention to partici-pate in the plan carried out by others. Thus, in traditional ethical analysis, not just causal efficacy but the intention to participate in causing harm can generate moral responsibility.

Much more can be said about the details of how we might assess the causal responsibility of the various participants in the raid on Dresden, but our focus here is on the difference between this kind of traditional causal analysis in ethics and that which is necessary in understanding causal relationships within the market. There are two fundamental differences.

Although one pilot acting alone would create a significant portion of the damaged caused by the raid, no single consumer in the absence of other consumers in the market would have any effect across the globe. More concretely, any one of us could drop out of the market completely without there being any reduction in the harms markets cause to others.

Second, unlike the pilots—both those who dropped their bombs and those who turned back—participants in the market generally have no intention to cause harm to others.

Thus our challenge is to articulate the moral responsibility that arises from our participation in markets even though none of us makes a percep-tible difference in the harms markets cause and none intends those harms in the first place. This challenge requires a shift in conceptual framework.

The traditional assessment of moral responsibility entails a sort of arithmetic estimate of causal responsibility, rooted as it is at the level of individual action. Yet as Douglas Porpora articulates in his chapter, our involvement in social structures occurs at the "higher" level of *social* reality. Thus an accurate assessment of moral responsibility within social struc-tures must be broadened to include a field of structured relationships—relationships not simply among individuals but among the preexisting social positions that individuals enter into. As Christina Traina put it in this volume, the shift required is something like that which occurred in physics in the move from Newtonian mechanics to the theory of relativity.

The more comprehensive view incorporates the earlier approach as a subset, while the earlier approach has no awareness of the more comprehensive vision. As will become clear, we must come to see social causality as more relational than arithmetic.

Sociological Resources

Mainstream economics is notoriously individualistic in its conception of economic life, and, as a result, social structures of all kinds (e.g., firms, government, markets) are undertheorized within economic science. In contrast, sociologists have paid consistent and careful attention to social structures and their impact in people's lives. Thus Christian economic ethics has much to gain from a conversation with sociology. In what follows, attention is focused on what sociology has to say about social structures (the relationships among people), largely ignoring its similarly helpful analysis of culture (what people think and say).

There are significant differences in how different schools of sociology understand institutions. Some approaches have put so much emphasis on the influence of structural forces that the actions of persons are understood to be largely determined by their context.[2] Persons are seen as little more than carriers of those forces, pushed around by what sociologist Margaret Archer has termed "hydraulic pressure." That is, persons retain little if any moral autonomy in a world where their actions and even their thinking are heavily conditioned by forces beyond their control. Christian ethics cannot work with such a deterministic understanding of the interaction of persons and social structures; it is empirically inaccurate and undermines any possibility for a full moral life.

A quite opposite approach is taken by the more individualistic perspectives within sociology—typically called methodological individualism—that understand social structures as little more than the aggregation of the actions of individual persons.[3] From this perspective, only individuals have real causal impact, and, in the extreme, our descriptions of social organizations (e.g. the firm, the family, the government) are little more than convenient verbal summaries for the effects that individuals have when they act in cooperation with others.[4] From the point of view of Christian ethics, there is indeed a clear place for individual moral responsibility, but by not adequately portraying the causal impact of institutions in the lives of individuals, this perspective actually overstates the causal and moral responsibility that individuals have for ordinary life.

Consider electoral politics.[5] In the United States, every member of the House of Representatives is up for election every two years. When the election is over, we say "the people have spoken." And while there is much truth to this, it is also seriously misleading. There are a number of difficulties in ensuring that the views of citizens eventuate in a Congress that reflects those views. The effect of money in campaigns is well known, but here let us focus on the phenomena of gerrymandering.

Consider a hypothetical example where all voters in the United States are unwavering members of one of the two main political parties; all are either Democrats or Republicans. Presume further that 60% of all citizens are committed Republicans but that the vast majority of Republicans live in heavily Republican congressional districts (e.g., districts where 75% of voters are Republican). If most Democrats live in less heavily Democratic districts (say with only 60% of voters being Democrats), the Congress will be made up of a majority of Democrats in spite of the Republicans' 60% majority in the nation. This fundamental fact of electoral politics leads the majority party in state governments (where election districts are defined) to strive to draw the boundaries of election districts to favor their own party's candidates for both state and national elections.

As this example makes clear, interpreting election outcomes as simply the result of the voting by individuals conceals structural forces at play and far overstates the causal efficacy of the action of individual voters. In the same way, an individualistic conception of agents acting in a market that does not attend to the market as a social structure provides an empirically inaccurate description. Like the deterministic approach within sociology, the individualistic perspective cannot provide to Christian ethics an adequate analysis of economic life.

Much more could be said about the options available within sociology, but the point here is that Christian ethicists hoping to employ sociological analysis to clarify issues of moral responsibility in markets must make a choice among the options available. It is the contention of this essay that the most fruitful option is the critical realist school of sociology. The epistemological and ontological assumptions of this school are, in my opinion, closest to those of the Catholic tradition and even to Christian ethics more broadly.

In the critical realist school, sorting out the relationship between structure and agency is essential. From this perspective, only humans are agents, but social structures have a causal impact in the lives of those agents. To understand this, it is important to understand how social structures "emerge" from the actions of individual humans, and this in turn requires attention to the fundamental notion of emergence as a scientific concept.

Emergence as an Ontological Reality

There are few notions in science as fundamental as emergence and few as helpful to Christian ethicists. In his book, *What Is a Person?*, sociologist Christian Smith defines emergence as "the process of constituting a new reality with its own particular characteristics through the interactive combination of other, different entities that are necessary to create the new entity but that do not contain the characteristics present in the new entity."[6] Perhaps the most telling example of emergence is water. Arising from the combination of hydrogen and oxygen, water has characteristics quite different from the characteristics of either of those two elements. Most basically, while both oxygen and hydrogen feed a fire, water will extinguish it. It would be a severe form of reductionism to claim that we can understand water simply by analyzing the two elements that come together to form it. For our purposes, because the market "emerges" from the actions of individual market participants, and because the market is often reductively understood as nothing more than the sum of all the actions of individual market participants, understanding how emergence works is essential to any moral analysis of markets.

Smith explains that emergence involves four things:

> First, two or more entities that exist at a "lower" level interact or combine. Second, that interaction or combination serves as the basis of some new, real entity that has existence at a "higher" level. Third, the existence of the new higher-level entity is fully dependent upon the two or more lower-level entities interacting or combining, as they could not exist without doing so. Fourth, the new, higher-level entity nevertheless possesses characteristic qualities (e.g., structures, qualities, capacities, textures, mechanisms) that cannot be reduced to those of the lower-level entities that gave rise to the new entity possessing them.[7]

From protons and neutrons, which are emergents from up quarks and down quarks at the subatomic level, to lawnmowers, which are higher level emergents from blades, wheels, pistons, and a variety of other items, the reality of emergence is ubiquitous in both nature and social life. And as lawnmowers, computers, and refrigerators indicate, emergence is often the result of careful human design, but it does not need to be so.

Once we understand the reality of emergence, we understand more clearly why reductionism is such a serious problem, since it attempts to explain phenomena by reducing them to the elements that generate those phenomena. One can no better understand water by understanding the characteristics of hydrogen and oxygen than one can understand a human person by understanding the biological or physical elements and forces that make human persons possible. From the perspective of Christian theology, this insight demonstrates the futility of the efforts of many sociobiologists to explain human moral behavior by means of certain hypothesized tendencies of our genes. More to the point for this essay, emergence makes clear the futility of an individualistic interpretation of social life.

Understanding Social Structures

Social structures are fundamental to any understanding of social life, and critical realist sociologist Douglas Porpora has helpfully outlined the four basic options within sociology. Some schools of sociology have seen structures as simply "patterns of aggregate behavior," while others describe them as "law-like regularities that govern the behavior of social facts." Others see them as largely "collective rules" structuring human behavior. Yet the critical realist approach, taken by Porpora, understands social structures as "systems of human relationships among social positions."[8]

Consider the example of a social structure known as a university. It comprises many sorts of relationships, but the most basic is that between teacher and student. The standard route to becoming a member of a university faculty is to earn a doctoral degree. But a degree cannot make one a teacher; only having students can do that. Being a teacher is not simply a characteristic of an individual but is a relationship among preexisting social positions.

Although university faculty members have considerable influence over the social dynamics within their classrooms, those relationships are structured by both expectations and explicit rules built into the professor/ student relationship. Students arrive on the first day expecting to receive and complete assignments, and faculty members expect to provide information and structure classroom conversations to lead students to greater knowledge of the content of the course. Consider now the enablements, restrictions, and incentives that are implicit in the preexisting relationships into which persons enter when they take on the roles of college student or professor.

The social structure we call a university enables students to learn from well-informed persons and enables professors both to channel student effort in ways conducive to learning and to have time and support for scholarly writing. Simultaneously, however, students are restricted by their professors' course requirements and faculty members themselves are restricted by the expectation of their department, for example, to give students grades and to publish research in professional journals. Both groups face incentives embodied in the social structure (i.e., in the relationship). Students want to perform well to receive good grades that will enable them to achieve a job or a place in a graduate program. Faculty members want to do well in order to keep their jobs, gain tenure, and enjoy a reputation as good teachers and scholars.

Returning now to our question about the causal impact of social structures, we can see that structures exercise their causal influence through enablements, restrictions, and incentives that individual actors confront when they enter into the preexisting relationships that constitute those structures. But, as we saw earlier, this influence is not deterministic; it does not operate as if by hydraulic pressure. Instead, this influence only has an effect insofar as it affects the choices individual agents make in trying to accomplish their goals while facing those enablements, restrictions, and incentives.

The Economic View of Markets

Economists are well known for their enthusiastic endorsement of markets, due to the remarkable effectiveness of markets in coordinating the activity of untold numbers of market participants. In his graduate economics courses, that great proponent of markets Milton Friedman regularly relied on the example of a simple pencil. The various parts of a pencil come from different regions of the earth, but anyone of us can buy a pencil for a few cents, and, most important, we do not have to concern ourselves with the complexities of coordination and distribution systems that brought these various inputs together to produce this quite practical writing instrument.

The function of prices is so central to the market system that economist sometimes refer to the market itself as "the price system." Consumers react to changes in prices quite often, for example, moving from a newly more expensive product to another that is cheaper and provides more or less the same benefits. Many Pepsi drinkers buy Coke when it's on sale, and higher gasoline prices lead people to buy smaller cars. But even more important to the efficiency of the economic system is the reaction of producers to changes in the price of inputs to production.

If the price of petroleum rises because new oil wells are in places where it's more expensive to drill, many industrial users of petroleum products will simply have to pay the higher price because there may be no feasible substitute, but some will find it attractive to switch to, say, natural gas to produce energy. And as the prices of wind turbines and solar collectors fall with economies of scale in their production, we may anticipate that power companies will in the long run shift away from fossil fuels toward renewables. Yet it is not simply long-term trends that the price system mediates. Even short-term changes—such as a rise in the price of coffee due to a freeze in Columbia or the drop in the price of natural gas due to the new technology of fracking—is conveyed to consumers and other producers rapidly through a change in price.

Although a change in price typically leaves some market participants with less attractive options, it also typically leaves others with more attractive ones. If petroleum becomes more expensive, the demand for both coal and renewable energy sources rises, benefitting producers there. If the price of coffee rises, consumers will drink more tea, improving the economic prospects of those who grow and market tea. And while those producers and consumers made worse off by a rise in price will frequently scale back their use of that product, those other market participants made better off by that price change will typically expand their production.

The mainstream economic view of all this is fundamentally individualistic. When prices change, individual market participants—whether consumers or producers—face a new set of options and make changes in their economic activity, to take advantage of new opportunities or to make the best of a newly bad situation. Particularly with global markets, economic life is characterized by long chains of exchanges, but economic theory focuses on how individuals react. As Pierpaolo Donati has argued in this volume, the mainstream economic paradigm treats the market as a sort of "black box" within which offers to buy and sell by producers and consumers interact with each other. The box is opaque because economists spend little time examining how those exchanges actually occur and instead stress the decision that each market participant has to make when market conditions change. This, of course, is like thinking about elections as the results of individual voters' decisions without asking about the shape of the election districts.

The problem here from the point of view of Christian ethics is that this individualistic construal of all economic exchange leaves each market participant free of moral responsibility for the harms that markets cause, since those harms are ascribed to the market "mechanism" that allocates goods and services to their highest valued use and each individual transaction is a morally legitimate voluntary transfer of resources.

If we hope to forge a link from economic analysis to a more adequate sociological understanding of the market as a social structure having an independent causal impact, we need to find a way to speak of the effects of prices as causal forces. The proposal of this article is to understand prices as bearing a kind of coercive power embedded in the market. Thus the next necessary step is to attend briefly to a vocabulary of power.

Power in the Social Life

Power has an unfortunately bad reputation within Christian theology and ethics. It has received some positive treatment in the form of "power to"[9] and "power for,"[10] but to understand the function of prices in the market we need to attend to more carefully "power over" others, which has most frequently addressed disparagingly.

In his book, *The Forms of Power*, Thomas Wartenberg provides a "field theory" of power.[11] "It treats an agent's power over another agent as a field *within* whose effect the subordinate agent acts."[12] This notion of power as a field of influence runs parallel to that of a magnetic field, where the magnet alters a space, causing motion for susceptible objects. Similarly, persons with power over others typically exercise that power through their influence on the actions of "third persons" who make up the social space surrounding the person subject to that power. In classic example, tyrants and mob bosses have power over others because their enforcers will carry out any threats they make. The set of our choices, what Wartenberg calls our "action-environment," is altered. So the definition of power is this: "a social agent A has power over another agent B if and only if A strategically constrains B's action-environment."[13]

Wartenberg identifies three types of power: force, coercion, and influence. Force is a physical intervention by one person to prevent another from doing something. You yourself might physically restrain a hysterical neighbor to prevent her from reentering her burning home to look for a missing child. Influence is the effort to persuade someone to think or do something while that other person is also subject to one's coercive power. The efforts of university professors to persuade their students of the truth of some principle are complicated by the power of coercion implicit in the professors assigning of a grade for performance. Our focus is on the third type of power: coercion.

Coercive power occurs when one person threatens a penalty unless another person acts in a certain way. Coercion itself occurs if the second person chooses to change his or her behavior instead of paying the penalty. That is, coercive power is the power of a threat; coercion itself is a successful threat. One can "resist coercion" by deciding not to change one's behavior and instead pay the penalty, but the penalty is the result of coercive power.

The words "coercion" and "threat" are replete with negative connotations, and many ethicists unfortunately use them as if it were always morally objectionable. But most threats are quite moral. Parents regularly tell their children that they must do this or that or the child will pay some penalty. College professors announce an implicit threat with every syllabus they distribute, indicating that the student will receive a failing grade if he or she does not complete the course requirements satisfactorily. Your local police force threatens you with a speeding ticket if you exceed the speed limit on the way to a meeting you're late for. And just about every club threatens you with eviction if you do not pay your dues.

It is important to note that many of these threats are never articulated orally and sometimes not even in writing; they are simply understood as the rules of the game, embodied in social structures, in the preexisting relationships we enter into. This is an important part of the civility and morality of coercive power when exercised well. Parents, teachers, police officers, and club secretaries would all prefer that ordinary human relationships go on smoothly without any need to enforce penalties. Thus coercive power is part of the software of all organizations, allowing daily life to boot up. It is a sign of dysfunction of those very organizations when penalties are so frequently imposed that the coercive power moves from a background condition rarely noticed to a foreground reality. In a well-ordered nation, for example, citizens voluntarily submit truthful tax returns, knowing that they could be severely penalized if they do not, but they pay the taxes they owe with no more angst than accompanies the need to pay the bill for lunch in a restaurant.

Thus we can extend Wartenberg's insights and recognize the presence of an implicit threat—coercive power—as one form of the restrictions created by social structures that constrain the opportunities of persons within them, that is, within the relationships that persons have when they take up preexisting social positions, such as diner/waitress, citizen/government, or professor/student. In ordinary social life, coercive power in the form of such tacit threats is nearly ubiquitous, generating incentives to act in one way or another. This does not mean that this coercive power is the dominant feature of these many relationships but simply that it is present, typically in the background, and that in most cases it operates morally as an ordinary part of daily social life.

Coercive Power in the Market

As we have seen, when a particular price rises or falls, signaling a change in market conditions, there are some market participants who have more attractive options and others who have less attractive ones. Neither group is forced to change the pattern of their behavior by any sort of hydraulic pressure, but the former can improve their economic well-being by such a change (at a minimum, a drop in price of a particular good means one's budget will stretch farther), while the latter can typically reduce the damage threatened to their economic well-being by making changes (since the damage caused by a rise in price of a good can usually be mitigated by buying less of it). It is easy to appreciate markets in the former case, for example, as technological change has brought about a long-term downward trend in the price of computers. Yet economists also appreciate how markets bring about adjustments in the latter. For example, a long-term upward trend in the price of a particular mineral due to its growing scarcity leads those employing that mineral to look for cheaper substitutes or to invent a new technology altogether. A key insight of economics, then, is that prices help make the economy more productive by inducing market participants to make changes in their behaviors to avoid greater loss. It is in this latter case—where a change in market conditions threatens to make one worse off—that the notion of coercive power can be helpfully applied to bring the insights of sociology into economic analysis.

In the same way that we can understand universities to exercise coercive power in the implicit threat that each professor's syllabus makes to each student in every classroom, we can similarly recognize the coercive power that markets exert implicitly through the price system: Either change your behavior to reduce the damage about to be caused by some particular change in price or this change will make you considerably worse off.

When the price of gasoline doubled and then doubled again during the 1970s due to the restriction of global petroleum supply by the Organization of Petroleum Exporting Countries, drivers were faced with a very real threat. Either they needed to consume less gasoline or they would have considerably less disposable income to spend on all the other goods and services they purchased each month. The individual consumer immediately tried to drive fewer miles per week, and over the longer run opted to buy smaller cars, and, when a change of residence was in the offing, they looked for a place to live that was closer to their worksite. Similarly, producers who were big users of petroleum products for heating or factory power found their profits—and in some cases their economic survival—under threat and looked both for ways to use less energy and for alternative sources of energy that would cost less.

Extending the sociological analysis outlined earlier, we can understand the coercive threat caused by the rise in the price of petroleum as a restriction generated by the social structure of the market, recognizing the market as a set of relationships among preexisting social positions. Consumers as drivers are in relationship with the producers of gasoline. This market relationship is complex and entails long chains of interactions. It includes all the consumers of gasoline, as well as those who run gas stations, the trucks and pipelines that transport gas, the refineries that create gas from crude oil, the tankers that bring crude across the ocean, and the oil wells. All these actors are interdependent in the market, through a long chain, each in a relation with the others.

This chain of market relationships may at first appear far more complex than the relationship that make up a university, but recall the "field" character of coercive power. The newly minted PhD who joins a university faculty enters into a set of preexisting relationships, with untenured colleagues, tenured colleagues, department chair, tenure committee, dean, provost, president, governing board, and many others. She will encounter many enablements, such as financial support for travel to scholarly conferences. But parallel to our focus on the threats made in the market, consider the role of coercive power in the professor's life.

The professor's implicit threat of a lower grade for weaker student performance is effective for many students precisely because of the field of her influence: Students know that countless employers and graduate school admissions committees will be looking at their transcripts. But the professor herself is subjective to coercive power. There is an implicit threat in the expectations others have for what and how well she should teach and the number and quality of publications necessary for advancement or to gain a position at a more prestigious university. One's future is to a large extent in the hands of unknown numbers of editors and journal referees whose decisions about whether to publish the professor's work influence on-campus decisions about tenure and promotion. Thus it turns out that markets are not different in kind because of the complexity of market relationships, even though conditions within market relationships typically change more frequently than do those in academe.

Markets, Power, and Harms Done to Distant Others

We can now relate these insights into social structures and coercive power to the underlying question at the beginning of this essay: how to understand the responsibility of an average consumer for the harms markets cause to distant others. I focus here on the hardest case—where persons make voluntary decisions, usually to take a job, that eventuate in harms to themselves caused by markets. The same empirical and moral analysis outlined above can also be applied to other forms of market harms, for example, environmental degradation.

When I bought the shirt that I am currently wearing, I entered into a preexisting relationship. As a consumer, I was in relation with the clerk and department store when I was looking for a good quality shirt at a low price. And both the clerk and the store occupied preexisting positions in the industry that produces and markets clothing. Thus I was in a long chain of relationships not only with other buyers of shirts but with the clerk, truck drivers, and other employees of the department store that sells them; the brand-name firm that provides them to the store; the shipping company transporting them from Asia; the subcontractor that turns bolts of cloth into shirts; the firm that wove thread into that cloth; and so on, including employees of each of those firms. Thus I am indeed in relationship with the Asian woman who sewed the stitches into my shirt, and we both are subject to enablements, restrictions, and incentives arising from these market relationships. At each stage, a change in price of a substitute input to production could spell bankruptcy for a firm or loss of a job for an individual—or improved profits and higher wages and a better shirt for me at a lower price.

Participants at each stage in this process have found their opportunities either enhanced or restricted by the market. It is in this latter case of restriction that harms arise. Although the seamstress who made my shirt may be glad to have her job, the coercive power of the market may well have left her under threat of losing that job unless she puts up with forced overtime or a lack of bathroom breaks or any number of other indignities, violations of rights, or life-threatening factory conditions made worse by market pressures to cut expenditures on safety equipment. Except in truly unusual situations close to slavery, she no doubt has opted to work at the factory. But as Albino Barrera has persuasively argued in *Economic Compulsion and Christian Ethics*,[14] this decision ought not simply be considered a "free choice," as so many economists presume.

Barrera employs a helpful example from Aristotle to clarify this point. The captain who decides to throw the ship's cargo overboard in order that he and his crew survive a terrible storm has indeed chosen but has chosen "against his will." This is a "mixed" choice. Barrera argues that markets impose analogous constraints on market participants and that, in cases of extreme harm, "economic compulsion" occurs. This he defines as

> a condition in which market participants unavoidably incur profound opportunity costs. People give up nontrivial interests in order to satisfy, safeguard, or procure their other vital claims that are at even greater risk. In other words, economic compulsion leads people to voluntarily accept a significant deterioration in their welfare in order to avert what would have otherwise been an even more catastrophic decline in their well-being.[15]

Although Barrera uses the term "coercion" differently than I propose, his conclusion is one I support. Put in the terms of this essay, the coercive power of prices in the social structure we call the market typically has good effects, even when imposing costs on market participants. However, when those costs are high enough and paid by people whose well-being is threatened severely in paying them, we must conclude that economic compulsion has occurred and that consumers as market participants, even at a great distance from that last link in the chain where the compulsion occurs, are morally responsible for the harm caused.

This is not to say that only consumers are responsible. There are many persons involved in the long chain of relationships that constitute the market, and each one must decide how to react to the enablements, restrictions, and incentives that their social position in this chain presents. Individualist analysis is surely wrong to attribute all the harms caused to the personal vices of the agents involved, but there are indeed harms that need to be attributed to vice. The manager who extorts sexual favors from his female workers and the factory owner who pays a bribe to local authorities to avoid proper fire inspections are cases in point. Nonetheless, each manager in each firm in this long chain of production is subject to expectations, rules, and requirements imposed on anyone who would hold that role. Even the CEOs of multinational firms often see their power of discretion quite limited, understanding most decisions as clearly indicated by market conditions. Personal virtue is necessary for a morally adequate market system, but it is not sufficient. Market pressures, information about which is delivered in the form of a change in prices, are responsible for significant damage to human well-being, and market participants are responsible for the market relationships they enter into.

Conclusion

Much more would need to be said to take the next step in this analysis and to address how markets might be structured more adequately from a moral point of view. For now, however, the purpose of this chapter has been to provide a conceptual structure for understanding how and why individual market consumers are morally responsible for harms that markets cause to distant others.

In summary, every social structure emerges from the prior interaction of humans and is constituted by a set of preexisting relationships that human persons enter into. Only persons are agents, but social structures exert causal impact through enablements, restrictions, and incentives, which in turn have an effect only through the decisions people make in response to them. Markets, thus, are fundamentally sets of relationships entered into by producers and consumers. When market conditions change, this information is conveyed to market participants by a change in price, with each change in price leaving some groups better off than before and others worse off. Focusing as we have done here on the harms markets cause, we look on the function of prices as exercising a kind of coercive power, a threat that affects market participants and tells them they should change their behavior in order to reduce the harms that this change in price would otherwise cause. These "price signals" are delivered through the very chain of economic relationships that constitute the link between consumers and the producers of the products consumers buy. Most of the effects of these price signals, even those that impose costs on market participants, are fully just. Yet when the harms caused to others are sufficiently threatening to their well-being, as too often happens in the lives of those with few options in life, they require redress. The moral character of my clothing purchase depends not simply on how the department store clerk and I treated each other but also on the moral character of the long chain of relationships connecting me to the Asian seamstress who sewed the shirt I am wearing.

NOTES

1. Christopher Kutz, *Complicity: Ethics and Law for a Collective Age* (New York: Oxford University Press, 2001), 117–124.
2. See, for example, "Methodological Collectivism" in Margaret S. Archer, *Realist Social Theory: The Morphogenetic Approach* (Cambridge, UK: Cambridge University Press, 1995), 46–54.
3. See, for example, Archer, "Methodological Individualism" in Margaret S. Archer, *Realist Social Theory: The Morphogenetic Approach* (Cambridge, UK: Cambridge University Press, 1995), 34–46.
4. For an extreme view here, see F. A. von Hayek, "Scientism and the Study of Society," *Economica*, New Series, 9.35 (August 1942): 267–291.
5. I am indebted to Margaret Archer for this example.
6. Christian Smith, *What Is a Person? Rethinking Humanity, Social Life, and the Moral Good from the Person Up* (Chicago: University of Chicago Press, 2010): 25–26.
7. Smith, *What Is a Person*, 26.
8. Douglas V. Porpora, "Four Concepts of Social Structure," *Journal for the Theory of Social Behavior*, 19.2 (1989): 195–212.
9. Christine Hinze, *Comprehending Power in Christian Social Ethics* (Atlanta, GA: Scholars Press, 1995).

10. Anna Mercedes, *Power For: Feminism and Christ's Self-giving*, (New York: T&T Clark, 2011).
11. Thomas E. Wartenberg, *The Forms of Power: From Domination to Transformation* (Philadelphia: Temple University Press, 1990).
12. Wartenberg, *Forms of Power*, 71.
13. Wartenberg, *Forms of Power*, 85.
14. Albino Barrera, *Economic Compulsion and Christian Ethics* (New York: Cambridge University Press, 2005).
15. Barrera, *Economic Compulsion*, 4–5.

REFERENCES

Archer, Margaret S. "Methodological Collectivism." In Margaret S. Archer, *Realist Social Theory: The Morphogenetic Approach*. Cambridge, UK: Cambridge University Press, 1995, 46–54.

———. "Methodological Individualism." In Margaret S. Archer, *Realist Social Theory: The Morphogenetic Approach*. Cambridge, UK: Cambridge University Press, 1995, 34–46.

Barrera, Albino. *Economic Compulsion and Christian Ethics*. New York: Cambridge University Press, 2005.

Hinze, Christine. *Comprehending Power in Christian Social Ethics*. Atlanta, GA: Scholars Press, 1995.

Kutz, Christopher. *Complicity: Ethics and Law for a Collective Age*. New York: Oxford University Press, 2001.

Mercedes, Anna. *Power For: Feminism and Christ's Self-giving*. New York: T&T Clark, 2011.

Porpora, Douglas V. "Four Concepts of Social Structure." *Journal for the Theory of Social Behavior*, 19.2 (1989): 195–212.

Smith, Christian. *What Is a Person? Rethinking Humanity, Social Life, and the Moral Good from the Person Up*. Chicago: University of Chicago Press, 2010.

von Hayek, F. A. "Scientism and the Study of Society." *Economica*, New Series, 9.35 (August 1942): 267–291.

Wartenberg, Thomas E. *The Forms of Power: From Domination to Transformation*. Philadelphia: Temple University Press, 1990.

Index